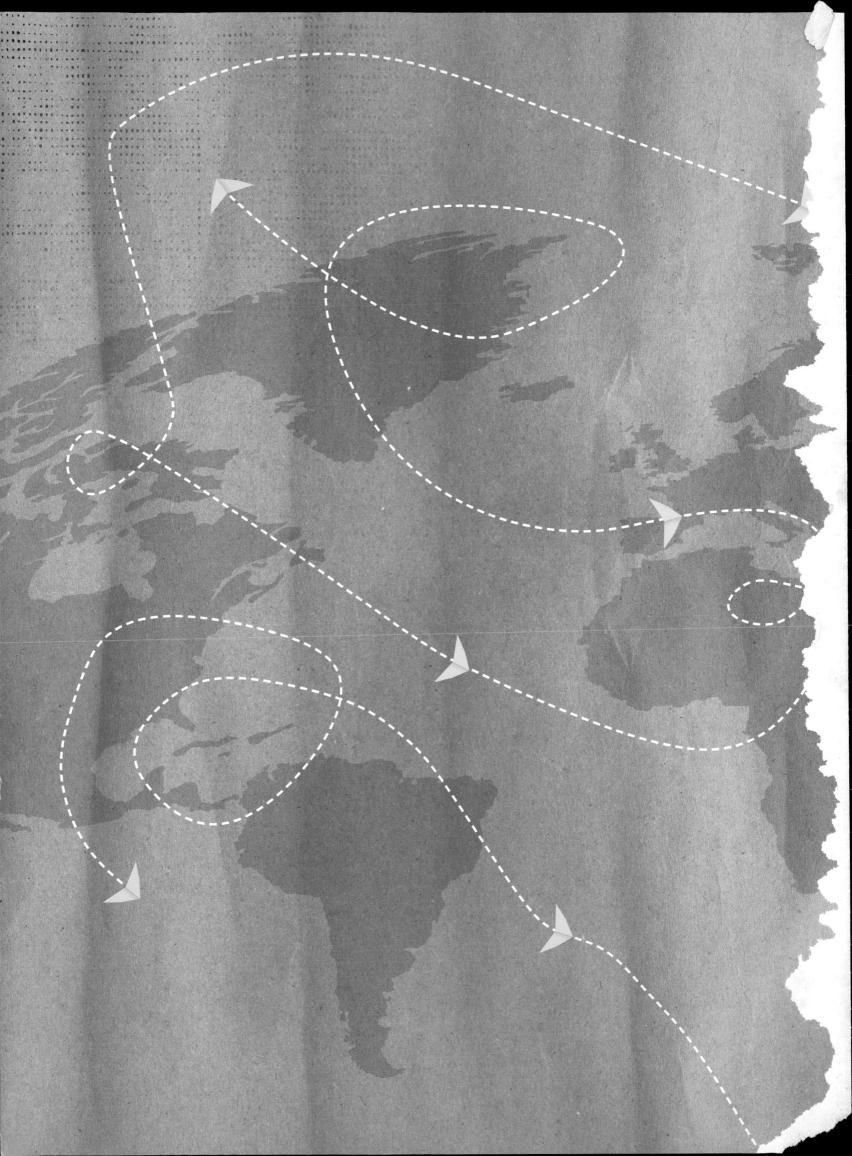

NATIONAL GEOGRAPHIC KiDS

weird but true!

WORLD 2023

Incredible facts, awesome photos, and weird wonders— for this year and beyond!

NATIONAL GEOGRAPHIC
WASHINGTON, D.C.

CONTENTS

I mustache you to keep reading!

CONTENTS

CHAPTER 9
SENSATIONAL
SEA AND SPACE 264

CHAPTER 8
AMAZING ANTARCTICA 244

INTRODUCTION

EVER HEARD THE SAYING "TRUTH IS STRANGER THAN FICTION"?

Well, we're here to show you that it's 100 percent true! There's a whole wide world of strange, shocking, spectacular sights out there, just waiting to surprise you. That's why we've collected some of the weirdest stuff the world has to offer. In these pages, you'll take a weirdly wonderful journey around our planet, stopping at every continent along the way.

You'll encounter unbelievable places, wacky festivals, and kooky creatures from around the world. You'll see spectacular buildings and peek inside oddball museums. And you'll learn some mind-blowing weird-but-true facts while you're at it!

Who are you calling weird?

I'm on top of the world!

FINDING YOUR WAY AROUND

Before you begin your journey around the globe, check out what's weird for this year in Chapter 1. Every year, we're crowning the world's top weirdos—including animals, places, photos, and news. Then it's time to see the world, one continent at a time, from the North American Arctic to the islands of Oceania.

In each chapter, you'll find breathtaking images of **Weird Wonders**, discover incredible stats in **By the Numbers** special features, and glimpse some not-so-normal sights to find out "What's Weird About This?" You'll also find quizzes that test your trivia chops and reveal silly secrets about your personality. And you'll meet adorable animals so weird, they're cute! And that's just the tip of the iceberg. So buckle up—we're going around the world,

Weird But True style!

WEIRD in the WORLD

Our home **PLANET** is bursting with **WEIRDNESS**—from the depths of its **OCEAN** to the peaks of its **TALLEST MOUNTAINS.**

Chile's **ATACAMA DESERT** is the **DRIEST NONPOLAR PLACE** on Earth, with an annual rainfall of just **.03 INCH (0.8 MM).** Bizarrely, it's situated next to the Pacific Ocean, the **BIGGEST BODY OF WATER IN THE WORLD!**

ARCTIC

NORTH AMERICA

ATLANTIC OCEAN

Mauna Kea

PACIFIC OCEAN

SOUTH AMERICA

Atacama Desert

SOUTHERN

That's weird!

The **TALLEST** mountain from **BASE TO PEAK** isn't Mount Everest—it's **MAUNA KEA IN HAWAII, U.S.A.,** but most of it is below sea level!

The time it takes for Earth to spin on its axis is **INCREASING EXTREMELY SLOWLY.** In **50 BILLION YEARS,** a single day on the planet could last **1,000 HOURS.**

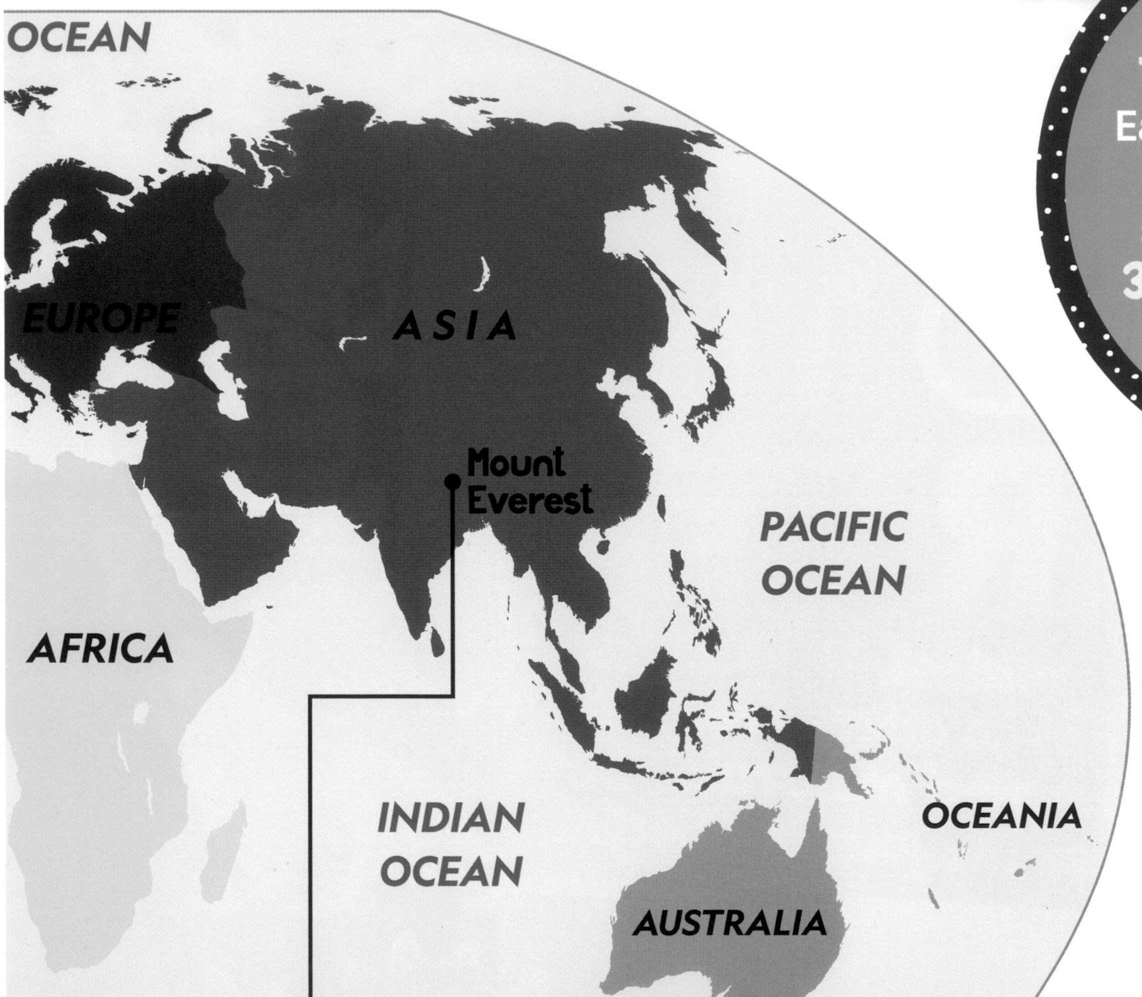

Sounds like you've had a long day.

If you could **DIG A HOLE ALL THE WAY THROUGH** Earth and jump into it, it would take you slightly longer than **38 MINUTES** to travel all the way through the planet!

OCEAN

EUROPE

ASIA

Mount Everest

AFRICA

PACIFIC OCEAN

INDIAN OCEAN

OCEANIA

AUSTRALIA

Earth is the **ONLY KNOWN PLANET** with **LIQUID WATER** on its surface—and the **ONLY PLANET** to **MAINTAIN LIFE.**

OCEAN

ANTARCTICA

1

WEIRD THIS YEAR

It's a wide world of weird!

Want the latest, greatest, WEIRDEST stuff the world has to offer? From trash-eating waterwheels to naked mole rats, Earth has it all. Let the journey begin!

SAVE THE DATE 2023

Whatever you enjoy doing, there's probably a day devoted to it. Here are some weird and wacky events happening in 2023!

JANUARY 1

POLAR BEAR PLUNGE DAY
Nope, this doesn't involve going swimming with the awesome Arctic Circle animals. Instead, tens of thousands of people jump into icy-cold lakes and seas worldwide. After that challenge, the rest of the year will be a cinch!

FEBRUARY 17

RANDOM ACTS OF KINDNESS DAY (U.S.)
Mow a neighbor's lawn. Pay a compliment to a friend. Put money in a vending machine so someone enjoys a free snack. This day of goodwill is celebrated at different times around the world. Why not be kind and celebrate them all?

MARCH 26

MAKE UP YOUR OWN HOLIDAY DAY
Annoyed that there isn't a Carry a Potato in Your Pocket Day or a Read a Poem Backward Day? Don't worry ... now you can invent your own special celebration! How many people can you get to join in?

APRIL 8

SUPERHERO DAY
Mask up! Cape on! Why not create a secret identity for yourself and draw a picture of your crime-fighting activities? Real-life heroes, such as nurses, firefighters and police officers, are celebrated today, too.

MAY 14

DANCE LIKE A CHICKEN DAY
Hold your hands at your sides. Move your elbows in and out. Jerk your head back and forth. Strut around the room. Now lay an egg. Well, maybe not that last one, but if you can do the others, you're dancing like a chicken!

That's weird!

JUNE 3

REPEAT DAY REPEAT DAY REPEAT ...
If something is worth doing once, it's worth doing again. And again. And again. Today you can have breakfast—and then eat exactly the same meal. Or repeat back everything your parents say to you. That won't be annoying, will it? That won't be annoying, will it ... ?

JULY 31

UNCOMMON MUSICAL INSTRUMENT AWARENESS DAY

Put down that guitar. Step away from the piano. Today is all about playing and listening to unusual instruments, such as the hurdy-gurdy—a stringed instrument played by turning a handle. Or there's the hyperbass flute, which has almost 50 feet (15 m) of piping. PAAAAARP!

AUGUST 13

INTERNATIONAL LEFT-HANDERS DAY

It's a right-handers' world—lots of products from scissors to notepads are designed with them in mind. So it's only fair that the 10 percent of the population who are left-handed have one day dedicated to them. And today, it's definitely right to be left!

SEPTEMBER 19

INTERNATIONAL TALK LIKE A PIRATE DAY

Ahoy, me hearties! Here is the chance for all landlubbers to get a taste of life on the high seas. Create an exciting pirate name for yourself and become a buccaneer. Just don't try to make anyone walk the plank or your crew might leave you marooned!

OCTOBER 6

WORLD SMILE DAY

Artist Harvey Ball certainly liked to smile. In 1963, he designed the smiley—the happy yellow face known around the world. 26 years later, he invented World Smile Day, encouraging people to make others smile. So tell a joke ... tickle a friend's feet ... it's a day for fun!

NOVEMBER 8

TONGUE TWISTER DAY

Can you say "Peter Piper picked a peck of pickled peppers"? If that's easy, today is your day! The tongue is one of the strongest muscles in the body, so it's all set for a good workout. But remember ... tricky tongue twisters typically tend to twirl tongues terribly!

DECEMBER 5

DAY OF THE NINJA

Ninjas were Japanese spies. They were active between the 14th and 19th centuries and were specialists in survival skills and staying out of sight. You can experience the ninja vibe by dressing in black and doing good deeds—without anyone knowing you were even there ...

WEIRD WAYS TO SAVE THE WORLD

With global temperatures on the rise and more plastic pollution in the ocean than ever, it's a tough time for planet Earth. Thankfully, do-gooders around the world are tackling the issues. Here are four super-weird ways to save the world in 2023!

Mr. Trash Wheel

If there's a river full of litter, then a sustainably powered trash interceptor could be the answer. In other words ... you need a trash wheel! Mr. Trash Wheel, to give him his official title, has been keeping the mouth of Jones Falls river in Baltimore, Maryland, U.S.A., clean since 2014. He sits in the water, using solar and hydro power to collect garbage from the harbor. Inside his gaping mouth is a conveyor belt, strong enough to transport mattresses and trees. At the top of the belt, the trash falls into a dumpster on a barge. When it's full, it's taken away to be burnt, generating electricity.

THESE THREE WASTE WARRIORS HAVE GOBBLED UP MORE THAN 1,470 TONS (1,334 T) OF TRASH.

Nom nom nom

MR. TRASH WHEEL HAS BEEN JOINED BY PROFESSOR TRASH WHEEL AND CAPTAIN TRASH WHEEL!

The Bubble Curtain

Limiting the spread of plastic litter or oil spills in water is not easy. Now a new method is being developed to deal with these tricky tasks—curtains! But these aren't large, soggy pieces of fabric hanging down from poles. These curtains are made from ... bubbles. Hoses connected to a compressor are submerged several yards underwater. Holes in the hoses release a wall of bubbles, which rise up, dragging the surrounding water with them.

Phytoplankton

These microscopic organisms live at or close to the surface of the ocean and need iron to grow. Some scientists have wondered if giving the phytoplankton a helping hand could repair the damage done by climate change. They tried dumping iron into the ocean, which caused the number of phytoplankton to increase and carbon dioxide levels to drop in that area. However, other scientists think this would take decades to work—and aren't sure how else it would affect the ecosystem. Studies on iron fertilization are continuing around the world, but all the scientists have one ultimate aim—to keep the population of amazing phytoplankton healthy and growing.

The WasteShark

The whale shark is the largest living fish. This massive shark can grow to be about 40 feet (12 m) long! Despite its size, it filter-feeds on tiny plankton and small fish by sucking prey into its enormous mouth. Thankfully, they don't pose any danger to humans—and have even inspired an invention that will help us instead! The WasteShark filter-feeds, too, except that its diet is trash! Designed for use in harbors, ponds, and canals, this small machine weighs about the same as a man and can collect up to 126 pounds (57 kg) of trash a day. It can also be used to collect biomass, such as algae and rootless plants, to keep waterways clean. The WasteShark isn't harmful to fish, which usually swim away from it, and doesn't emit any pollution.

SURPRISING STATS

The world's LARGEST FUNCTIONAL PENCIL was unveiled in New York, U.S.A.—it's **76 FEET 2.75 INCHES** (23.23 M) long, the height of a SEVEN-STORY BUILDING.

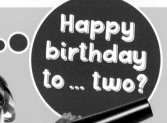

...Happy birthday to ... two?

A theory called the **BIRTHDAY PARADOX** states that if there are **23 PEOPLE IN A ROOM**, there is a **50 PERCENT CHANCE** that at least two of them will share the **SAME BIRTHDAY!**

TAE KWON DO MASTER **MUHAMED KAHRIMANOVIĆ** holds the record for breaking **23 PAIRS OF COCONUTS** by **HAND IN ONE MINUTE.**

ABOUT THE NUMBER 23

FRENCH CLOWN **FRANÇOIS "JESTER COCO" CHOTARD** HOLDS THE WORLD RECORD FOR **SPINNING HATS ON POLES** ONE-HANDED, WITH **23 ITEMS** OF **HEADGEAR** IN MOTION AT THE SAME TIME.

2023 is weird down to its digits!

23 DRESSES covered in candies, pastries, and truffles were paraded on the catwalk at the 2008 Salon du Chocolat fashion show in Paris, France.

Basketball legend **MICHAEL JORDAN** chose his famous **JERSEY NUMBER** after playing with his older brother Larry on his high school team. Larry wore the **NUMBER 45 SHIRT,** so Michael halved it and rounded it up to **23!**

SOME PEOPLE, INCLUDING A GROUP CALLED THE **23RDIANS,** BELIEVE THAT THE NUMBER **23** HAS **MAGICAL QUALITIES.**

WEIRDEST PLACES TO LIVE
RUNNERS-UP ...

Looking to move this year? We've got you covered. Why settle for the ordinary when you could live in one of the weirdest places on the planet? Without further ado: Here are the top oddball abodes for 2023!

Cat Island, Japan

If you find Tashirojima tricky to say, you can just use its nickname—Cat Island! Home to around 100 people, it's estimated that they share the island with up to 600 furry felines. Between the mid-18th and mid-19th centuries, Tashirojima was a center for silk production. Cats were brought in to chase away mice that ate the valuable silkworms. Another popular industry was fishing—the fishermen would share their catch with the cats and the feline population grew.

THERE ARE ABOUT A DOZEN ISLANDS AROUND JAPAN WITH MORE CATS THAN HUMAN RESIDENTS.

IN JAPAN, CATS ARE BELIEVED TO BRING GOOD LUCK AND MONEY.

Thames Town, China

Cobbled streets ... a fish-and-chip shop ... a statue of British prime minister Winston Churchill. It might look like a typical English location, but Thames Town is actually in China! Built in the early 21st century, this unusual development was designed to encourage people to move from busy Shanghai to the less crowded suburbs. It was planned as one of nine towns copying architecture from different countries. Germany, Italy, and Spain have also been used for inspiration.

That's weird!

THAMES TOWN'S LAMPPOSTS WERE IMPORTED FROM ENGLAND!

Monowi, Nebraska, U.S.A.

MONOWI 1

Monowi has never been huge—in the 1930s, it boasted a population of 150. Over the years, people moved away. And in 2004, there was just one resident left there, making it the smallest town in the U.S. Elsie Eiler was only one and a half years old when she moved there with her parents in the 1930s, and she has lived in Monowi for nearly all of her life. Since 1971, she has been running the town's café, which is open six days a week for truck drivers and people from nearby towns who meet up there.

Matmata, Tunisia

With underground homes burrowed vertically into the rock, Matmata feels like it could belong on another planet. Movie director George Lucas certainly thought so—the Hotel Sidi Driss in Matmata was used for the home of Luke Skywalker and his aunt and uncle in the original *Star Wars* film! People have been living here for centuries; no one knows exactly how long. But it's easy to see why they chose to live here. Living underground means an escape from the intense heat of the sun. It's estimated that 15,000 people once made the underground dwellings their home, but by the 1960s, most were abandoned as families left to seek jobs in nearby towns.

WEIRDEST PLACES TO LIVE

And the Winner Is ...

That's weird!

WINNER

Júzcar, Spain

If you're feeling blue, head to Júzcar—you'll feel right at home! This village in southern Spain is home to several hundred people who used to live in traditional whitewashed houses. That's until 2011, when *The Smurfs* was released and the film company wanted a fun way to promote it. So they paid to have the buildings in Júzcar painted Smurf blue. When they returned in 2012 to turn the village white again, the locals didn't want to change back. This was partly due to an increase in tourism—the number of sightseers rose from the hundreds to around 80,000 in the year after the color change! Although the statues of the movie characters still remain, Júzcar is now known as the blue village, rather than as the first ever Smurf town!

IT TOOK AROUND 1,000 GALLONS (ABOUT 4,000 L) OF BLUE PAINT TO COVER THE WHOLE TOWN!

TO GET AN AERIAL VIEW OF THE VILLAGE, YOU CAN TAKE A ZIP LINE ACROSS THE VALLEY!

JÚZCAR IS ALSO HOME TO A MUSHROOM MUSEUM.

What a blue view!

23

WEIRDEST ANIMALS
RUNNERS-UP ...

Need a peculiar pet for your new home? Look no further. OK, so these guys aren't pets. But they definitely ARE peculiar. Here are the year's top five weirdest animals!

Immortal Jellyfish

Ever imagined what it would be like to live forever? Well, some animals can do exactly that! And the immortal jellyfish is leading the way. Once found mainly in the Mediterranean Sea, this extraordinary animal is now appearing all over the world. The jellyfish starts life as a tube-shaped larva that attaches itself to a rock. It then enters the polyp stage, blooming like a flower, and the buds on the polyp become baby jellyfish! The adult, known as the medusa, is only about the width of a grown-up human's fingernail. While most jellyfish have a fixed lifespan, the immortal jellyfish can revert back to its polyp stage at any time—and do it again and again!

SCIENTISTS FOUND ONE COLONY OF IMMORTAL JELLYFISH THAT WAS REBORN 11 TIMES IN JUST TWO YEARS!

Naked Mole Rat

It's clearly not going to win any cute critter competitions, but the naked mole rat is a truly remarkable rodent. It never travels above ground, living in groups of around 75 animals in a network of burrows. Just one burrow system can cover around three miles (4.8 km) in total. That's the length of 250 bowling lanes! A naked mole rat is well adapted for digging, using its large, protruding teeth to break up hard earth. These stick out over the top of its lips, which it keeps shut to avoid swallowing any dirt.

Pignose Frog

Commonly called the purple frog, this amazing amphibian is also known as the pignose frog for obvious reasons! It feeds on termites and lives mostly underground, which is probably why it wasn't properly identified until 2003. It actually spends only two weeks of the year aboveground, when it surfaces to mate! The female frogs, which are three times as long as the males, can lay 3,000 eggs at a time. When the tadpoles are born, they cling to algae on submerged rocks, using suckers in their mouths to keep from being washed away.

Read my lips!

Red-Lipped Batfish

A fish that isn't good at swimming sounds like the punch line to a joke. But it's actually a description of the red-lipped batfish! It can swim, but its fins are better adapted to walking along the ocean floor instead, so it's not the speediest marine creature. This might be a problem when it comes to chasing fast-swimming prey, but the bat-fish isn't worried—it lets its dinner do all the hard work! Reaching up to 16 inches (40 cm) in length, this unusual creature belongs to the order of anglerfish, which have special appendages to lure prey.

WEIRDEST ANIMALS

And the Winner Is ...

WINNER

Proboscis Monkey

If you want to make a big noise—you need a big nose! At least, that's how it works for the proboscis monkey. This peculiar primate is famous for its substantial snout. A male's nose can be longer than four inches (10 cm) and hang lower than its mouth. This fabulous facial feature works as an echo chamber to increase the volume of the monkey's call. This helps to attract a mate and to frighten off rival males. Proboscis monkeys have a surprising talent— they're good swimmers! Their webbed feet and hands help them swim up to 66 feet (20 m) underwater and escape one of their main predators— crocodiles. If a proboscis monkey needs to make a swift getaway, it "nose" what to do!

PROBOSCIS MONKEYS HAVE A SPECIAL HONK TO COMFORT INFANTS.

That's a honk from the heart.

27

WEIRDEST PHOTOS
RUNNERS-UP ...

Sometimes seeing is believing—and these photos will have you doing a double take! Check out our top five to see if you agree that these reign supreme.

Atacama Desert, Chile

This is most definitely not a picture of snowmen watching a tennis match. These weirdly shaped blocks of snow and ice—all facing in the same direction—form in the dry, cold air of the Andes, in high-altitude areas exposed to strong sunlight. Sometimes reaching up to 16 feet (5 m) high, the icy spires are named "Penitentes" after the kneeling, praying crowds of Spanish Holy Week.

STUDYING THE ATACAMA'S EXTREME ENVIRONMENT HELPS SCIENTISTS UNDERSTAND WHERE LIFE MIGHT BE FOUND ON MARS.

Baby Lionfish

Is it a flower? Is it a snowflake? Is it a fairy? No, it's a baby lionfish. Aaahhh! Known as fry, these almost transparent tiddlers hatch from eggs, then live and feed at the surface until big and strong enough to swim deeper down. As they grow, they develop the fabulous colors, patterns, and feather-like spines that adult lionfish are famed for. But don't get too close—the spines are venomous!

Lake Retba, Senegal

Anyone for a strawberry milkshake? Well, don't try a glass of this—it's not milk and there's not a strawberry in sight. This amazing photo shows the salty waters of Lake Retba in Senegal, Africa. The incredible pink color is caused by *Dunaliella salina* bacteria in the lake that produce a red pigment.

HARVESTERS CAN GET 24,000 TONS (22,000 T) OF SALT FROM THE LAKE IN JUST ONE YEAR.

Romanesco Cauliflower

You may think you've stumbled across an alien life-form here, but this wonderfully weird photo is definitely from planet Earth! It's actually something you could eat—as long as you like your greens. Called Romanesco cauliflower, or Romanesco broccoli, it's delicious roasted, steamed, or raw, but it's the shape that gets the weird-o-meter buzzing. It's an example of something called a natural fractal. The buds are arranged in a spiral, gradually getting smaller at the spiral's center—and those buds are formed by smaller buds in other spirals!

WEIRDEST PHOTOS

And the Winner Is ...

Denise's Pygmy Seahorse

WINNER

And the top prize for weirdest photo of the year goes to, um, some kind of crispy corn snack? Take another look! Sitting among the twisting yellow branches, there's a tiny seahorse in hiding. The knobbly orange-yellow body of Denise's pygmy seahorse makes it a master of disguise among the lumpy, bumpy corals of the western Pacific Ocean, where it makes its home.

AT THE SIZE OF A NICKEL, THIS TINY SEAHORSE IS THE WORLD'S SMALLEST!

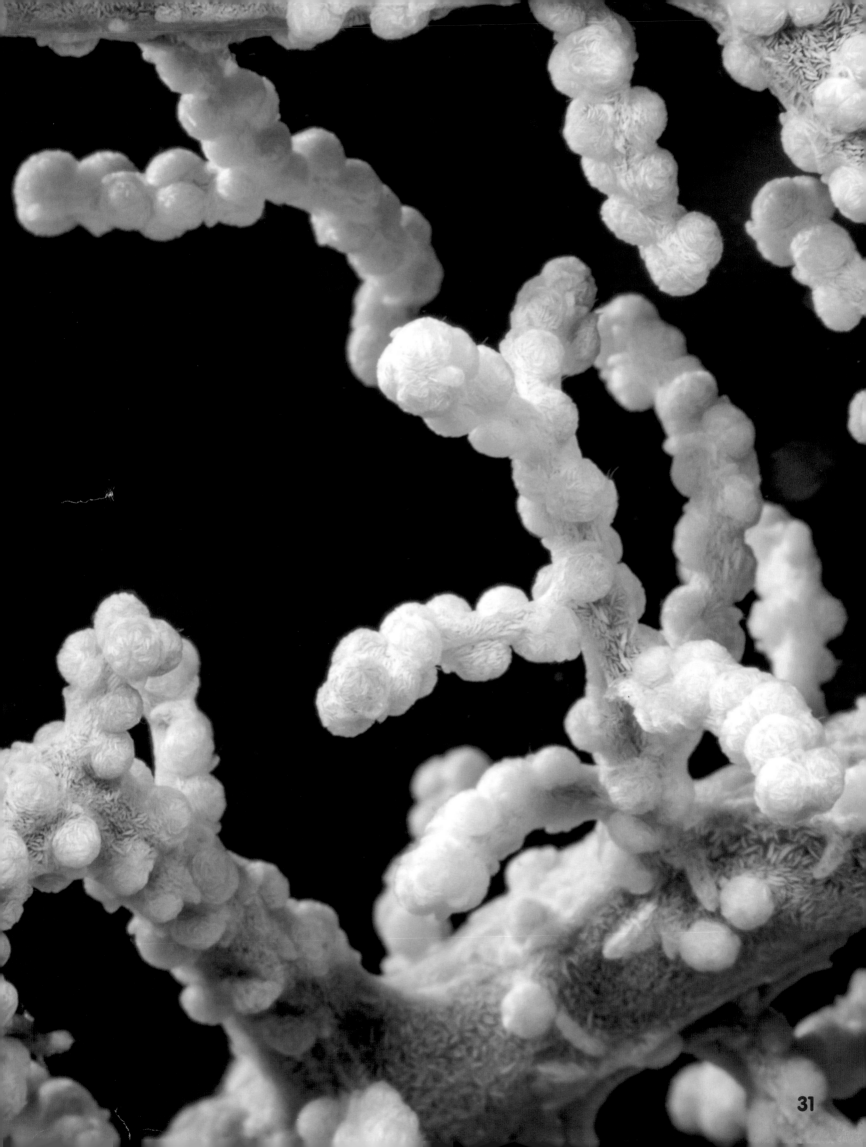

BY the NUMBERS

It's been a year of weird for the whole world. And that means it's been a year of weird for you, too! Don't believe us? Check out these strange stats. You are 31,536,000 seconds older than you were on this day last year! In that time ...

YOUR HAIR HAS GROWN **4 TO 6 INCHES** (10 TO 15 CM)— ABOUT THE LENGTH OF A SODA CAN.

YOU'VE SPENT ABOUT **24 HOURS** BRUSHING YOUR TEETH. (THAT'S A WHOLE DAY!)

YOUR TOENAILS HAVE GROWN ONLY **HALF AN INCH** (1.3 CM)— ABOUT THE LENGTH OF A SUNFLOWER SEED.

YOU'VE **BLINKED** APPROXIMATELY **4 MILLION** TIMES.

YOUR FINGERNAILS HAVE GROWN **1.5 INCHES** (4 CM)— ABOUT THE LENGTH OF TWO CANDY CORNS!

YOU HAVE LIKELY **TOOTED** SOMEWHERE BETWEEN **5,000** AND **8,000** TIMES!

WEIRD NEWS FROM AROUND THE WORLD

Think your town is weird? Check out these super-strange headlines from around the world!

Fan-tastic!

ROBOT FANS

FUKUOKA, JAPAN

When the COVID-19 pandemic meant that Japanese baseball team Fukuoka SoftBank Hawks weren't allowed to admit fans to their stadium, they chose the ideal replacement ... dancing robots! In 2020, more than 20 humanoids were in the stands as the Hawks took on the Rakuten Eagles. Some of the metal supporters even wore caps and waved flags!

REAL-LIFE CARTOONS

ATLANTIC OCEAN

During a 2021 ocean expedition, the U.S.A.'s National Oceanic and Atmospheric Administration (NOAA) stumbled upon a yellow sponge and a pink sea star that looked shockingly similar to characters SpongeBob and Patrick from the hit 'toon *SpongeBob SquarePants*. Unfortunately, these ocean critters aren't best friends in real life. More likely, the sea star was preparing to make a meal of the deep-sea sponge!

ORGAN MUSIC

HALBERSTADT, GERMANY

Music lovers enjoyed a rare treat in February 2022. A keyboard piece called "Organ²/ASLSP (As Slow As Possible)" by composer John Cage is being played on a church organ in Germany. The performance is due to last for 639 years! On February 5, 2022, a new chord was played. The previous note change had taken place on September 5, 2020!

ANIMAL ELECTIONS

CALIFORNIA, U.S.A.

A California neighborhood held an election in 2020 to become the mayor of 55th Street, but all the candidates were cats and dogs! Shiba Inu Mimi campaigned using the slogan "She'll bark when it matters." Macy, a pit bull mix, promised to "Keep Oakland ruff," while Wally the cat revealed that he was pro-speed bump!

ELECT BATTY
MAYOR OF   55TH STREET
CHANGE MEOW
PAID FOR BY OAKLAND PURRRGRESSIVES

ICONIC LANDMARK

DOHA, QATAR

Let's hear it for 2022—a year of fancy footwork in Qatar, the venue for the FIFA World Cup! And if you're celebrating an important year, you need an important building! The 2022 Iconic Landmark is the first building in the world to be designed using a year's number as its shape. It was opened on December 2, 2019, exactly nine years after Qatar was named as the World Cup host.

SCULPTURE SAFETY NET

ROTTERDAM, NETHERLANDS

When a raised tram in Rotterdam crashed through barriers and past the end of the track in 2020, it would have plummeted to the ground—if there hadn't been a whale to catch it! The front of the tram ended up suspended on a statue depicting two marine mammals. The sculpture, which isn't part of the railway, was renamed "Saved by a Whale's Tail" after the accident.

Who are you squawking at?

You, bird brain!

RUDE PARROTS

LINCOLNSHIRE, ENGLAND, U.K.

In 2020, five parrots ruffled a few feathers when they arrived at Lincolnshire Wildlife Park. The birds—named Billy, Eric, Tyson, Jade, and Elsie—started squawking rude words at visitors. Unfortunately, when people laughed in response, it encouraged the parrots to swear even more. The foulmouthed fivesome had to be separated into different areas of the park!

35

2

INCREDIBLE
NORTH
AMERICA

Home is where the weird is.

Spectacular salamanders, wondrous waterfalls, marvelous mansions, and more!

Axolotls can REGROW BODY PARTS— and even bits of their BRAIN!

There are more than 350 SHIPWRECKS off the coast of Canada's Sable Island, in Nova Scotia.

The United States is home to more than 700 ROLLER COASTERS.

In 2019 alone, North Americans reported about 6,000 UFO SIGHTINGS.

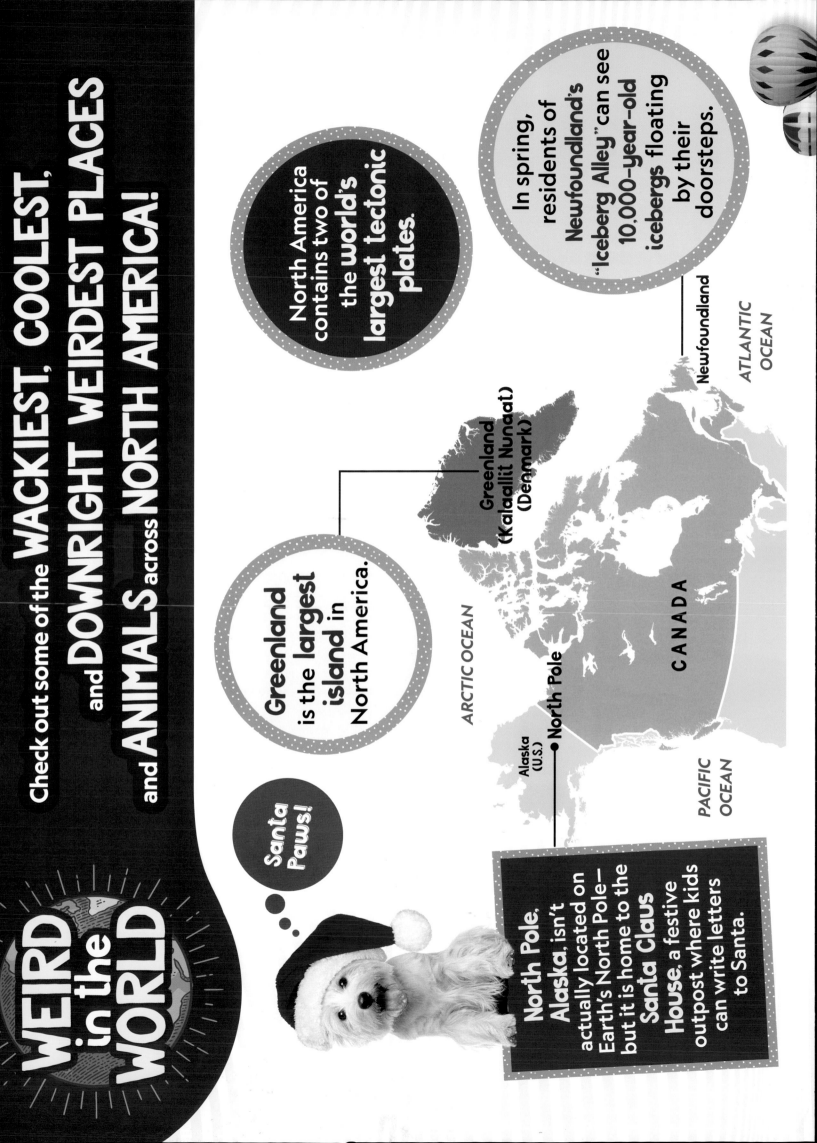

WEIRD in the WORLD

Check out some of the WACKIEST, COOLEST, and DOWNRIGHT WEIRDEST PLACES and ANIMALS across NORTH AMERICA!

North America contains two of the world's largest tectonic plates.

In spring, residents of Newfoundland's "Iceberg Alley" can see 10,000-year-old icebergs floating by their doorsteps.

Greenland is the largest island in North America.

Santa Paws!

North Pole, Alaska, isn't actually located on Earth's North Pole—but it is home to the Santa Claus House, a festive outpost where kids can write letters to Santa.

Greenland (Kalaallit Nunaat) (Denmark)

Newfoundland

ATLANTIC OCEAN

ARCTIC OCEAN

North Pole

Alaska (U.S.)

CANADA

PACIFIC OCEAN

BY theNUMBERS

Get ready for a supercharged ride!

Kingda Ka at Six Flags Great Adventure in New Jersey, U.S.A., is not only the world's tallest roller coaster—it's the world's second fastest, too! Hang on tight and check it out ...

HEIGHT:

456 FEET
(139 M)

That's as tall as a **45-STORY** building!

DROP:

418 FEET (127 M)

129-FOOT-TALL (39-M)
CAMEL HUMP

SPEED:

128 MPH (206 KM/H)

RIDE:

50.6 SECONDS

LENGTH:

3,118 FEET (950 M)

BONKERS BUILDINGS

Biomuseo
Panama City, Panama

At the entrance of the Panama Canal, the Biomuseo stands proud in all its colorful glory. The angular building is by world-famous architect Frank Gehry. It is as if the building is rising up from the water. The design reflects the way that Panama began forming millions of years ago as it rose out of the sea, uniting North and South America in the process. This natural history museum is dedicated to Panama's biodiversity and its incredible variety of unique wildlife. Positioned in a 5.9-acre (2.4-ha) botanical park, the building's vivid color attracts clouds of butterflies and moths. Yep, even the bugs are enjoying the vibrant architecture!

THE TEMPERATURE INSIDE THE HOTEL IS ALWAYS BETWEEN 27° AND 41°F (MINUS 3° AND 5°C).

Hôtel de Glace
Québec, Canada

Imagine rebuilding a hotel every year. Sounds impossible, right? But that's exactly what happens at Hôtel de Glace. Made entirely from snow and ice, this enchanting crystal palace melts away each spring as temperatures rise, and is then rebuilt in a new form the following winter. A team of around 50 to 100 artists and engineers from all over the world work together to create the new masterpiece, using up to 30,000 tons (27,000 t) of snow and 500 tons (450 t) of ice to build features such as ice sculptures, snow arches, and even an ice slide! Sleeping there isn't as cold as you'd expect thanks to sleeping bags, rugs, and mattresses—some rooms have fireplaces, too.

Museum of Pop Culture

Seattle, Washington, U.S.A.

On the inside, this museum celebrates everything from rock-and-roll to science fiction—but it's the outside that's got everyone talking! It would be hard not to notice this striking structure, with its dazzling metallic glow. It is made from 140,000 square feet (13,006 sq m) of stainless steel and painted aluminum—21,000 pieces in all—which catch and reflect the light like a giant disco ball! Another creation by Frank Gehry, he designed the building's ripples and curving lines to reflect the way that music and culture are always changing and flowing.

Locals have nicknamed the museum "the Blob."

Color-Coded Buildings

Greenland

The colors of Greenland's rainbow villages are part of a secret code! Each building was originally painted depending on its function—green for police and post offices, yellow for hospitals, and so on. Houses were even painted according to the jobs of the people living there. This system was introduced in the 1800s after wooden kit houses had been sent from Scandinavia to Greenland to construct new settlements. The color-coding was thought up to help people find their way around before houses were numbered or streets had names. It was also done to make the settlements visible from the sea.

FOOD FRENZY

Mashed Potato Wrestling
Barnesville, Minnesota, U.S.A.

Potatoes are a mealtime favorite in many countries, but potatoes in a wrestling ring ... now that's quite a mash-up! It turns out that mashed potato wrestling is a thing, and these spud-tacular events happen in various parts of America, including at the annual Barnesville Potato Days Festival. The action takes place in a ring made from hay bales, filled with potato flakes, water, and leftover potato scraps. Yummy! Contestants compete in two rounds, each lasting three minutes, to pin down their opponent the most times. Other challenges include potato peeling contests and mashed potato sculpting. You might be thinking that all this sounds like a waste of food, but think again—local cattle gobble up the leftover mush.

Ben and Jerry's Flavor Graveyard
Vermont, U.S.A.

Do you want to know what happens to Ben and Jerry's ice-cream flavors that go extinct? If they're lucky, they wind up buried in the Ben and Jerry's Flavor Graveyard, where fans can pay their respects in person. Perhaps a flavor isn't popular anymore, or the ingredients become too expensive. Whatever the reason for retirement, they're remembered in this graveyard for the "dearly de-pinted." Just like a regular graveyard, this one has headstones with messages, but in this case the inscription is for each flavor. They have even taken things to the next level by holding a Flavor Funeral. For ice cream, extinction isn't always the end: Popular flavors may be brought back!

Other recently retired flavors include Wavy Gravy and Dastardly Mash!

COOL BRITANNIA
Vanilla ice cream with strawberries and fudge-covered shortbread

COOL BRITANNIA
A flavour so smashing-
& yet it fouled out;
Strawberries & shortbread-
a love match devout
But sadly it missed
all the fame it deserved,
A bit too much English
put into the serve.
1989-1990

Strange Sodas

**Lititz,
Pennsylvania, U.S.A.**

If you love soda but are bored of the same old flavors, Candy*ology in Lititz, Pennsylvania, is the perfect shop for you! The walls are lined with weird and wonderful options including Blue Cheese Dressing Soda, Dirt Soda, and Grass Soda. These are all odd for sure, but would you have the stomach to sip Dog Drool or Unicorn Yack? The labels claim these are actually regular flavors—orange lemon and raspberry orange cream—but can you believe them?

IF SODA ISN'T YOUR THING, THE STORE ALSO STOCKS BACON-FLAVORED LIP BALM AND HAM CANDY CANES!

Bubblegum Alley

**San Luis Obispo,
California, U.S.A.**

The alley wall, known as Bubblegum Alley, is 15 feet (4.5 m) high, 70 feet (21 m) long, and completely covered in chewed-up gum! OK, it may sound gross, but the effect is actually pretty special. Tourists add wads to the wall every day, so it's always changing and evolving. Some believe it could have started as far back as the 1940s as part of a school graduation, while others think it was a result of rivalry between a local high school and a university in the 1950s. Of course, the gum wall is not loved by all—some locals think it's unhygienic and should be cleaned off. But when the wall is scraped clean, it doesn't stay gum-free for long!

COOL CAVES

Stalacpipe Organ
Luray Caverns, Virginia, U.S.A.

These caverns in Virginia are part of a working musical instrument known as the Great Stalacpipe Organ. It uses rubber mallets to tap and play the stalactites that hang naturally from the cavern ceilings, which make different sounds depending on their size! A scientist and mathematician named Leland W. Sprinkle built the instrument over three years in the 1950s, and it is now a popular tourist stop. It's even played by an organist for wedding ceremonies.

Covering 3.5 acres (1.4 ha) this is the largest musical instrument in the world.

Ra Paulette's Caves
New Mexico, U.S.A.

This may look like a palace, but it's actually a hand-carved desert cave. And it's all the work of American sculptor Ra Paulette. Found in the desert, north of Santa Fe, it's just one of his sandstone masterpieces, transporting visitors to another world. To build them, Paulette tunneled into the soft cliffs by digging and chiseling. Some of his epic templelike creations are 40 feet (12 m) tall—that's as high as a four-story building—with intricate textures and patterns. Each cave is unique, and includes features such as skylights, special spots for candles, and columns. So peaceful are these spaces, some have been used as spiritual retreats for meditation and healing.

It's crystal clear that this cave is weird!

SCIENTISTS ESTIMATE THE CAVES' **LARGEST CRYSTAL** HAS BEEN GROWING FOR OVER **500,000 YEARS.**

Naica Crystal Caves,
Chihuahuan Desert, Mexico

These 36-foot (11-m)-long beauties are among the largest natural crystals ever to be discovered. Each one weighs up to 55 tons (49 t), which is about as heavy as nine adult male African elephants. In 2000, a team of miners found the gigantic gypsum crystals 1,000 feet (300 m) beneath Naica mountain in Mexico, inside a cave now known as the Cave of Crystals. Over thousands of years, a mineral called selenite formed these colossal crystals, thanks to the optimum conditions found within the cave. Immersed in hot, mineral-rich water, the crystals grew and grew to the breathtaking size they are today.

HORSETAIL FALL'S
FIREFALL

Yosemite, California, U.S.A.

WEIRD WONDERS

See the optical illusion that turns water into fire!

This narrow waterfall tumbles a dizzying

2,000 FEET (610 M)

down El Capitan's rocks.

This incredible sight is becoming one of Yosemite National Park's most popular attractions. For 11 and a half months of the year, a small waterfall on the side of the 3,000-foot (910-m) rock formation known as El Capitan goes mostly unnoticed. But then, in the last two weeks of February, if the conditions are just right—meaning a clear sky and the presence of enough snow to make the waterfall flow—the setting sun lights up the water so the fall glows bright orange, as if it's on fire. The amazing sight has come to be known as a "firefall," and attracts photographers and visitors from all around the world.

No wonder this site is so flame-ous!

MADCAP MUSEUMS

Neon Museum
Las Vegas, Nevada, U.S.A.

Las Vegas is famed for the vibrant signs that line the Strip, but what happens when those signs are no longer wanted? Many of them end up in the Neon Boneyard. It might sound like a Scooby-Doo location, but it's actually one of the outdoor areas at the Neon Museum. This museum, established in 1996, is dedicated to preserving these sparkling signs from recent history. The boneyard, which is packed with huge light installations from the 1930s to the present day, is best wandered at night, when the restored signs can be seen in their full glory.

The Troll Hole Museum
Alliance, Ohio, U.S.A.

Trolls—magical, cave-dwelling creatures with mops of wild hair—may come from Scandinavian folklore, but thousands of these cute, furry little figures have found their way to the small town of Alliance, Ohio. As of 2018, the Troll Hole Museum was home to a record-breaking 8,130 troll dolls, and the collection has been growing ever since. Today, troll dolls and related memorabilia of all shapes, sizes, and colors fill 14 rooms to the rafters. Here, you can learn everything there is to know about the origins of these fabulous furballs, and meet a host of troll-ified musicians, celebrities, and athletes in a variety of wacky settings, from a pop concert to a pro-football hall of fame.

Mmuseumm

Manhattan, New York, U.S.A.

Want to see something cute? Check out this teeny-tiny museum inside an elevator shaft. Yep, it's so compact that only three people can visit at a time! Mmuseumm is New York City's smallest museum. It displays ordinary everyday objects (the kind people don't pay much attention to a lot of the time!) in order to tell a story about the world that we live in today. Some of the museum's collections are permanent, but others change each year. It is all about creating an organized space in a chaotic life. The museum may be miniature, but there is lots to take in— there is even an audio guide for visitors to learn more about the collections!

One **exhibition** featured items from the closet of the museum **owner's grandmother!**

Gopher Hole Museum

Torrington, Alberta, Canada

If you want to find out what stuffed gophers look like dressed in full costume, then this is the museum for you. Meet the gophers of Torrington, Alberta! The taxidermy has been posed in different mini scenes with beautifully painted backdrops. There are dozens of gophers, all displayed in weird and wonderful costumes in order to show the daily life and history of the town. The creatures wear all kinds of different outfits complete with props, too.

FASCINATING FACTS ABOUT THE

weird but true!

THE WHITE HOUSE, located in Washington, D.C., is the **official workplace** and **residence** of the **president of the United States.**

The White House's hot tub, outdoor shower, and pool are **HEATED BY SOLAR ENERGY.**

Legend has it that the **ghost** of **President Lincoln haunts** the Lincoln Bedroom.

The White House has a

PRIVATE THEATER

where the **FIRST FAMILY** can **WATCH MOVIES** and **TELEVISION.**

The White House has employed a crew of **CALLIGRAPHERS**— who pen everything from dinner invitations to menus—**since 1801.**

PRESIDENT GERALD R. FORD'S SON JACK TOOK **SCUBA-DIVING LESSONS** IN THE WHITE HOUSE POOL.

Friends and family can **SEND LETTERS** directly to the **PRESIDENT** and **FIRST LADY** using a **TOP SECRET PERSONAL ZIP CODE.**

WHITE HOUSE

The White House has a kitchen **DEDICATED ONLY to SWEETS.**

MICHELLE OBAMA'S SECRET SERVICE **CODE NAME WAS "RENAISSANCE."**

President Woodrow Wilson's second wife, Edith, earned **the nickname "FIRST LADY PRESIDENT"** when she **took over MANY PRESIDENTIAL DUTIES** after her husband fell ill.

That's weird!

President **Herbert Hoover's son** had **PET ALLIGATORS** that crawled around the **WHITE HOUSE GROUNDS.**

What's **Weird** About This**?**

It may sound like make-believe, but on the Pitch Lake in Trinidad and Tobago, you can walk on water. This 100-acre (40-ha) lake is in fact the world's largest natural deposit of asphalt—10 million tons (9.1 million t) in total! The lake is a peculiar mixture of liquid and solid. Be careful before taking a stroll, though. Some areas are like quicksand, making it incredibly dangerous. The surface of the lake is patchy with some areas feeling totally solid, others springy like sponge, and even parts that are more like lake water. The deepest part of the Pitch Lake is estimated to be 250 feet (76 m). As well as being popular with tourists, the lake is mined for its asphalt, which is used for building bridges, roads, and paving.

BY the NUMBERS

GENERAL SHERMAN

HEIGHT:

275 FEET (83 M)

6.8 FEET
(2.1 M) IN DIAMETER

VOLUME:

52,500 CUBIC FEET
(1,487 CUBIC M)

BASE:

OVER 36 FEET (11 M) IN DIAMETER

Meet the biggest living tree on the planet.

It may not be the tallest, but General Sherman is the world's biggest tree by volume—which is the total amount of space that it takes up. The enormous redwood is a giant sequoia, and you can find this beast of a tree in the Giant Forest at California's Sequoia National Park. It's estimated that this tree is 2,000 years old. Some giant sequoias have lived to be more than 3,000 years old, so this tree may still have another thousand years of living and growing to do.

Approximately
2,000 YEARS OLD

WEIRD DAYS OUT

Bug Carousel

Bronx, New York, U.S.A.

This bug-themed carousel at the Bronx Zoo puts a unique spin on the traditional fairground horse. You can ride on anything from a praying mantis to a grasshopper! Of course, a carousel wouldn't be complete without cheerful fairground music, would it? The Bug Carousel goes one step further with tunes composed using real insect sounds. Each colorful critter has been carved from basswood and beautifully painted in accurate detail, meaning visitors can learn while they enjoy the ride.

The **Bug Carousel** features **64 different types** of insects.

Underwater Music Festival

Key West, Florida, U.S.A.

Diving gear is essential at this music festival on Looe Key in the Florida Keys—it happens 20 feet (6 m) below the water's surface! Underwater speakers pump out an ocean-themed playlist, including songs like "Yellow Submarine" by the Beatles and "Fins" by Jimmy Buffett, while the band mime along with instruments created by a local artist. Music fans can dive down to enjoy the tunes as they explore the reef, while those who prefer dry land can enjoy the underwater beats from the radio. The festival is a ton of fun, but it's got a serious message. It aims to remind people about the importance of preserving the coral reef.

Cow Dung Throw

Prairie du Sac, Wisconsin, U.S.A.

Forget throwing a javelin or a discus, at the Wisconsin State Cow Chip Throw, contestants lob cow chips (aka cow dung)! The festival continues a tradition that started in the 1970s. The idea is pretty simple: Adult competitors start with two chips (children compete with one chip each) and see who can throw it farthest. Oh, and gloves are banned! That's right, you've really got to go for it. If they so choose, players are allowed to lick their fingers before picking up their dung. Why? Word has it that this technique helps with that all-important grip!

THE RULES STATE THAT AN INDIVIDUAL COW CHIP MUST BE A MINIMUM OF SIX INCHES (15 CM) IN DIAMETER.

Radish Sculpting

Oaxaca, Mexico

Pumpkins are carved at Halloween, so why not radishes at Christmas? Noche de Rábanos means Night of the Radishes, and it's when the red-skinned veg is carved into everything from intricate figurines to miniature churches. Radish carving is a pre-Christmas tradition in Oaxaca, Mexico. It was started by local farmers who would display their carved radishes as a way to showcase their produce at the market. Customers loved the displays, and many bought them to decorate their table at Christmas. In 1897, December 23 was officially made Night of the Radishes, and it is still celebrated with a radish-carving competition.

PERSONALITY QUIZ

Your perfect day out in North America would be ...

Take this quiz and keep track of your answers to reveal your results.

1 What word describes you best?
a. Curious
b. Adventurous
c. Brainy
d. Calm

2 Your favorite subject in school is ...
a. Music
b. Physical education
c. History
d. Science

3 In your friend group, you're the ...
a. Creative one; you're full of ideas and love experimenting.
b. Bold one; you're the person that's always up for an adventure.
c. Studious one; people come to you for homework help.
d. Listener; you're always there for your friends.

MOSTLY A's
Your perfect day out would be ... the underwater music festival in Florida! Since you're not afraid to try new things, grab that snorkel and get groovy. This is the ideal way to satisfy your creative curiosity and indulge your passion for music, so what's not to love?

MOSTLY B's
Your perfect day out would be ... the Kingda Ka roller coaster in New Jersey, so climb on board and get ready to hold on to your hat! What better way to indulge your thirst for fun and fascination with the way things work—all while scoring a supercharged thrill.

4. Which of these are you most likely to attend?

a. Festival
b. Sports club
c. Book group
d. Yoga class

5. What is your favorite type of TV show?

a. Drama
b. Action
c. Documentary
d. Travel

6. What's your dream job?

a. Rock star
b. Engineer
c. Explorer
d. Biologist

7. In your spare time, you're mostly ...

a. Being creative
b. Out and about
c. Reading
d. Connecting with nature

8. Pick your dream vacation activity

a. Scuba diving; exploring the ocean would be amazing!
b. Anything as long as it will give me a thrill!
c. Exploring a new city
d. Peaceful nature walks spotting wildlife

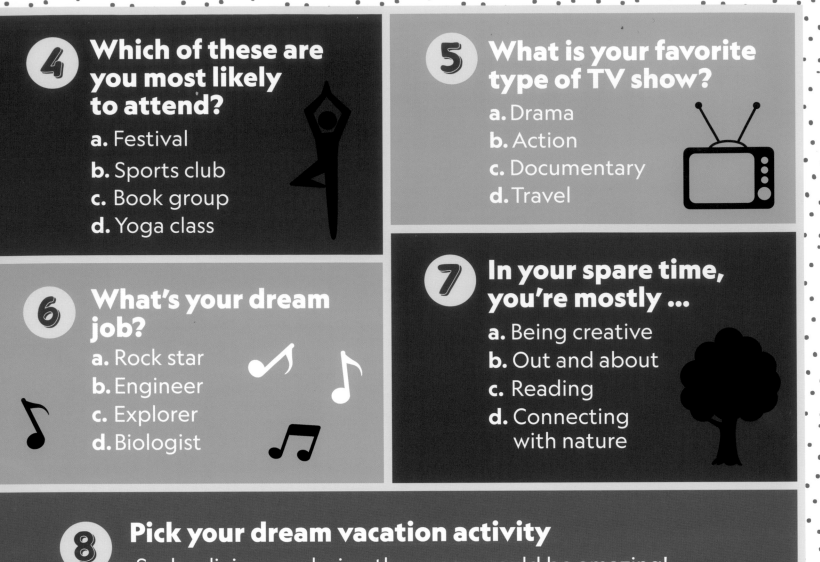

MOSTLY C's
Your perfect day out would be ... a trip to Greenland to explore the color-coded buildings. You love history and you get excited when you can find out cool new things. What could be more fun than wandering around rainbow streets?

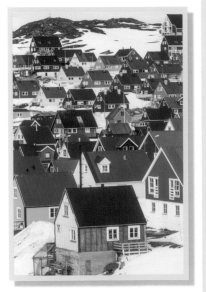

MOSTLY D's
Your perfect day out would be ... a walk to see the General Sherman in real life! You are happiest away from the city, surrounded by peaceful nature. Soak up the tranquil surroundings and explore this ancient beast of a tree.

CATCH A WAVE

Bermuda Triangle
North Atlantic Ocean

Over the years, there have been countless tales of boats and planes disappearing without a trace over this ominous area in the Atlantic Ocean. There are heaps of conspiracy theories including everything from alien abductions to fire crystals from the lost city of Atlantis. But it turns out that the mystery of the Bermuda Triangle could all be put down to some great big waves! This part of the Atlantic (between Bermuda, Puerto Rico, and Florida) experiences many storms and hurricanes, and with them come "rogue waves," caused by storms colliding from many directions. They're so powerful they could destroy whole vessels without leaving a trace.

"ROGUE WAVES" IN THE BERMUDA TRIANGLE CAN BE UP TO 100 FEET (30.5 M) TALL!

$$\sum_{k=0}^{n}$$

The Wave
Coyote Buttes, Arizona, U.S.A.

This rippling red sandstone formation began forming 190 million years ago as the sand dunes calcified and turned into solid, compact rock. Wind and rain have eroded its surfaces over time, creating beautiful sweeping shapes and lines, earning the rocks their name—the Wave. These breathtaking formations of orange and red can be seen in the Coyote Buttes North area of the Utah-Arizona border, 5,225 feet (1,600 m) above sea level.

Museo Soumaya
Mexico City, Mexico

This glimmering gallery has been making waves in Mexico City since it was built in 2011. Inside the futuristic building are 66,000 pieces of art, mostly from Central America and Europe. Curvy and wavelike in shape, the Museo Soumaya covers an area of 170,000 square feet (15,800 sq m) and is six stories high. The metallic silver tiles that cover the building glint like fish scales as they catch sunlight at different angles. But not everybody is a fan of this eye-catching construction. Some have even described the design as "tasteless."

Dog Surfing
California, U.S.A.

From wacky waves to waggy waves—welcome to the world of dog surfing! Adventurous pooches and their owners come together to compete at the World Dog Surfing Championships. Canine competitors have 12 minutes each to ride as many waves as they can. They're judged on things like how long they stay on the board, the size of the wave, and technique—tricks are a bonus! Along with the headline event, there's also a costume contest for humans and dogs. And it all happens on the Northern California coast.

Canine competitors wear a life vest known as a canine flotation device to keep them safe.

Quirky CREATURES!

Resplendent Quetzal
Mexico

Is this the world's most beautiful bird? Just look at the luminous emerald green feathers of the resplendent quetzal. These vibrant birds live in Central America's tropical forests. Ancient Maya and Aztec peoples considered them sacred and wore their fabulous feathers during ceremonies.

Crab Invasion
Bay of Pigs, Cuba

Every spring, red-black-and-yellow crabs swarm Cuba's Bay of Pigs for weeks at a time. The pincered creatures take over the town as they travel from the forests to the sea. This happens after mating season. The migration causes chaos for local traffic! But it's not a walk in the park for the crabs, who face obstacles including swimming pools and cars.

Baird's Tapir
Central America

Baird's tapir can grow as big as eight feet (2.4 m) and weigh up to 660 pounds (300 kg)—making it Central America's largest native animal. Tapirs are distantly related to horses and rhinos but have stubby legs and round bodies. This doesn't stop them from being speedy and thriving in a variety of environments, from rugged mountains to rainforests. With their long snout, they look like a mix between a cow and an elephant. But its substantial schnoz has an important purpose: It helps the tapir grab hard-to-reach food.

I nose there's food around here!

Star-Nosed Mole
North America

Star-nosed moles have a burst of tiny tentacles on their nostrils. These are always moving to help them figure out their surroundings and find prey. The moles' tentacles help make them the world's fastest eaters—they can find and devour a meal in less than a quarter of a second!

Rhinoceros Beetle
Central America

It doesn't take a genius to figure out why this critter is called a rhinoceros beetle! It's also known as the Hercules beetle, after the mythological hero who was famed for his strength—and not without reason! This beetle is the strongest insect in the world relative to its body size.

Adams River Salmon Run
British Columbia, Canada

Adams River's brilliant ruby red hue doesn't come from the water. It's the color of over a million sockeye salmon migrating—also known as the Adams River salmon run. After two to three years of living in the high seas of the northeast Pacific ocean, the fish make the two-to-three-week journey home. They navigate through canyons and rapids to their spawning areas 310 miles (500 km) from the ocean. The river only turns red every fourth year, when the number of salmon migrating is very high.

Gila Monster
Southwestern United States and Northwestern Mexico

Meet the largest native lizard in the United States. The Gila (pronounced HEE-luh) monster can grow as big as 22 inches (56 cm) long. Its eye-popping markings make it easy to spot, which is handy because it has a venomous bite—pretty rare for a lizard!

HUMAN-MADE MASTERPIECES

Dr. Seuss House
Talkeetna, Alaska, U.S.A.

Over 20 years ago, a man in Alaska built a log cabin. Nothing strange about that, but he didn't stop with just one cabin. He kept on building upward, cabin upon cabin ... upon cabin! The mega-cabin now has between 14 and 17 floors, some of which are only accessible by ladder, and the entire structure reaches 185 feet (56 m) into the sky. It has been nicknamed the "Dr. Seuss House" after the children's author and cartoonist—it looks like it has come right out of one of his books! This towering construction can't get any higher into the sky because 200 feet (61 m) is officially federal air space.

From the top of the Dr. Seuss House, you can see for 300 miles (480 km)!

Leaves me alone. I want to sleep!

Moss Lady
Victoria, Canada

This mega Moss Lady lies tucked under a soft blanket of moss, with living plants sprouting like hair from the top of her head. Snoozing peacefully, she measures 35 feet (10 m) long—that's about as long as a school bus. The sculpture is made from a combination of boulders, wire, cement, and pipes. It was built in 2015 by an artist named Dale Doebert, who was inspired by a similar sculpture at the Lost Gardens of Heligan in Cornwall, U.K.

Sunken Pirate City

Port Royal, Jamaica

Back in the 17th century, Port Royal was an infamous pirate city, built on sand. When a huge hurricane and tsunami waves hit Jamaica in 1692, Port Royal was swallowed by the sea. In total, around 33 acres (13 ha) of the city sank beneath the waves. Up until the 1900s, locals claimed the city's ghostly roofs were still visible beneath the water's surface.

Enchanted Highway

Regent, North Dakota, U.S.A.

You may have heard of enchanted forests, but what about an enchanted highway? Well, that's exactly what this North Dakota highway is, now that it's been filled with record-breaking sculptures. The metallic masterpieces lining Highway 21 were all created by a former school principal. A self-taught scrap metal sculptor, Gary Greff wanted to find a way to attract visitors to the town to stop it from being forgotten, so he decided to build a series of sculptures. But not any old sculptures—these are the world's largest metal sculptures.

67

ROCKY WONDERS

Stone Spheres
Diquís Valley, Costa Rica

These boulders may decorate the gardens of many modern Costa Rican homes, but their history dates back centuries. Nobody knows what the mysterious stone spheres, or Diquís Spheres, were made for. They were discovered by workers clearing land in the Diquís Valley back in the 1930s, and they vary in size from ones you can hold in your hand to examples that are eight feet (2.5 m) in diameter. It is thought that ancient makers would chip away at them, using stone tools to create their almost perfect spherical shape.

Devils Tower is so huge that it is visible from space.

Devils Tower
Black Hills, Wyoming, U.S.A.

Devils Tower was formed underground when magma from Earth's mantle rose up between gaps in sedimentary rock and became solid. As the magma cooled, it formed pentagonal- and hexagonal-shaped columns. Despite its massive height— 867 feet (264 m)—Devils Tower was hidden for millions of years! Over time, wind and water wore away areas of sedimentary rock to leave behind the harder igneous rock columns. This extraordinary formation, also known as Bear Lodge, is sacred to many Native American tribes.

Hidden Beach
Marieta Islands, Mexico

Playa del Amor, or Hidden Beach, sits beneath a crater on one of Mexico's uninhabited Marieta Islands. To get there, visitors must either swim or kayak. With its white sand, sparkling water, and hidden location, this secret beach is picture perfect! While the islands formed as a result of volcanic activity, the craters are thought to be damage caused by military testing. The good news is that today the island is swarming with marine life. The area is now protected as a national park and UNESCO reserve.

Fly Geyser
Nevada Desert, Nevada, U.S.A.

This rainbow-colored wonder in the middle of the Nevada desert is human-made—albeit by mistake! So how did this beautiful accident occur? It all started around 100 years ago when residents were looking for water for their crops. They drilled a well and found 200°F (93°C) boiling water—much too hot for what they wanted—so it was abandoned. Decades later, a geyser (or hot spring) formed at the spot. Then, in 1964, an energy company built another well nearby. But the water wasn't hot enough for what they needed. This well was abandoned, and the hot water burst out to form a second geyser—Fly Geyser. It "stole" the water pressure from the original geyser and can fire boiling water five feet (1.5 m) into the air! Fly Geyser is always growing as the minerals from the water solidify into weird shapes.

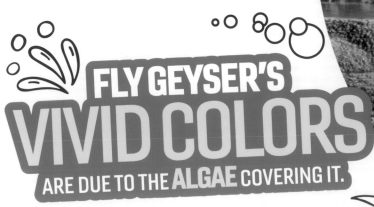

FLY GEYSER'S VIVID COLORS ARE DUE TO THE ALGAE COVERING IT.

QUIZ WHIZ

Think you're a whiz at Weird But True?
Test your knowledge with these head-scratchers!

1 Horsetail Fall's Firefall in California, U.S.A., glows bright orange because:

a. It is made of lava.

b. It contains bioluminescent bacteria.

c. A rare combination of environmental conditions causes the setting sun to light up the water.

d. Scientists are shining lasers through it.

2 What is one of the best ways to reach the Museo Subacuático de Arte?

a. Scuba diving

b. Hiking

c. Hot-air balloon

d. Dogsled

3 A mysterious crash that occurred outside of Roswell, New Mexico, U.S.A., in 1947 was most likely caused by:

a. A weather balloon

b. A top secret government project

c. An alien spaceship

d. Pranksters creating a hoax

4 The White House in Washington, D.C., features:

a. A solar-powered pool
b. A kitchen devoted to sweets
c. A private theater
d. All of the above

5 Which creature overruns Cuba's Bay of Pigs each spring?

a. Pigs
b. Sharks
c. Crabs
d. Vultures

6 Lake Kliluk's multicolored spots are caused by:

a. Tiny colorful fish
b. Mineral deposits
c. Reflections of the northern lights
d. A human artist

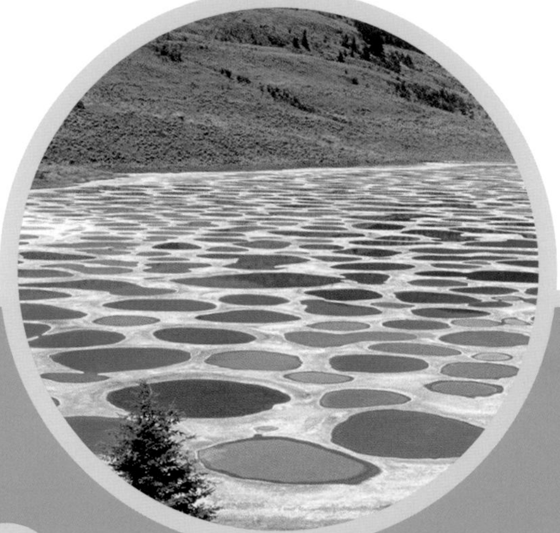

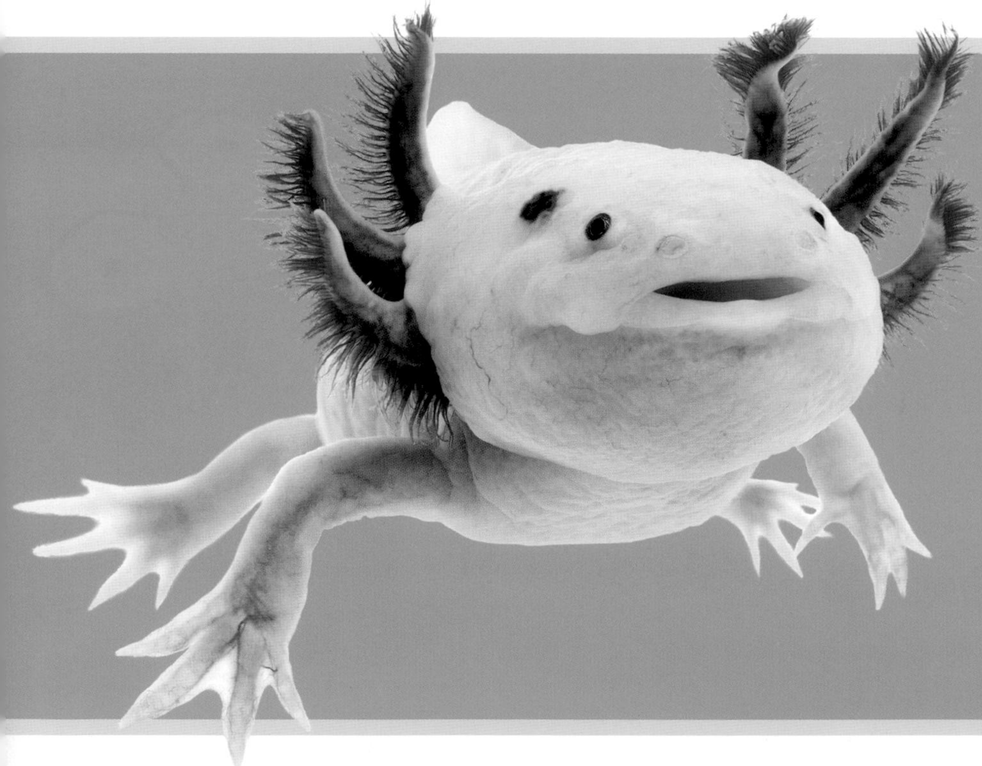

7 What is this creature?

a. Fringed sea lizard
b. Nudibranch
c. Smiling pinkfish
d. Axolotl

8 The grasshopper mouse often communicates by:

a. Howling
b. Singing
c. Fancy dance moves
d. Scent

Answers: 1. c, 2. a, 3. b, 4. d, 5. c, 6. b, 7. d, 8. a

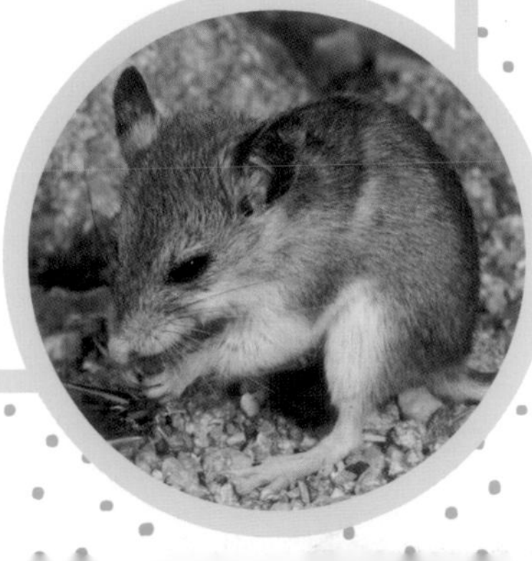

Keep an eye out for weird.

SPECTACULAR SOUTH AMERICA

Colorful carnivals, bizarre bugs, mysterious mummies, and strange sights galore!

Some South
American mummies
are more than
2,000 YEARS
older than the
Egyptian ones.

The kinkajou
is also called
HONEY BEAR,
but it is
actually related
to raccoons.

WEIRD in the WORLD!

Explore some of the WILDEST and WEIRDEST PLACES, CREATURES, and SIGHTS in SOUTH AMERICA!

Millions of years ago, South America's east coast was connected to the west coast of Africa. Check them out on a map and you'll see they match up!

South America is made up of just 12 countries but is home to about 450 recorded languages!

255 MILLION YEARS AGO

PANTHALASSA (PANTHALASSIC OCEAN)

Asia

North America

Europe

South America

Africa

PALEO-TETHYS OCEAN

TETHYS OCEAN

Southeast Asia

Australia

Antarctica

NORTH AMERICA

AFRICA

SOUTH AMERICA

ANTARCTICA

Pacific Ocean

Atlantic Ocean

ATLANTIC OCEAN

Caribbean Sea

COLOMBIA

VENEZUELA

GUYANA

SURINAME

French Guiana (France)

ECUADOR

Galápagos Islands (Ecuador)

PERU

A m a z o n   r a i n f o r e s t

BRAZIL

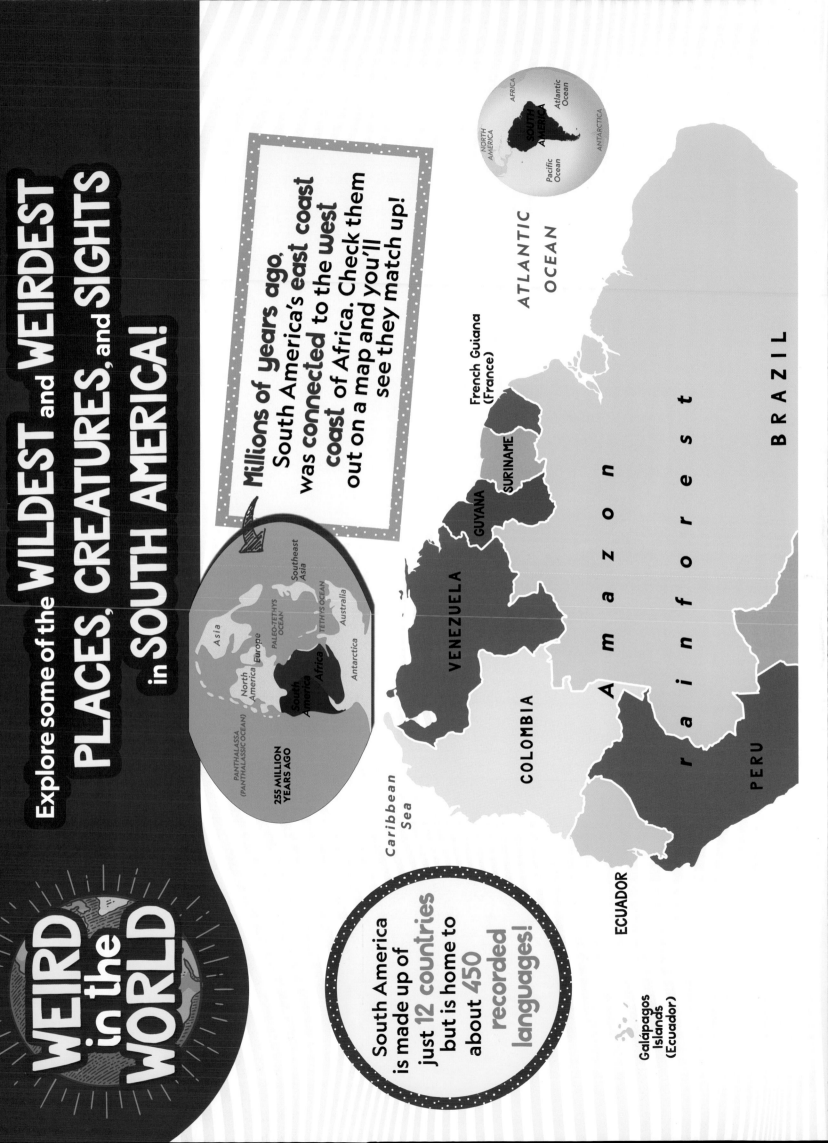

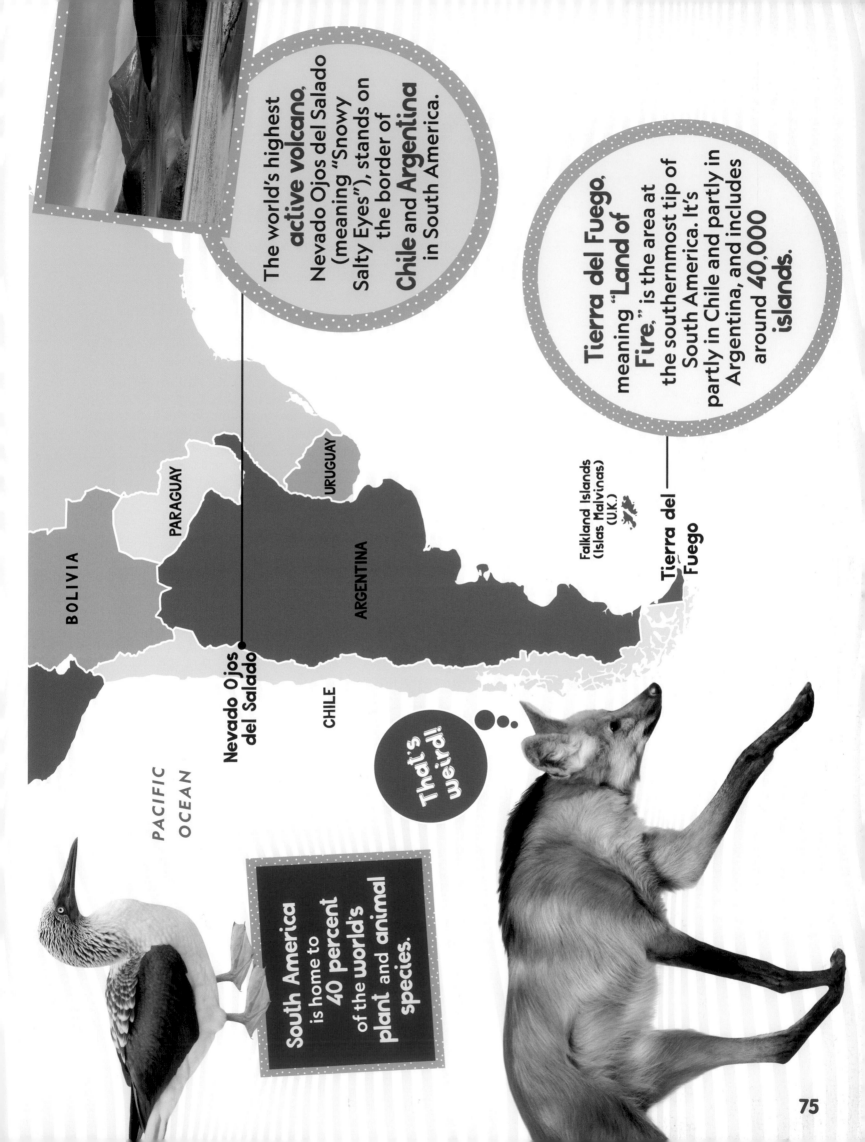

The world's highest **active volcano**, Nevado Ojos del Salado (meaning "Snowy Salty Eyes"), stands on the border of **Chile and Argentina** in South America.

Tierra del Fuego, meaning **"Land of Fire,"** is the area at the southernmost tip of South America. It's partly in Chile and partly in Argentina, and includes around **40,000 islands**.

URUGUAY

PARAGUAY

BOLIVIA

ARGENTINA

Falkland Islands (Islas Malvinas) (U.K.)

Tierra del Fuego

Nevado Ojos del Salado

CHILE

PACIFIC OCEAN

That's weird!

South America is home to **40 percent** of the world's **plant and animal species**.

PECULIAR PLACES

El Ojo Floating Island
Buenos Aires, Argentina

In a wild, marshy area near the city of Buenos Aires there is a small lake that is so perfectly circular it seems as if it couldn't be natural. Even stranger, there's a floating, circular island in the lake that rotates! Known as el Ojo, or "the Eye," the mysterious lake has become famous, and some say it must have been made by ancient peoples. However, experts think it is a natural phenomenon. Floating islands are rare, but they can form in marshlands from mats of floating plants. As the island spins in the current, it bumps against the edges of the lake, shaping both the lake and itself into circles.

The floating island is 387 feet (118 m) in diameter—about as long as a football field.

The Equator! (Or Is It?)
Quito, Ecuador

Just north of Quito, the capital of Ecuador, you can stand on the Equator—the imaginary line that runs all the way around the widest part of the planet, dividing the northern and southern hemispheres. At the Mitad del Mundo, or Middle of the World, there's a yellow Equator line painted on the ground, leading up to a towering monument. Here, tourists can stand with their feet on either side of it for photos. There's just one problem—they put the line in the wrong place! Modern satellite measurements reveal that the Equator is 328 to 492 feet (100–150 m) farther north. The nearby ancient ruins of Catequilla, built 1,200 years ago by Native peoples, sit exactly on the Equator!

Caño Cristales
Meta, Colombia

In a remote region of the Serranía de la Macarena (a mountain range in Colombia), an hour's trek into the wilderness, there's a rainbow-colored river that only appears for a few months each year, sometime between June and December. The Caño Cristales, meaning "crystal channel," has a variety of vibrant colors, especially a bright, pinkish red. That might sound like something out of a sci-fi movie, or perhaps the result of a worrying pollution problem—but it's actually neither. It's completely natural. When the combination of the water level and the warm sunshine is just right, a riverweed that grows in the water blooms bright red. Along with the yellow sand, green mossy rocks, turquoise water, and dark river depths, it creates a breathtaking display known to locals as the "liquid rainbow."

OLIVEIRA'S STORE HOLDS A GUINNESS WORLD RECORD FOR HAVING THE MOST ICE-CREAM FLAVORS IN THE WORLD.

Heladería Coromoto
Merida, Venezuela

Would you like to try beef or garlic ice cream? You can taste these, and a whole lot more, at Heladería Coromoto, a world-famous and extremely weird ice-cream parlor in Venezuela. Ice-cream maker Manuel da Silva Oliveira started the store after perfecting his skills in other ice-cream companies. He began with normal flavors like vanilla and chocolate, but wanted to create something different. After inventing a recipe for avocado ice cream, he caught the bug for creating ever wackier flavors. On any particular day, you can choose from around 60 different types of ice cream, but Oliveira has created 860 of them altogether. Some of them are based on popular Venezuelan foods, such as pabellón criollo (beef with rice and black beans), mushroom, chili, and hot dog flavors!

77

COULD IT BE MAGIC?

Bichacue Yath
Cali, Colombia

This magical nature garden, called Bichacue Yath, lies just outside the city of Cali, Colombia. Visitors come to enjoy some peace and quiet, see the beautiful flowers, and spot wild animals. But as they peer through the bushes, they'll also notice some strange faces staring back at them! Hidden among the plants are dozens of fairies, elves, gnomes, and goblins. They might look real for a moment, but they're actually carved from wood or shaped from the soil, with flowers and leaves all around them. Colombian folktales and local beliefs tell of countless magical spirits and fairy beings, often said to guard forests, streams, and other wild places. Here at Bichacue Yath, they are celebrated alongside the natural world.

Campanopolis
González Catán, Argentina

Campanopolis is one seriously weird village. It's recycled from old buildings, resembles a set from a medieval fantasy movie, and no one actually lives there! The whole village is the work of Antonio Campana, a wealthy businessman who owned a chain of supermarkets. In 1976, he was told he had only five years to live. So he quit his job, bought some land, and started creating his dream village, using reclaimed materials. His wacky designs include curly chimneys, cobbled streets, castle towers, secret alleyways, and spiral staircases that lead nowhere. Houses are decorated with coins, old typewriters, and metal flowers. Around the village there are lakes with wooden bridges and a forest full of fairy cottages. As for Campana, he beat his illness and lived another 24 years!

Alasitas Festival

La Paz, Bolivia

Every January, in La Paz, the capital of Bolivia, you can buy everything your heart desires for just a few pennies. Why so cheap? Because the items are tiny! At the month-long festival of Alasitas, the market squares are filled with stalls selling miniature versions of everything—from washing machines, cameras, computers, and clothes, to cars, boats, and even whole houses. People buy themselves, or each other, mini versions of whatever they wish for. Then they take their purchases home and hang them on a little statue of Ekeko, a traditional local god of good fortune and happiness in the home, in the hope that he'll grant them their wish in the coming year.

AT THE FESTIVAL, YOU CAN EVEN BUY A MINIATURE "DIPLOMA" FROM A TOP UNIVERSITY!

Weirdly Cute!

Pink Fairy Armadillo

Where's my wand?

It's not really a fairy, but the pink fairy armadillo is a rare, magical sight in the sandy deserts of Argentina. It's hard to spot one, as they mostly stay under the sand and only come out at night. They're also tiny! Some armadillos can grow to five feet (1.5 m) long, but the pink fairy variety only measures between five and six inches (13–16 cm). Under its soft, pinkish shell, it's covered in fluffy white fur, with a cute snout, tiny eyes, and big claws for digging in the sand. It can also disappear like magic, burrowing under the ground in seconds.

WEIRD WONDERS

This salt lake covers over

4,086 SQUARE MILES
(10,582 sq km)

on a plateau high up in the Andes.

Can you figure out what's happening in this photo? At first glance, this person seems to be riding their bike in the sky, or perhaps cycling on water. In fact, they are crossing the breathtaking Salar de Uyuni in Bolivia. It's the world's biggest salt flat—a vast, white, almost totally flat expanse of salt, 80 miles (130 km) wide, left behind after an ancient lake dried up. In the rainy season, from January to April, it's covered in a shallow layer of still water, transforming it into the biggest mirror anywhere on Earth.

SALAR DE UYUNI

Uyuni, Bolivia

But where's the pepper?

WEIRD VACATION DESTINATIONS

Skylodge Pods
Cusco, Peru

If you're scared of heights, look away now! To get to this hotel, you have to trek up a 1,300-foot (400-m)-high mountainside and inch your way along a *via ferrata*—a climbing path with metal ladders and cables bolted to the rock to cling on to. When you finally reach your room, it's a see-through metal and plexiglass pod fixed to the side of a cliff! The Skylodge Adventure Suites, as they're called, dangle above Peru's Sacred Valley, close to the ancient Inca ruins of Machu Picchu. Each lodge contains a dining area, bathroom, and beds. Of course, the view is fantastic, both down to the valley floor, and up to the night sky. Whether you'll be able to relax enough to fall asleep is another matter!

Palacio de Sal
Salar de Uyuni, Bolivia

Bolivia's Salar de Uyuni salt flat (see previous page), high in the Andes mountains, is popular with tourists, so it makes sense to build a hotel there. The problem is, there aren't many trees or other building materials in the area. So instead of carting tons of concrete to the site, the builders used what they had on hand—salt! They created the Palacio de Sal, or Salt Palace, from about one million blocks of salt cut from the ground, each about the size of a microwave oven. There was a problem with the building material though—salt dissolves in water! Each year, during the rainy season, some parts of the hotel crumbled and had to be rebuilt. Eventually, the original hotel was closed due to sanitation issues, but a new one was built 15 miles (25 km) away.

It's not just the walls that are made of salt— there are salt sculptures for decoration, too.

Supersize Swimming Pool
Algarrobo, Chile

Stay at Chile's luxurious San Alfonso del Mar resort and you can take a dip in its stunning swimming pool—one of the biggest in the world! Surrounded by hotel buildings on one side and the Pacific Ocean on the other, the artificial 3,323-foot (1,013-m)-long lagoon stretches along the seafront. You can swim in various parts of it, but other areas are set aside for water-skiers, kayaks, and even small yachts. Why build such a big pool right next to the sea? It's because the ocean here, though beautiful, is pretty cold, with dangerous currents, so you shouldn't actually swim in it!

SAN ALFONSO DEL MAR'S **SUPERSIZE POOL** TAKES UP MORE SPACE THAN **60 OLYMPIC-SIZE SWIMMING POOLS!**

Montaña Mágica Lodge
Neltume, Chile

Imagine staying inside a miniature magic mountain, covered in rainforest plants, with a real waterfall cascading past your window! Head to the Montaña Mágica Lodge in Chile, and you can! Although it looks like something conjured up by a wizard, the lodge is actually a building made of stone and wood, not a real mountain. It's in a nature reserve, surrounded by rainforest where you can spot amazing wild animals, such as the 13-inch (33-cm)-tall pudu, the world's smallest deer, as well as birds, butterflies, condors, and cougars. To get into the lodge, you have to cross a rope bridge from a treetop walkway.

BY the NUMBERS

AMAZON RIVER

The mighty Amazon River flows almost all the way across South America, through Ecuador, Colombia, Peru, and Brazil, surrounded by the huge Amazon rainforest. Though it's not the world's longest river, it is the widest, not to mention the wildest!

LENGTH:
4,000 MILES (6,400 KM)

It all looks different from up here!

SPECIES OF FISH:
2,257

NUMBER OF BRIDGES:
(ACROSS ENTIRE WIDTH)
0

MAXIMUM WIDTH:
(IN THE RAINY SEASON)
25 MILES (40 KM)

AMOUNT OF WATER FLOWING INTO THE SEA PER SECOND:
7,740,000 CUBIC FEET
(220,000 CUBIC M)

WEIRD WONDERS

Take a ride on a swing miles from the nearest playground!

THE SWING AT THE END OF THE WORLD

Baños, Ecuador

Hold on tight! The famous "swing at the end of the world" doesn't look all that special at first glance—but it swings out over the edge of a steep mountain cliff. Thrill-seeking tourists line up to take a turn on the swing and fly out into the emptiness over the valley far below. The swing is attached to a tree house, which is used as a monitoring station to check on a nearby active volcano, Mount Tungurahua. A man who worked there made the swing for his own family to use, but photos of people dangling out over the abyss spread around the world and put the swing on the map!

DRY AS A BONE

Where Rain Never Falls
The World's Driest Desert

If you're going for a trek in the Atacama Desert, don't forget a water bottle! This beautiful, mountainous desert in northern Chile is the world's driest place, apart from Antarctica, where it doesn't rain much and it's too cold for ice to melt! As a whole, the Atacama receives about half an inch (15 mm) of rain per year. But there are places in the middle where not a single drop has ever been recorded. These areas are so dry that there are no plants, not even cacti—just red, gray, and golden rocks, carved into shapes by the wind. Moviemakers often come here to film scenes set on the moon!

Archaeologists believe that there are **thousands** more **mummies** buried beneath the **Atacama Desert's** sand.

Atacama Mummies
Arica, Chile

You've probably heard of the mummies of ancient Egypt—but the Atacama Desert has mummies, too, and they're even more ancient! From around 7,000 years ago, the Chinchorro people mummified their dead and buried them in the dry desert sand. There they lay preserved for thousands of years, only being discovered in 1914. To make a mummy, the Chinchorro stuffed the body with animal hair, dried plants, and sticks, then covered it with mineral paste, adding a wig and a clay mask over the face. Hundreds of mummies have been found so far. You can see some of them in museums in Arica, on Chile's coast, where most of them were discovered.

Mano del Desierto

Antofagasta, Chile

Close to the Pan-American highway—which stretches from Tierra del Fuego all the way to Alaska—there's a ginormous hand reaching up out of the ground. It's the Mano del Desierto, or Hand of the Desert, a 36-foot (11-m)-tall sculpture located outside of Antofagasta, Chile. It's a breathtaking sight for those who stop to take a look up close. Though it's built from iron and concrete, it resembles the desert rocks, making it seem to be a living part of the Atacama itself. It's the "handiwork" of Chilean sculptor Mario Irarrázabal.

Talk to the hand!

THE GIANT MANO DEL DESIERTO IS TWICE THE HEIGHT OF A GIRAFFE.

Weirdly Cute! Viscacha

What is this chilled-out, chubby, yet slightly grumpy-looking creature? It appears to be a cross between a rabbit and a squirrel, with its big ears and long, bushy tail. It's actually a viscacha, a cat-size animal often spotted in the less dry parts of the Atacama, where there are a few desert plants to eat. Viscachas make their homes under and in between desert rocks. During the day, they relax on top of the rocks to catch some rays. At night, when the desert temperature can drop to almost freezing, their thick fur keeps them warm.

HAIR-RAISING!

Catatumbo Lightning

Lake Maracaibo, Venezuela

If you like watching lightning storms, you'll love Lake Maracaibo! The area where the Catatumbo River flows into the lake, close to Venezuela's Caribbean coast, is known for having more lightning than anywhere else in the world. Weather experts think it's caused by warm, wet air rising from the tropical lake mixing with cold winds from the mountains. Thunderclouds form there almost every day, and on more than half the nights of the year, the lake is lit up by almost constant lightning flashes—in fact, there are thought to be more than a million lightning bolts per year.

Lightning bolts are so bright, sailors out at sea once used them to find their way!

Troll Doll Bug

Suriname

This bizarre bug is a baby planthopper from the rainforests of Suriname. When it was first discovered, scientists thought it looked like a troll doll, with its big, sticking-up mass of hair. However, this bug's bouffant actually sticks out of its butt instead of its head! The "hair" is made of strands of wax extruded out of the bug's back end, similar to how spiders spin their silk. It acts as a distraction to predators, and might put them off gobbling up the tiny bug, which is only about a quarter of an inch (6 mm) long.

Emperor Tamarin
Peru, Bolivia, and Brazil

From hair-raisingly scary, to just hairy! The emperor tamarin, a monkey from the Amazon region, is the proud owner of the most fabulous mustache in the animal kingdom. It's white, silky, perfectly pointed, and wider than the tamarin's own head! Both males and females have mustaches, which they probably use to help them spot other emperor tamarins in the jungle. This species was named after the German emperor Wilhelm II, who was also famous for his large mustache—although even his wasn't this impressive!

TODAY, BOLIVIA'S YUNGAS ROAD IS MAINLY USED AS A CYCLE RIDE FOR THRILL-SEEKING TOURISTS.

Don't look over the edge!

Yungas Road
Bolivia

The mountains of Bolivia are home to one of the most hair-raisingly scary roads on the planet. In some parts, the famously deadly Yungas Road is cut into the side of a sheer cliff, with a single track just 10 feet (3.2 m) wide. And it's often flooded with rain and waterfalls. For decades, it was the only road connecting the city of La Paz to the lower-lying region of Yungas. Cars, trucks, and buses drove up and down it daily, squeezing past each other with inches to spare, and sometimes falling off. It was so dangerous that it was eventually replaced with a new, much safer road on a different route.

Bizarre BUGS!

... and spiders!

Goliath Birdeater

When you hear that an animal has the name "birdeater," you might imagine a snake, crocodile, or wild cat. But the Goliath birdeater is none of these. It's actually the world's biggest, heaviest spider. It can grow to the size of a dinner plate, and with its powerful legs and large fangs, it really does sometimes catch birds to drag back to its burrow for its next meal. More often though, it preys on insects, worms, frogs, lizards, and mice.

Peanuthead Bug

The name says it all! This large Amazon rainforest bug has a head that looks like a giant, unshelled peanut. However, scientists think it frightens predators away because to them, it resembles a lizard's head. This makes the bug look like a bigger and more dangerous animal than it really is. If that doesn't work, it spreads its wings, revealing an even bigger decoy—a set of scary fake eyes!

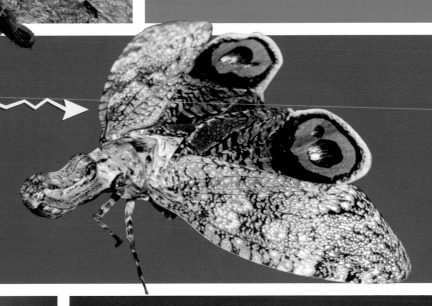

Brazilian Treehopper

No one is sure why this tiny tree-dwelling bug has what looks like a set of weird, lumpy helicopter rotors sticking out of its back. Maybe they put off predators by making the bug look painful to eat. Another theory is that they mimic a type of killer fungus that some-times takes over insects' bodies, making pred-ators think the bug is already dead and would taste gross. Either way, they're no good for flying—the bug uses its wings for that!

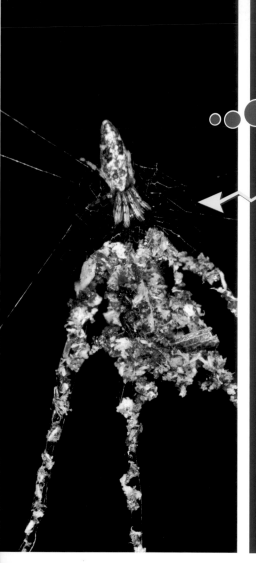

Decoy Spider

This sneaky spider, discovered in a remote part of Peru, has a genius way of scaring off its enemies. The arachnid is tiny, only about 0.2 inch (5 mm) long, and is in danger of being eaten by other spiders, large bugs, frogs, and lizards. So it uses dead flies, bits of leaf, and skin it has shed to build a much bigger fake spider in the middle of its web! By moving around on the web, it can even make its creation twitch and shake, so hungry predators will think it's alive and steer well clear.

Panda Ant

Is it an ant? Is it a tiny, six-legged panda? No, the panda ant is neither of these things! It's actually a type of wasp from Chile and Argentina, which was given the name "panda ant" for obvious reasons! Its black-and-white patterns, which only the female has, act as a warning to predators. The wasp also has a horribly painful sting, earning it another nickname, "cow-killer"—though the sting isn't actually bad enough to kill a cow. Phew!

Giant Silkworm Moth Caterpillar

What's the most dangerous creature on this page? Maybe you think it's the giant bird-eating spider? Think again! The creature you should really steer clear of is this silkworm moth caterpillar found in several South American countries. Its delicate bristles make it look strangely beautiful ... but it's a creepy-crawly killer. One touch of its stinging spines injects deadly venom that's strong enough to kill a human.

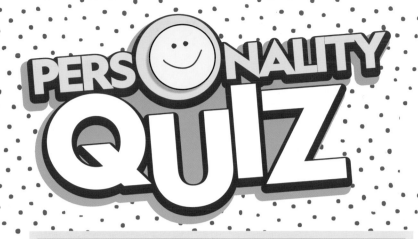

PERSONALITY QUIZ

Which South American Creature Are You?

Write down your answers for each question, **and see which letter you** picked the most often.

1 ***Mmm*, you're feeling hungry! Pick a dish from today's menu:**

a. Leafy salad
b. Roast guinea pig with a fruit garnish
c. Fresh sardines
d. Seaweed surprise

2 Are you a good swimmer?

a. People don't expect me to be, but I am!
b. Not really, but I'll swim if I have to.
c. Not bad—but you should see me dive!
d. Yes, I go swimming every day!

3 How do you like to exercise?

a. Exercise? No thanks!
b. Going for a lovely long run
c. Making moves on the dance floor
d. Scuba diving

4 How would you escape from a hungry jaguar?

a. My only chance is to hide in a tree and hope it doesn't see me.
b. No sweat! It'll never catch me!
c. Jaguars can't fly, so I'd take to the air.
d. I'd run for my life and jump into the sea.

5 You're at a friend's party. Where can you be found?

a. In the yard, just chilling with the plants
b. Singing along with my favorite song!
c. On the dance floor, of course!
d. With a big group of friends

6 Choose a superpower!

a. Turning my head almost all the way around
b. Rotating my ears
c. High-speed flight
d. Sneezing salt out of my nose

7 What's your most noticeable feature?

a. My adorable face
b. My very long legs
c. My fabulous feet!
d. My spiky hairdo

Mostly A's
**You are ...
a three-toed sloth!**
Hanging upside down in a tree, you munch leaves all day, moving ve-ee-ery slowly from branch to branch. You'll venture down to the ground once a week to go to the bathroom. You also drop out of your tree into a river to go for a swim!

Mostly B's
**You are ...
a maned wolf!**
Resembling a tall, fluffy wild dog with a strange bark, you're a unique creature. You roam the grasslands in search of mice, rats, rabbits, guinea pigs, and armadillos to eat, along with your favorite snack, the wolf apple fruit!

Mostly C's
**You are ...
a blue-footed booby!** Check out those feet, baby! In between flying out on sea fishing trips, you love dancing on the seashore, showing off your brilliant blue webbed feet, and posing for many photos.

Mostly D's
**You are ...
a marine iguana!**
The only lizard found in the sea, you're a fabulous swimmer and diver, and a fast runner. When not basking in the sun with your friends, you dart in and out of the waves to collect seaweed and algae from the rocks.

OUT OF THIS WORLD!

Niterói Contemporary Art Museum

Niterói, Brazil

The first time you catch a glimpse of this strange object, you might think, "What's that flying saucer doing there?" However, the space-age structure is actually an art museum, and it's firmly fixed to the ground in the city of Niterói. It's the work of the brilliant Brazilian architect Oscar Niemeyer, who created hundreds of beautiful and bizarre buildings in Brazil, from the 1930s to the 2010s. The circular museum is 165 feet (50 m) wide and stands on a narrow "stem" just 30 feet (9 m) across. It has three floors, and you enter via a swirling, spiraling walkway leading into the side.

The **planetarium** contains a **collection of meteorites** that fell in northern Argentina.

Planetario Galileo Galilei

Buenos Aires, Argentina

Here's another flying saucer! Or is it an actual alien planet or moon that's landed in the middle of Buenos Aires? In fact, this building does have something to do with outer space. It's the Galileo Galilei Planetarium, built in 1966 for Argentina's capital city. The inside of the dome is a screen where you can look up and watch movies about the stars and planets. The planetarium also has a space museum, whose exhibits include a piece of the moon, brought back from the first moon landings in 1969. And the outside of the dome is covered in LEDs, which light up the dome at night.

WEIRD WONDERS
Ancient mysteries—best seen from above.

THE NASCA LINES

Nasca Desert, Peru

In Peru's windless Nasca Desert, thousands of straight lines and geometric shapes form drawings of animals: a spider, a monkey, a hummingbird, and many more. The Nasca people, who lived in the area around 2,000 years ago, made these drawings by removing the desert's top layer of pebbles to reveal paler soil underneath. The designs are huge—some of the lines stretch up to 30 miles (48 km) long. You can see them from nearby hills, but the best view is from the air. Archaeologists think the lines were probably made to mark religious sites, or as messages to weather gods.

WEIRD WONDERS

Willys Jeeps are known locally as

"MULITAS MECANICAS"

(or mechanical mules).

For Colombia's coffee farmers, a Willys Jeep is a prized possession. These jeeps were used for military purposes during World War II, then sold off to other countries after the war. In Colombia, they were perfect for the steep mountain roads in the coffee-growing Quindío region. They're old now, but still working and being used to carry crops, farm equipment, and whatever else needs transporting. And every year, the locals pile their jeeps as high as they can with stuff, and drive them through the streets in the *yipao* (meaning "loaded-up jeep") parade. There are prizes for the most overloaded jeeps and the most artistic arrangements of household items, local crafts, or farm crops. Popular items to stack on your vehicle include furniture, paintings, electrical goods, houseplants, pets, and children!

WITHDRAWN

PERPLEXING PLANTS

Yareta Plant

Andes Mountains

Go trekking high in the Andes mountains, and you might see something that looks like a giant green booger stuck to the rocks! This strange, alien-like blob is actually a yareta, a tough mountain plant. It grows a thick mass of stems, topped by thousands of tiny, leaves and flowers that form a dense, solid mat. It may look soft and kind of slimy, but the yareta is actually firm like wood. You can even sit down on one and it won't get squashed! Growing like this helps the yareta to hold in water and warmth, and stops it from getting blown away by the icy mountain winds. Yaretas grow very slowly, and some are believed to be up to 3,000 years old!

The **yarenta plant** can grow to **20 feet** (6 m) across—the size of a **large car.**

Floralis Genérica

Buenos Aires, Argentina

There's definitely something strange about this flower—it's made of metal, it's 75 feet (23 m) tall, and each of its six huge stainless-steel petals is 43 feet (13 m) long. It's a flower the size of a seven-story apartment block! You can see it in the middle of the busy city of Buenos Aires, the capital of Argentina. In 2002, Argentine architect Eduardo Catalano designed and paid for the spectacular sculpture as a gift to his city. It stands in a park in the middle of a circular pool that reflects it like a mirror. Every night at sunset, it slowly closes its petals, and a red light glows from inside. In the morning, at 8 a.m., it opens again for the day.

Shy Plant
Tropical South America

Can a plant be shy? The *Mimosa pudica,* also called the shy plant or touch-me-not plant, has an amazing ability. If you touch it, or just brush past it, the leaves suddenly droop and fold up. This makes it harder for some animals, such as caterpillars, to eat them. Plants aren't known for their speedy moves, so how does the mimosa do this? It has special water-filled cells at the base of each leaf. Touching the leaf makes the cells empty out their water and become floppy, like a deflated balloon—and the leaf collapses. But these plants are smart too! Scientists have tried playing harmless tricks on mimosas, like sprinkling them with water. At first, they close up, but after the trick is repeated a few times, they "learn" that there's no danger and stop reacting!

Cajueiro de Pirangi
Natal, Brazil

You're lost in a forest in Brazil, surrounded by thick, gnarly tree trunks, with a leafy green canopy overhead. But don't panic! You're not in the middle of the jungle, miles from anywhere. You're in a park in the seaside village of Pirangi, and the forest you're in is actually just one single tree! It's the famous Cajueiro de Pirangi, or Cashew of Pirangi. Something went wrong with the tree as it grew, making its branches spread out sideways instead of growing into the sky. Where they touch the ground, many of the branches sprout roots, making them look like separate trunks. In this way, the curious cashew tree has managed to spread out over two acres (0.8 ha) of ground.

THE CASHEW TREE OF PIRANGI TAKES UP SLIGHTLY MORE SPACE THAN A SOCCER FIELD.

STRANGE STRUCTURES

Sacsayhuamán
Cusco, Peru

Take a close look at these walls. They were built around 600 years ago, near the city of Cusco in Peru, by the Inca people. They're made of solid stone blocks, some up to 28 feet (8.5 m) high—and no mortar or cement. Instead, the blocks were all cut to fit together exactly. Although many are oddly shaped, they fit so perfectly that you can't even slide a piece of paper between them. They were also carved into rounded shapes, making them look a little like giant pieces of bubble gum that have been squished together. The Inca built three huge, zigzagging walls like this to defend the hilltop fort of Sacsayhuamán.

These ancient walls are so well constructed that they've survived centuries of earthquakes.

Plastic Bottle House
Puerto Iguazú, Argentina

Thrown-away plastic bottles are a big problem in many parts of the world. But there is an ingenious way to get rid of them: turn them into houses! This house in Argentina has been built from thousands of plastic drinks bottles, stacked up inside sturdy frames to make the walls. The homeowner has made sofas and beds from old bottles too, and there's even a curtain made of strung-together bottle tops! This particular house is open to the public for tours, but many more bottle houses are being built as normal, everyday dwellings.

Post Office Bay
Galápagos Islands, Ecuador

At first glance, this jumble of wood doesn't look special. But it's actually a post office! Not only that, it's one of the oldest post offices in the world—and one of the strangest, since no one works there. It's on a beach on one of Ecuador's remote Galápagos Islands. In the 1700s, ships used to stop here to collect food and water, and the sailors decided to set up a postal system, installing a barrel as a postbox. Anyone could leave letters in it for their loved ones back home. At the same time, they'd pick up letters addressed to where they were headed and deliver them. And it still works! Tourists post letters in the barrel and collect any that they can take home to deliver.

Amazon Tall Tower Observatory
Amazon Rainforest, Brazil

Want to take a trip up the tallest tower in South America? Then head to the jungle! Oh, and you'll have to be a scientist, a technician, or a visiting journalist to be allowed up. This skyscraping structure isn't a modern office building in a big city, but a special science research base, deep in the Amazon rainforest. Named the Amazon Tall Tower Observatory (ATTO), it was built in 2015 and rises 1,066 feet (325 m) into the sky. Yet it's only 10 feet (3 m) from side to side! It takes an hour to climb to the top. On the way up, there are platforms where scientists can work, as well as a deck right at the summit. The tower is also covered with high-tech sensors for measuring pollution, temperature, humidity, and climate change above the rainforest.

LUCKILY FOR THE EXPERTS WHO WORK ON THE AMAZON'S OBSERVATORY TOWER, THERE'S AN ELEVATOR!

Going up?

KOOKY COLORS!

The Colors of Guatapé
Colombia

Welcome to Guatapé, the world's most colorful town! Though it may resemble a dream world or a film set for a fantasy movie, this is a real place in Colombia, where people live and work—and spend a lot of time painting their houses. The tradition started around 100 years ago, when people put 3D-tiled and painted panels around the base of the buildings. Gradually, they began painting the rest of the buildings in bright colors, too—and now every street is a rainbow of patterns and pictures, and the town has become a tourist attraction. The locals take great pride in their colorful homes, and are often seen out on the streets cleaning and retouching their paintwork.

Paint the town all the colors of the rainbow!

THE **MURALS** ON THE **BUILDINGS** TRADITIONALLY TELL THE **HISTORY OF THE FAMILY OR BUSINESS** THAT OWNS THEM.

Peru's Potato Park

Cusco, Peru

Chips, fries, wedges, and mash: People all over the world love potatoes. But did you know that potatoes originally come from South America, and they're not all the same brownish color you might be used to? In the Andes mountain region, there's the Potato Park, where Quechua people grow hundreds of different varieties, and scientists test the best types for different climates and areas. There you'll find strange-looking potatoes in countless shapes: knobby, banana-shaped, flat, and round, plus a range of colors from black and purple to blue, red, yellow, white, and bright pink!

The part of the potato we eat is the root, but potato flowers and fruits are poisonous.

Weirdly Cute! Blue Anole

I'm feeling a little blue.

This could be your only chance to see a blue anole, one of the world's rarest (and bluest!) lizards. It's only found on the small island of Gorgona, off the coast of Colombia, where it darts around in the forest catching insects to eat. Owing to deforestation and people capturing it for the exotic pet trade, the blue anole is critically endangered and at risk of dying out. But the island where it lives has now been made into a nature reserve, giving the little lizard a chance of survival.

weird but true!

MALE RIVER DOLPHINS, or *botos*, found in the Amazon's waterways are often an **UNUSUAL PINK COLOR** ... and according to local folklore, they can shape-shift into **HANDSOME HUMAN MEN!**

The peculiar-looking **POTOO BIRD** can **disguise itself** as a **tree stump**—but only when it **closes** its **BULGING, BRIGHT YELLOW EYES.**

THE GLASS FROG HAS **TRANSPARENT SKIN,** WHICH MEANS YOU CAN **SEE ITS BONES AND ORGANS AND WATCH ITS HEART BEATING!**

The **common basilisk lizard** can **ESCAPE FROM DANGER** by spreading out its toes and running across water.

Catch me if you can!

AMAZONIAN ANIMALS

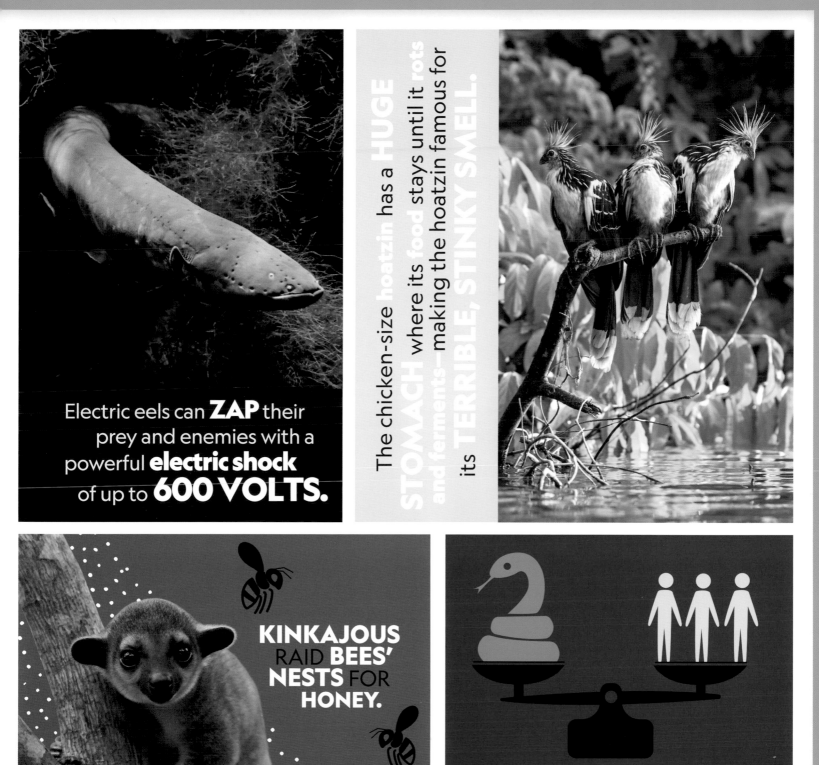

Electric eels can **ZAP** their prey and enemies with a powerful **electric shock** of up to **600 VOLTS.**

The chicken-size **hoatzin** has a **HUGE STOMACH** where its **food** stays until it **rots and ferments**—making the hoatzin famous for its **TERRIBLE, STINKY SMELL.**

KINKAJOUS RAID **BEES' NESTS** FOR **HONEY.**

A **FEMALE GREEN ANACONDA** can grow to **17 FEET (5 M) LONG** and weigh as much as **THREE ADULT HUMANS.**

QUIZ WHIZ

Now that your brain is bursting with weird-but-true South America stuff, take this quick quiz and see how you do!

1 **What runs down the outside of Chile's Montaña Mágica Lodge?**

a. A ski slope
b. Rainforest mice
c. Local joggers
d. A waterfall

2 **What does Nevado Ojos del Salado mean?**

a. New egg salad
b. Beware of the Sun Octopus
c. Snowy Salty Eyes
d. Salt-flavored ice cream

3 **What is special about the common basilisk lizard?**

a. It is blue.
b. It can fly.
c. It can walk on water.
d. It has no tail.

4 What does it feel like to sit on a yareta plant?

a. Spiky and painful
b. Slimy and slippery
c. Firm and supportive
d. Soft and fluffy

5 Why was the emperor tamarin named after Emperor Wilhelm II?

a. They both have amazing mustaches.
b. The tamarin has a crown-like crest on its head.
c. They both resemble emperor penguins.
d. They both have enormous noses.

6 Which of these is NOT one of the Nasca Lines drawings?

a. A hummingbird
b. An astronaut
c. A dog
d. A teapot

7 Where can you find a giant hand sculpture sticking up out of the ground?

a. The Amazon rainforest
b. The Atacama Desert
c. The Andes mountains
d. Patagonia

8 What type of things do people buy at Bolivia's Alasitas festival?

a. Red things
b. Recycled things
c. Tiny things
d. Things carved from pebbles

Answers: 1. d, 2. c, 3. c, 4. c, 5. a, 6. d, 7. b, 8. c

CHAPTER

4

UNIQUE EUROPE

Ready for some underground adventures, ghostly goings-on, and mind-bending monuments? Then you've arrived at the right destination ...

Lake Lucerne was formed 12,000 YEARS AGO, at the end of the ice age.

The Hubble Space Telescope has CAPTURED AURORAS similar to Earth's on JUPITER, too.

WILLKOMMEN, BIENVENUE, and WELCOME TO EUROPE!

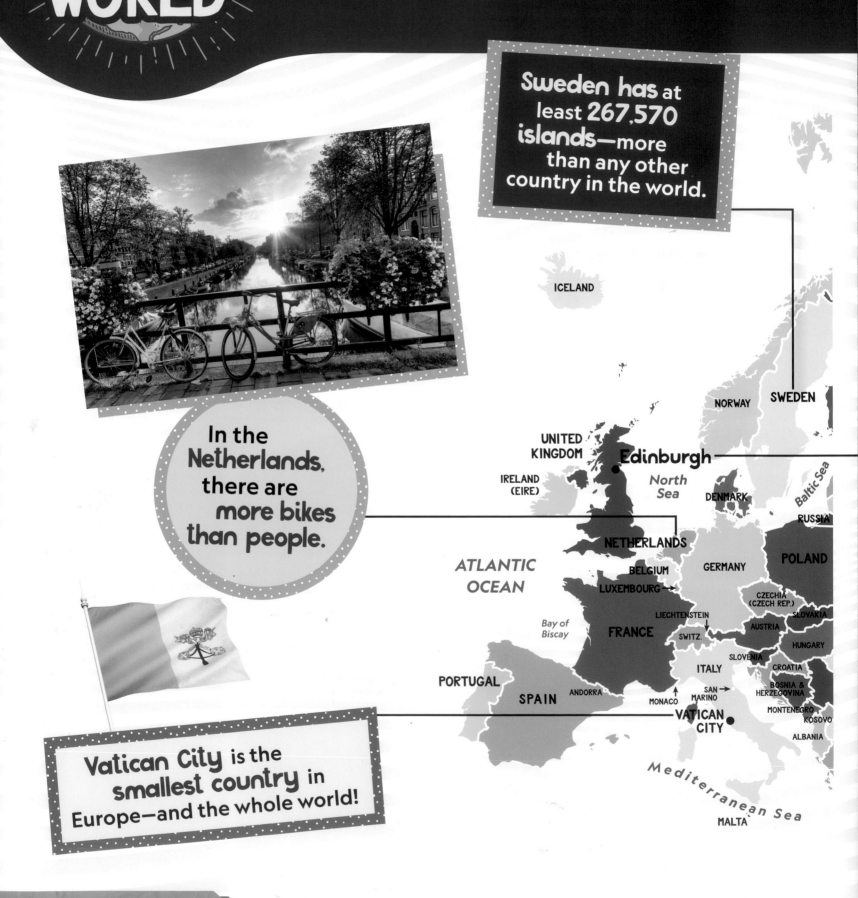

Sweden has at least 267,570 islands—more than any other country in the world.

In the Netherlands, there are more bikes than people.

Vatican City is the **smallest country** in Europe—and the whole world!

ICELAND

NORWAY

SWEDEN

UNITED KINGDOM

Edinburgh

IRELAND (EIRE)

North Sea

DENMARK

Baltic Sea

RUSSIA

NETHERLANDS

ATLANTIC OCEAN

BELGIUM

LUXEMBOURG →

GERMANY

POLAND

CZECHIA (CZECH REP.)

SLOVAKIA

LIECHTENSTEIN

AUSTRIA

HUNGARY

Bay of Biscay

FRANCE

SWITZ

SLOVENIA

CROATIA

PORTUGAL

ITALY

ANDORRA

SAN → MARINO

BOSNIA & HERZEGOVINA

SPAIN

MONACO

VATICAN CITY

MONTENEGRO

KOSOVO

ALBANIA

Mediterranean Sea

MALTA

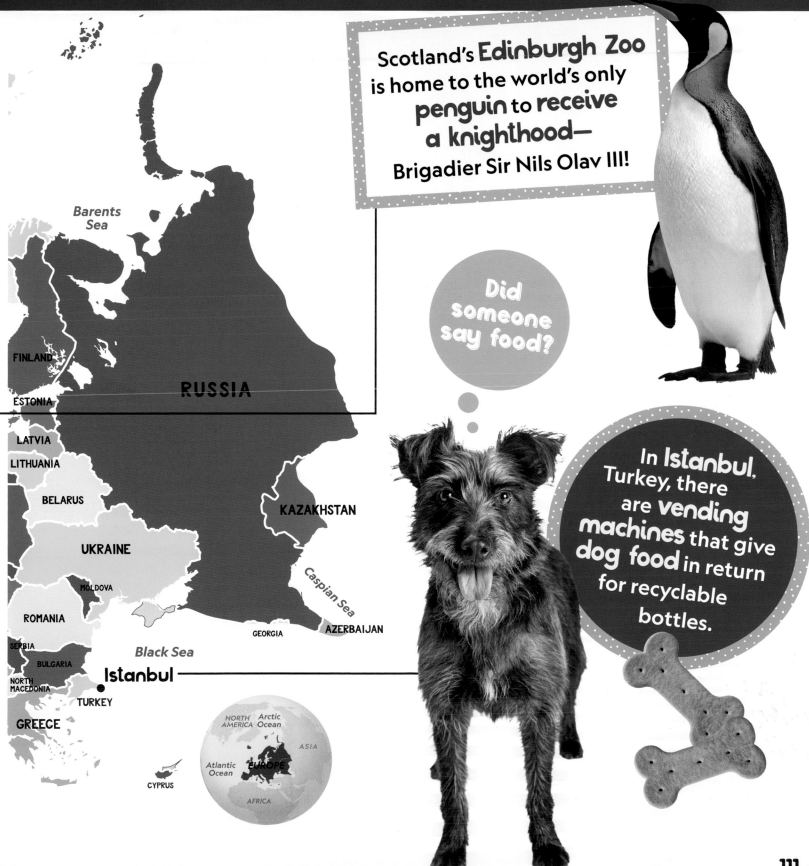

Scotland's **Edinburgh Zoo** is home to the world's only **penguin** to **receive** a **knighthood**— Brigadier Sir Nils Olav III!

Did someone say food?

In **Istanbul, Turkey**, there are **vending machines** that give **dog food** in return for recyclable bottles.

Barents Sea

FINLAND

ESTONIA

RUSSIA

LATVIA

LITHUANIA

BELARUS

KAZAKHSTAN

UKRAINE

MOLDOVA

Caspian Sea

ROMANIA

GEORGIA

AZERBAIJAN

SERBIA

Black Sea

BULGARIA

Istanbul

NORTH MACEDONIA

TURKEY

GREECE

NORTH AMERICA

Arctic Ocean

ASIA

Atlantic Ocean

EUROPE

CYPRUS

AFRICA

111

NATURALLY BIZARRE

Northern Lights
Tromsø, Norway

Who needs fireworks when you can watch the northern lights? Luckily, this spectacular nighttime display isn't exclusive to just one country. They can be seen in Canada, Greenland, Sweden, and lots of other places in the Northern Hemisphere. One of the best locations to witness the stunning light show is near Tromsø, Norway. It has perfect viewing conditions—with long, dark nights between September and March and little light pollution. Also called the aurora borealis, the spectacular colors are created when tiny particles called electrons come from the sun and mix with gases in Earth's atmosphere, making them glow. And you can never be certain what you're about to see.

Legend claims that there is a golden cave under Krupaj Spring guarded by a water spirit called Tartor.

Krupaj Spring
Milanovac, Serbia

Visiting Krupaj Spring feels like stepping into a fairy tale. Of course, first you have to find this vibrant, tucked-away turquoise lake. Between an old water mill and a hill is a small, easy-to-miss passageway. Take the narrow path through lush forest, past ponds full of fish, and you'll reach the stunning spring. After all that walking, you might be tempted to dive in. But with the water a chilly 50°F (10°C), you might want to think again! Still, there are mysteries to be explored under the rippling surface. Scuba divers have discovered a dizzying maze of underwater canals and have given the tunnels nicknames, such as "the Slide" and "the Stomach." It's no wonder that this fairy tale spring has inspired myths and stories.

Silfra

Iceland

At Silfra, scuba divers can touch two tectonic plates—at the same time! Tectonic plates are the gigantic pieces of land that make up the outer layer of Earth's crust. Just seven major tectonic plates make up most of the planet's surface. Iceland sits on two of them—the North American and the Eurasian plates. Silfra was formed by these two plates pulling apart, which they are still slowly doing. In parts of this beautiful lake, the plates are only a few feet apart! The lake water comes from Iceland's second largest glacier 31 miles (50 km) away and travels underground through porous lava rock. It can take up to 100 years to reach Silfra and is filtered by the rock, which makes it crystal clear. It's possible to see 330 feet (101 m) down between the canyon walls to the carpet of green algae at the bottom—the Statue of Liberty isn't even that tall!

Stuck between a rock and a hard place!

THE LAKE WATER IS **PURE** AND A **CHILLY** 36 TO 39°F (2 TO 4°C)!

Stone Mushrooms

Beli Plast, Bulgaria

These massive rocks are commonly known as the Stone Mushrooms—and they certainly wouldn't look out of place on a giant's dinner plate! They stand around eight feet (2.4 m) tall—the height of a soccer goal. They look like they've been carved, but that's not right. A local legend even claims that these bizarre rock formations are the severed heads of four sisters—and that's wrong, too! Their magnificent shapes were actually created naturally. The rocks were once mostly covered by water, which wore them down by erosion over thousands of years to create the thinner stalks. When the water dried up, the sun and the wind continued shaping them.

UPS AND DOWNS

Salina Turda
Romania

Sightseeing in an abandoned mine might seem weird on its own. But visiting one to play golf or have a beauty treatment? Now that's downright unusual! From Roman times to the early 20th century, salt was mined at Salina Turda in Romania. Today, visitors can enjoy an incredible theme park 394 feet (120 m) underground! The brightly lit attractions include a playground, a bowling alley, a mini-golf course, and a Ferris wheel. There's even a theater, a spa, a rowing lake, and a museum. Salina Turda has been used in other surprising ways over the years. During World War II, it even provided refuge as a bomb shelter for local residents.

In 1950, Salina Turda was used as a cheese warehouse.

Hammetschwand Elevator
Ennetbürgen, Switzerland

Going up ... and up ... and up! For sightseers with a head for heights, the Hammetschwand Elevator provides a speedy route to enjoy the views of Switzerland's Lake Lucerne. Carrying passengers 501 feet (152.7 m) up the mountainside, the structure holds the record for the highest outdoor elevator in Europe. It was also once the fastest elevator in the world. Opened in 1905, the original compartment was built out of wood and zinc and took nearly three minutes to travel to the top. Today, after lighter materials were used to rebuild it, the elevator's journey takes less than a minute. Race you to the top!

BY the NUMBERS

TERRIFIC TOWER

It's amazing that France's famous Eiffel Tower is still standing! Opened in 1889, it was only supposed to last 20 years before being dismantled. Thankfully, this magnificent metal monument is still attracting visitors today. Its famous look has even inspired other designs, including a scale model in Nevada, U.S.A., and the Tokyo Tower in Japan.

HEIGHT:

1,063 FEET (324 M)

THAT'S SIX TIMES AS TALL AS NIAGARA FALLS!

2.5 MILLION

RIVETS USED

1,665

STAIRS TO THE TOP

7 YEARS, 2 MONTHS,

AND 5 DAYS TO BUILD

7 MILLION

VISITORS EACH YEAR

ANIMAL ANTICS

My claws are as tough as nails!

Alpine Marmot
Alps and Apennine Mountains

Digging through frozen soil is a tough task, but Alpine marmots have just the tools for the job. These little guys are no more than 25 inches (64 cm) tall, but have strong claws and a specially adapted thumb with a nail on it—perfect for breaking through hard mountain ground to reach tasty worms and insects, which they feast on, along with leaves and grass. But these cute members of the squirrel family don't just use their impressive digits to hunt for food. They are also ideal for digging underground burrows. Alpine marmot families hibernate together in deep dens between October and March. To survive half a year of nap time, they fill their faces in the spring and summer. During the six months an Alpine marmot is awake, its weight usually increases by a hefty 50 percent!

Alpine marmots lived during **the last ice age.**

Runde Island
Norway

After a Dutch merchant ship sank in 1725 and lots of gold coins washed up on its shores, Runde was nicknamed "Treasure Island." Although it sounds like a great place to make your fortune, coins aren't the reason most people flock there now. Around 150 people live on Runde, but the human population is tiny compared to the number of birds that make a visit every year. During the nesting season, between February and August, the small island is home to more than 500,000 feathered friends. Over 230 species have been spotted there, including shags, gannets, and guillemots. But Atlantic puffins truly rule the Runde roost—in excess of 100,000 pairs nest there every year!

Duck Village
Il-Gżira Manoel, Malta

If you think it would be a hoot living next door to kooky neighbors, then take a trip to Manoel Island. This small island, off the east coast of Malta, is home to an incredible assortment of fowls and their friends. Duck Village was started by a volunteer as a shelter for ducks, chickens, and geese. The little homes are a hodgepodge of colorful buildings, and luckily the neighbors all seem to get along. Local residents bring food and cuddly toys as treats for the animals. The bad news is that building work may be planned for Manoel Island, which could threaten the future of this unique wild-life haven. If it goes ahead, it's hoped that the entire Duck Village will be moved to a new location.

DUCK VILLAGE IS ALSO HOME TO STRAY CATS, RABBITS, AND GUINEA PIGS.

Weirdly Cute!

Fire Salamander

The phoenix is supposed to die in fire and be reborn in the ashes. Of course, that's a myth, but fire salamanders are real amphibians—and centuries ago, people mistakenly believed that they were born in fires! That's probably because these animals hide under stones and wood to stay cool and keep their skin moist. When humans collected logs to build fires, these salamanders may have been hanging out inside. When the blaze began, they had to make a speedy escape! Although fire salamanders are experts at hiding, that does not mean they're pushovers for predators when they do venture out. Their striking yellow markings warn predators that their skin contains deadly toxins.

Dead WEIRD!

Turn out that light!

St. Michan's Mummies
Dublin, Ireland

St. Michan's Church was built on former swamp land and some think methane gas rising up from the soggy ground is the reason bodies are mummified. Notable residents include one corpse nicknamed the "Crusader," after the religious wars known as the Crusades. He was a tall man for the time, at 6.5 feet (2 m). His legs were broken and folded underneath, probably so he could be squashed into the coffin!

Kaplica Czaszek
Czermna, Poland

This chapel's walls and ceiling are covered with the skulls and bones of more than 3,000 people! It was created between 1776 and 1794 by a local priest. He put everything into the decoration—his skull even became part of the altar after he died! The crypt under the chapel contains another 21,000 skeletons!

The Catacombs
Paris, France

Deep underneath the busy Parisian streets lie the remains of more than six million people. In the 18th century, the cemeteries couldn't cope with the number of corpses, so they were moved to tunnels beneath the city. Some of the bones were simply stacked up, but others were arranged in patterns and designs. Today, more than several hundred thousand visitors line up each year to walk just over a mile (1.6 km) through the bone-lined passageway. The complete network of tunnels, however, covers around 186 miles (300 km)!

Hampton Court Palace
Molesey, England, U.K.

Once home to King Henry VIII, it's not surprising that at least two of the royal's six wives are said to haunt Hampton Court. Some claim the ghost of Jane Seymour—Henry's third wife—carries a candle near the room where she died. Catherine Howard—Henry's fifth wife, who was beheaded for treason—is said to run through the Haunted Gallery screaming for mercy!

Sedlec Ossuary
Sedlec, Czechia (Czech Republic)

In 1870, woodcarver Frantisek Rindt was hired for an unusual and gruesome task. When a local abbot brought soil from Jerusalem to the church at Sedlec, it became a popular place to be buried. The ossuary, a room under the church, soon filled up with the remains of tens of thousands of people. Rindt was hired to decorate the chapel with the bones. First, he bleached them to make them all the same color. Then he carved them to create some astonishing structures, including a family crest and a chandelier!

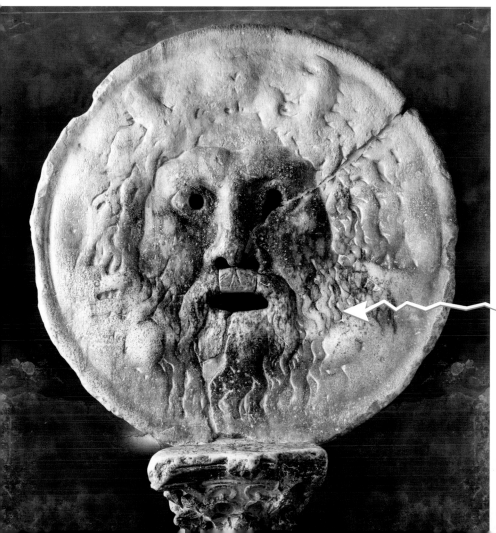

Bocca della Verità
Rome, Italy

An ancient legend claims that if you tell a lie when you stick your hand into this stone face's mouth, it will be bitten off! Some think that hundreds of years ago, the hands of lying lawbreakers were placed in the large stone disc and severed as a punishment.

PECULIAR PLANTS

Poison Garden
Alnwick, England, U.K.

What could be more relaxing than a walk through a plant-filled garden? Pretty much anything when all the vegetation in it could kill you! Behind these garden gates are around 100 plants you won't find at your local florists. In the collection, there's giant hogweed, which can burn your skin and give you blisters that last for up to seven years! Another one to avoid is aconitum, also known as wolfsbane. It may have pretty blue flowers, but it also has poisonous roots, poisonous stems, and poisonous leaves. And its berries? Yes, you guessed it ... poisonous. The gardeners that work here often have to wear protective suits, gloves, and visors. Visitors are told not to smell, touch, or taste the plants.

Each year people are said to faint from breathing in the garden's toxic fumes!

Crooked Forest
Gryfino, Poland

If you go into these woods, you're in for a big surprise—you'll find around 400 pine trees, all with the same bizarre bend at the bottom of their trunks. No one knows what caused the trees to grow this way. One idea is that a heavy fall of snow might have flattened the saplings, which then grew upward when the snow melted. A popular suggestion is that the crooked trees were created on purpose in the 1930s by foresters who wanted curved wood for shipbuilding or furniture-making. The outbreak of World War II interrupted their plans and the trees were left to grow upward again. Others believe the trees were flattened during the war by German tanks, when the local town, Gryfino, was destroyed.

What's **Weird** About This**?**

The dragon arum goes by many names: the dragon-wort, the Indian turnip—and the stink lily! That last name might describe this peculiar plant the best, because what really makes it unusual is its odious odor. To attract flies for pollination, it gives off a disgusting rotten meat smell. Thankfully, the stench only lasts for about 24 hours each year! Found in Greece, the striking dragon arum has large purple leaves, surrounding a dark purple column, called a spadix. It can grow to a height of more than 39 inches (1 m), so it's easy to spot—and avoid.

EYE-CATCHING ODDITIES!

Idiom
Prague, Czechia (Czech Republic)

Reading a book can transport you to a different place. And if you look inside the tower of books outside Prague Municipal Library, it really seems like they can send you on a long, magical journey! This impressive art installation is called "Idiom," or the "Column of Knowledge." Created by Slovakian artist Matej Krén, it's an impressive 17-foot (5.2-m)-high tower that climbs from the floor to the ceiling. A 10-foot (3-m)-tall tear-shaped slit on one side allows visitors to peer inside and enjoy an amazing view. Carefully positioned mirrors at the top and the bottom make it appear as if the colorful tunnel stretches on forever—in both directions. Each year some books are replaced to keep the tower in perfect condition. If you've ever been lost in a book, now you can experience what it feels like to be lost in thousands of them!

"IDIOM" IS CONSTRUCTED FROM AROUND 8,000 BOOKS!

Crooked House
Sopot, Poland

Would you walk inside a building that looks like it's about to fall down? Poland's Krzywy Domek, which translates as "Crooked House," looks like it's straight out of a cartoon! And that's not far from the truth. The architects who designed the building were inspired by the drawings of Per Dahlberg and Jan Marcin Szancer, who illustrated more than 200 books, including fairy tales. Built in 2004, the warped walls and glass are totally safe. Even though it might look like a bit of a squeeze from the outside, there's plenty of room inside. The Crooked House is part of a shopping center and covers 43,000 square feet (4,000 sq m), which is similar to the area inside a standard outdoor running track.

Chêne Chapelle
Allouville-Bellefosse, France

Tree trunks often provide homes for squirrels, owls, and many other animals. Churchgoers ... well, they're are a bit less common! But the Chêne Chapelle, which means "chapel oak" in French, has been used as a place of worship for centuries. In the 1600s, this oak was struck by lightning, causing a fire that hollowed out the trunk. The village priest decided it was a sign from God and built a shrine inside the oak at ground level. Later, another chapel was added farther up, which could be accessed using a staircase around the outside. The tree is still used for two church services and a pilgrimage every year, though the congregation has to wait outside, due to lack of space!

Each of the **tree's chapels** can hold only **three people.**

Rakotzbrücke Devil's Bridge
Kromlau Park, Germany

A devil's bridge might sound like it's part of a highway to hell, but it's not really scary! There are so-called devil's bridges all around the world. The name is used to describe any bridge built in a dangerous location or which looks impossible to construct—no human could create such a design, so it must be the work of the devil instead! Germany's Kromlau Park contains one of the best examples. Built in 1860 of local stone, thin jagged spires reach up to the sky at either end. But what's "impossible" about this bridge is only revealed when the lake is full and the water is still. That's when the reflection in the water creates the illusion of a perfect circle.

weird but true!

Visit Paris, France, for the world's only **VAMPIRE MUSEUM.** Exhibits include an **ANTI-VAMPIRE PROTECTION KIT,** just in case!

The art at the **Miniature Museum** in Ordino, Andorra, is **SO TINY** that it has to be **viewed through microscopes** to be seen!

AT THE **FAIRYTALE MUSEUM** IN NICOSIA, CYPRUS, EXHIBITS ARE TUCKED AWAY IN **SECRET ROOMS** AND **HIDDEN PASSAGES.**

Some of the officials that run the **CAT MUSEUM** in Minsk, Belarus, are **ACTUALLY CATS!**

MAGNIFICENT MUSEUMS!

Some of the games exhibited at the **MUSEUM OF SOVIET ARCADE MACHINES** in Moscow, Russia, were **built in secret,** at a time when **no official arcade machines** were being produced!

At the **NOSE ACADEMY** in Lund, Sweden, there are **MORE THAN 100 PLASTER CASTS** of acclaimed **SCANDINAVIANS' NOSES!**

Estonia's **MARZIPAN MUSEUM** in Tallinn is home to models of **ALL SHAPES AND SIZES,** including 12 life-size statues, made from the almondy paste!

At the **CORPUS MUSEUM** in Oegstheest, Netherlands, you can take a tour through a giant human body. **WALK INSIDE AN OPEN WOUND** on a knee and work your way up to **THE MASSIVE BRAIN!**

BIZARRE, BRILLIANT BRITAIN

Sultan the Pit Pony
Penallta Country Park, Wales, U.K.

The big patch of lumpy ground at Penallta Country Park may not seem special—until you climb up to the observation point. From this vantage point, you can see that the ground forms an amazing sculpture, best viewed from above. Penallta used to be a colliery, where coal was mined. Between the 18th and 20th centuries, most collieries used pit ponies to haul coal around the mine shafts in carts. The animals even slept in underground stables, only coming to the surface for short breaks. Artist Mick Petts spent three years creating the earth sculpture to honor these beasts. It is made from 60,000 tons (54,400 t) of coal waste, stone, and dirt, covered with grass, and was named Sultan by locals after one of the last ponies to work at the pit.

THE PIT PONY IS 656 FEET (200 M) LONG—LONGER THAN 20 BUSES END TO END.

Giant's Causeway
County Antrim, Northern Ireland, U.K.

The Giant's Causeway was named 'cause of the way a giant created it—or so legend has it! Irish giant Finn MacCool wanted to cross the sea to fight his rival, Benandonner, in Scotland. However, Finn fell asleep and his wife wrapped him in a blanket. When Benandonner crossed the causeway and saw Finn sleeping, he mistook the giant for his rival's baby. Imagining that Finn must be huge, he ran back home, destroying most of the rocks to stop Finn following him! The real explanation is just as exciting, though. The 40,000 interlocking columns were shaped by volcanic activity between 50 and 60 million years ago. As the lava cooled, the columns were formed. Most are hexagonal, but some have up to eight sides. The tallest columns are around 39 feet (12 m) tall—that's taller than two giraffes.

Birdman Competitions

Bognor Regis, England, U.K.

The aim of this kooky competition is to run off the end of a pier, travel for 328 feet (100 m), and cross the finish line markers—before hitting the water. For many people, though, it means dressing up in wacky costumes and enjoying a speedy, vertical drop! Birdman events have also been held in the U.K. towns of Worthing and Selsey, but the one at Bognor, now held every two years, is the best known. Thousands of spectators watch participants compete, dressed as anything from planes to animals to superheroes. There is a cash prize for entrants who hit the target, but the money is rarely won. One competitor at Worthing in 2009 came close, missing it by just 5.5 inches (14 cm)!

One Birdman contestant competed dressed as a chicken-and-mushroom pie.

Weirdly Cute!

I need to trim my bangs!

Highland Cattle

With their long, shaggy hair, Highland cattle look a bit like cuddly toys—although their formidable, curved horns might make you think again! However, these amazing-looking animals are usually friendly and have been known to approach people for attention. Highland cattle have an uncommon double coat of hair, with long, oily strands on top of a feathery undercoat. The two layers help keep them warm in cold winters—and their horns are perfect for pushing away snow to find food. There are 15,000 Highland cattle in the U.K., and thanks to their popularity, there are now herds in Finland, Australia, Canada, and the United States, too. Even the royal family are fans. Queen Elizabeth II brought the cows to her holiday home in Scotland in the early 1950s. The herd still thrives today, grazing in the fields nearby!

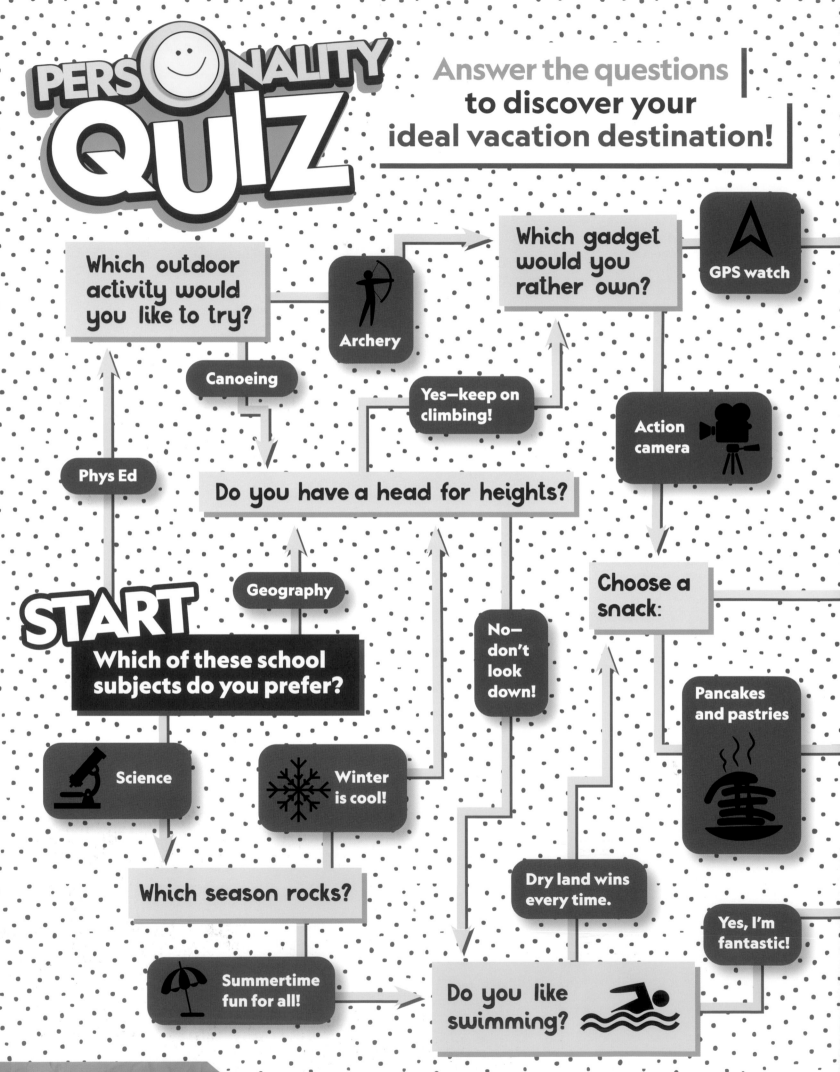

PERSONALITY QUIZ

Answer the questions to discover your ideal vacation destination!

Which outdoor activity would you like to try?

Archery

Canoeing

Which gadget would you rather own?

GPS watch

Action camera

Yes—keep on climbing!

Phys Ed

Do you have a head for heights?

Geography

START

Which of these school subjects do you prefer?

Science

Winter is cool!

No—don't look down!

Choose a snack:

Pancakes and pastries

Which season rocks?

Dry land wins every time.

Summertime fun for all!

Do you like swimming?

Yes, I'm fantastic!

Plenty of chill-out time!

Treehotel, Sweden

Hidden in a Swedish pine forest is a truly tree-mendous hotel. One room—the Mirrorcube—reflects the woodland around it. The Bird's Nest looks like it has been constructed from branches. And the Blue Cone ... is bright red!

What sort of vacation do you prefer?

Pizza and pasta

Action-packed

Bivacco Gervasutti, Italy

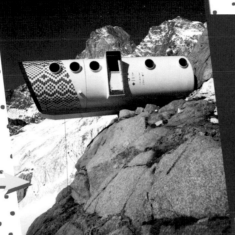

This is the perfect place for anyone who wants to live the high life—it sits 9,300 feet (2,835 m) above sea level on a glacier. Built to replace a drafty wooden shelter, some sections were flown into place by helicopter!

The more the merrier

Kemi SnowCastle, Finland

No two visits to this hotel are the same—that's because it's rebuilt every January with a new design. The hotel is only open for about three months, until the warmer spring temperatures turn it to slush.

Do you like hanging out with lots of people?

Just one or two friends at a time

Utter Inn, Sweden

There's something fishy about this two-person hotel! A ladder leads down to a room with two beds and windows providing an all-around view of underwater life. The hotel was designed as a reverse aquarium, so that fish could watch the guests!

ANNUAL ABSURDITIES!

Caga Tió
Catalonia

There are lots of Christmas customs: singing festive songs, leaving out cookies for Santa, feeding the log that poops out sweets ... Wait, what? The log that poops out sweets? That's right! Caga Tió is a hollow log with a happy face at one end—and it "poops" out sweets from the other! In the weeks before Christmas in Catalonia, children cover their festive friend with a blanket and feed him bread and orange peel. On Christmas Eve, Caga Tió delivers small presents. As encouragement, children whack it with a stick and sing a song, ordering the log to poop out gifts of sweets, nuts, and small toys!

Caga Tió means "poop log"!

Air Guitar World Championships
Oulu, Finland

If you have no great musical skill, but love to put on a performance, this could be the perfect event for you. Every year, competitors from around the world head to Oulu to pluck, strum, and get their groove on to their favorite tracks. It's open to all ages and you don't need any special equipment—just enthusiasm. The organizers think that if everyone in the world played air guitar at once, all bad things would vanish and it could lead to world peace. Now that's gotta be worth a try!

What's **Weird** About This **?**

Keep the noise down!

Once a year, fireworks light up the night sky on the Greek island of Chios. But it's not to entertain the local people—this is rocket-powered rivalry! For hundreds of years, an annual battle has taken place in the town of Vrontados. The targets are two churches on separate hills around 1,300 feet (400 m) apart. Bizarrely, no one seems to know why this colorful contest began! Local legend claims that until 1889 cannons were used, but after they were banned, homemade rockets took their place. Each year, up to 80,000 fireworks are fired between the two churches. The aim is to hit the opposing church's bell tower, although it's hard to see in all the chaos when that happens.

STADT.WAND. KUNST MURAL

Mannheim, Germany

WEIRD WONDERS

Don't let this brain-bending mural mess with your mind.

Artist Peeta's large murals usually take between **15 AND 20 DAYS** to complete.

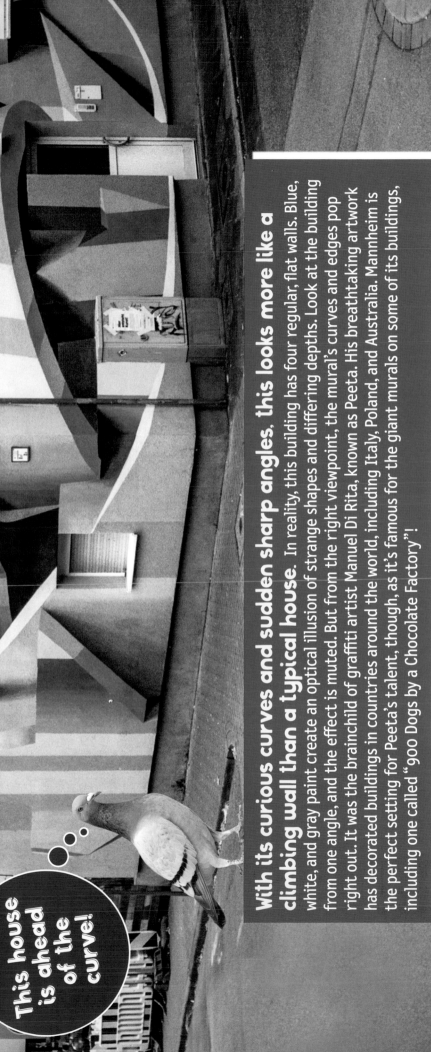

With its curious curves and sudden sharp angles, this looks more like a climbing wall than a typical house. In reality, this building has four regular, flat walls. Blue, white, and gray paint create an optical illusion of strange shapes and differing depths. Look at the building from one angle, and the effect is muted. But from the right viewpoint, the mural's curves and edges pop right out. It was the brainchild of graffiti artist Manuel Di Rita, known as Peeta. His breathtaking artwork has decorated buildings in countries around the world, including Italy, Poland, and Australia. Mannheim is the perfect setting for Peeta's talent, though, as it's famous for the giant murals on some of its buildings, including one called "900 Dogs by a Chocolate Factory"!

This house is ahead of the curve!

133

DISHING THE DIRT!

Museum of Soap and History of Dirt
Bydgoszcz, Poland

If reading about dirt and dung makes you feel a bit grimy, you might enjoy a trip to this sweet-smelling museum. Back in medieval times, people made a bit of a stink about bathing regularly and didn't think it was necessary. The Polish city of Bydgoszcz was different though—it has a long history of making soap and promoting the benefits of good hygiene. There was even a public bath in the 14th century where people could soak. They could also have any rotten teeth pulled out, but with much less sugar eaten than today, our ancestors had fewer dental problems than you might think! The tradition of keeping clean continues at the Bydgoszcz's Museum of Soap. Upon arrival, visitors must wash their hands. Workshops allow you to make your own bar of soap—choosing the color, shape, and scent—or learn about make up. The exhibits cover 5,000 years of cleanliness: You can find out about reusable toilet paper from the ancient world and a character called Doctor Plague from the Middle Ages!

World Bog Snorkelling Championships
Llanwrtyd Wells, Wales, U.K.

Participants in this bizarre competition are ready to make a splash! The course is a water-filled trench carved through marshy bogland. Wearing a snorkel, mask, and flippers, the contestants attempt to cover 360 feet (110 m) as speedily as possible—relying solely on flipper power! Neil Rutter has proved the snorkeler to beat recently, taking home the title in 2017, 2018, and 2019 and setting a world record of 1 minute 18.82 seconds on the way. Of course, many people compete for fun and plunge into the dirty water wearing costumes. Dinosaurs, pea pods, and sharks have all been seen battling the bog!

LLANWRTYD WELLS HOLDS A **BIKE BOG SNORKELING** COMPETITION WHERE YOU CAN RIDE ALONG THE COURSE ON A **CUSTOMIZED BICYCLE!**

Mud! Glorious mud!

Swamp Soccer
Finland

Any soccer players who complain about a damp field or a few drops of rain might want to pass on swamp soccer. This physically demanding sport is played on muddy bogs and players can find themselves buried up to their waists in sludge! The game originated in Finland in 1998 when 13 teams competed in the first tournament. In the 2019 World Championships, around 200 teams battled it out. Matches usually last just 24 minutes because charging through the mud is so exhausting. That might explain why goals aren't that common, too. Anyone who pays the entry fee can play in the world championships, but all players have one thing in common—they don't mind a good mud bath!

Treasure Seekers
Staffordshire, England, U.K.

Getting muddy is fun, right? Getting muddy because you've found buried treasure is even better! In 2009, a metal detectorist named Terry Herbert was searching a farmer's field when his detector beeped. At that point he had no idea what he had discovered. It was the largest ever find of Anglo-Saxon gold and silver—that means the items are around 1,500 years old. Over 4,000 pieces of jewelry and other objects were uncovered by the end of the year.

The hoard was valued at a staggering £3.285 million ($4.6 million)!

IMPROBABLE ITALY

The Park of the Monsters
Bomarzo, Italy

If you picnic at the Park of the Monsters, it might be you on the menu! These stunning gardens contain an astonishing assortment of statues and buildings. One sculpture nicknamed the "Hell Mouth" has a table inside it. But to reach it, you'll have to climb inside the mouth—in other words, diners have to be eaten before they eat! The mouth, which appears to be frozen in a scream, has the inscription *Ogni Pensiero Vola*, meaning "all thoughts depart." The park was commissioned by a 16th-century duke, Pier Francesco Orsini, to represent his grief after he suffered various tragedies in his life.

Open up and say aarrgghh!

The park's other **sculptures** include a **giant tearing a rival in half!**

Lake Resia
Curon, Italy

When an energy company wanted to build an artificial lake and dam in 1939, there was one major problem—there was a town already on the site. So residents were moved to new homes and the old houses were blown up. After delays caused by WWII, the area was finally flooded in 1950—but one building was allowed to survive. The bell tower, once part of a 14th-century church, now rises above the surface of the lake. It was restored in 2009, so it's still standing tall today. In winter, when the lake freezes over, visitors can walk right up to the tower. It's even rumored you can hear the bells ring on cold nights!

BY the NUMBERS

GARGANTUAN GAMES

The Colosseum was built between A.D. 72 and 80 in ancient Rome. Big enough to easily fit a soccer field inside, this amazing arena hosted some unusual events, which were free to watch, including gladiator contests, animal hunts, and prisoner executions. The Colosseum was sometimes even filled with water for mock naval battles!

36 TRAPDOORS
IN THE ARENA FOR SPECIAL EFFECTS, INCLUDING AMAZING SCENERY AND EXOTIC ANIMALS SUDDENLY APPEARING!

MORE THAN
6 MILLION
TOURISTS VISIT THE REMAINS EVERY YEAR.

164 FEET (50 M)
HIGH—THAT'S ABOUT THE HEIGHT OF A MODERN 12-STORY BUILDING.

620 FEET (189 M) LONG

AND
513 FEET (156 M) WIDE
MAKING IT THE LARGEST AMPHITHEATER IN THE WORLD

50,000 PEOPLE WATCHED THE SPECTACLES TOGETHER.

Going UNDER!

I'm getting tunnel vision!

Piusa Sand Caves
Piusa, Estonia

For almost 50 years, Piusa was home to a huge quarry. But when the workers left the 13.7-mile (22-km) network of caves and corridors, new residents moved in—bats! Between October and May, more than 3,000 of the flying mammals come to Piusa Caves to hibernate. That makes the caves the biggest wintering colony of bats in Eastern Europe. The caves are now protected, but you'd have to be batty to want to disturb these creatures!

Olms
Italy, Slovenia, and Croatia

These salamanders were first identified in 1689, when locals thought they were baby dragons! They've also been called "human fish" because of their pale pink skin. Olms have spent so long in dark caves that they're almost blind. Instead, they rely on their smell and hearing to catch prey.

Large Hadron Collider
Meyrin, Switzerland

There are a lot of big science projects taking place at CERN (the European Council for Nuclear Research). And you don't get much bigger than the Large Hadron Collider, which makes tiny particles travel at extremely accelerated speeds. It's a vast underground ring of magnets—16.8 miles (27 km) in circumference. That's the "large" part—and it's a collider because it smashes particles together up to one billion times every second! Ultimately, it will help scientists learn what the universe was like when it was created in the big bang.

British Museum Tube Station
London, England, U.K.

Announcements in London's metro system tell travelers to "mind the gap" between the train and the platform. But should some stations warn people to mind the spirits instead? Farringdon Station is said to have a "Screaming Specter," and it's claimed an "Elderly Angel" calls Aldgate Station home. Abandoned stations provide perfect haunting spots, too. The British Museum Station, open between 1900 and 1933, is supposed to be home to the ghost of either the Egyptian pharaoh Amun-Re, or his daughter—depending on who you ask. Legend says the ghost screams so loudly that the sound carries through the tunnels to other stations!

I miss my mummy!

Fingal's Cave
Isle of Staffa, Scotland, U.K.

The translation of this cave's original Gaelic name is the "Cave of Melody." The echoes of waves inside the huge, arched hollow inspired 19th-century composer Felix Mendelssohn to write *Fingal's Cave Overture*. Writers, poets, and artists have also visited the cave to be inspired.

Syri i Kaltër
Albania

When you gaze into this water, are you looking at it … or is it looking at you? Syri i Kaltër translates as "Blue Eye," and this beautiful pool lives up to its name. The dark waters in the center look like a pupil surrounded by a turquoise and green iris. No one knows exactly how deep it is. Divers have swum down 164 feet (50 m), but still couldn't see the bottom!

Škocjan Caves
Matavun, Slovenia

The Škocjan Caves make up one of the largest known underground canyons on Earth. The caves were inhabited from around 10,000 years ago, through the Stone and Bronze Ages, and the remains of an Iron Age temple have been discovered there, too. The caves are now home to a remarkable collection of plants and animals. The total length of all the cave passageways is around 3.7 miles (6 km), and visitors can marvel at the numerous pools and huge stalagmites within.

BIZARRE BUILDINGS

Giant Crossword
Lviv, Ukraine

4 across: L _ _ V: The place to go for anyone who enjoys a BIG challenge. The answer is Lviv—home to the world's largest crossword puzzle. Standing at more than 100 feet (30 m) tall and printed on the side of an apartment building, there are around 80 clues to crack. These are hidden on major landmarks, such as monuments and museums, all located around the Ukrainian city. Filling in the crossword teaches puzzle-solvers about Lviv's history.

Do you know the answer to 7 down?

THE SOLUTIONS APPEAR AT NIGHTTIME SO YOU CAN CHECK YOUR ANSWERS.

The Pan House
Zagaré, Lithuania

If you ever need to borrow a pan in Lithuania, a man named Edmundas Vaiciulis has quite a collection! The only problem is they are attached to his house. Vaiciulis prefers to do things his own way and doesn't always follow the rules. He only lasted one week in his first ever job because his boss didn't like his hairstyle or his footwear, and he refused to change either! When he bought half of a house, he wanted to rebuild all of it, but the owners of the other half were happy with the building as it was. Unable to renovate, Vaiciulis decorated the exterior with pots, pans, and old machinery parts instead. The Pan House, as it's known, is now one of the most photographed homes in Zagaré.

Kunsthofpassage
Dresden, Germany

If you've ever said it's too rainy to go outside, you probably don't live in Dresden! A sudden downpour is the ideal weather to take a trip to the Kunsthofpassage. Here you'll find five small, themed courtyards created by local artists, sculptors, and designers. In the Courtyard of Elements, the front of one building is covered with funnels, pipes, and gutters, which look like bizarre musical instruments. And that's exactly what they are! When the rain begins, so does the soggy symphony. The drops loudly pitter-patter off the metalwork and flow through the pipes, splattering on the paving slabs in the yard below. Local residents must need earplugs on a rainy night!

One courtyard features images of wild monkeys and giraffes on its walls.

Telefonplan Tower
Stockholm, Sweden

The thin, gray Telefonplan Tower looks pretty drab during the daytime. At 20 stories, it rises up above the surrounding buildings—but it's a far cry from being the world's tallest tower. The building transforms at night, when colorful lights shine through the windows of the top 10 floors. But a lot of buildings have fancy illuminations, don't they? Now take another walk past and you'll see that the colors in the windows have changed. That's because the lights can be controlled by phone or an app—and anyone can change them! This installation is called "Color by Numbers" and was only meant to run for one year. It has proved so popular, though, it has been lighting up the Telefonplan Tower since 2011. Color changes can be made by calling a phone number and using the keypad to select a floor and a color, or pressing the chosen selection by app. You can even watch a live feed of the transforming tints.

Call me anytime!

May I ask for this dance?

AWESOME AFRICA

Breathtaking landscapes, ancient mysteries, and a whole bunch of weird and wacky wildlife!

When the pyramids were first built, they had smooth and SHINY SIDES!

The tallest giraffe to ever live was about 19 FEET (5.7 M) TALL.

Pineapples aren't just a delicious fruit. Their LEAVES can be made into ROPES!

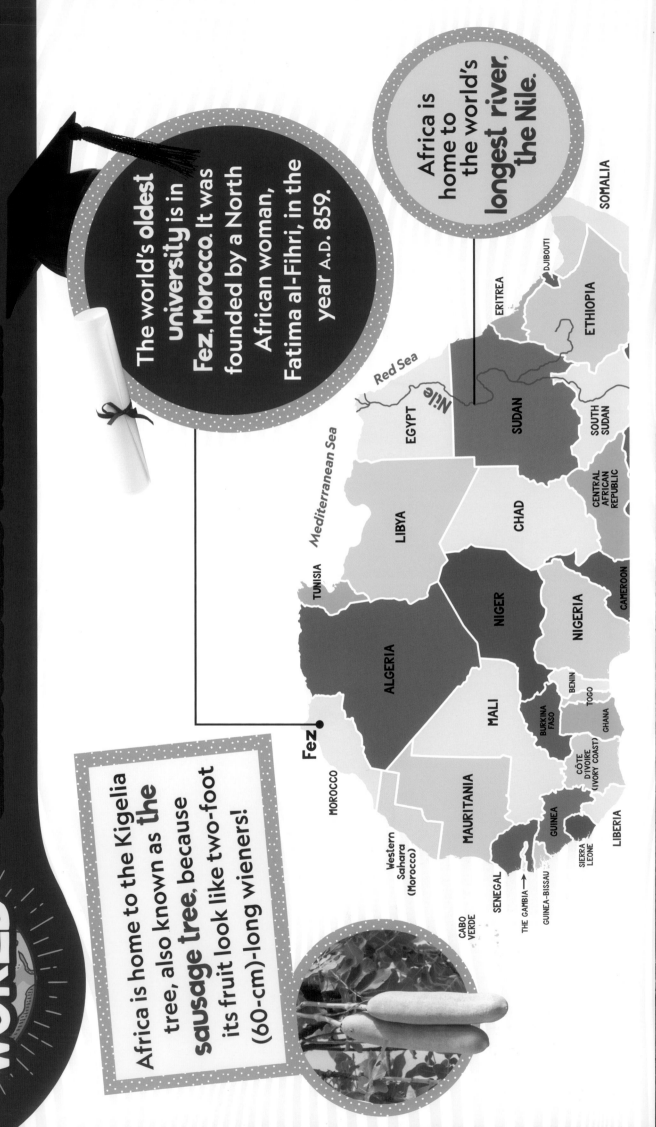

WEIRD in the WORLD

Explore an **INCREDIBLE CONTINENT** full of **STRANGE SIGHTS, AWESOME CELEBRATIONS,** and **FASCINATING ANIMALS.**

The world's oldest university is in Fez, Morocco. It was founded by a North African woman, Fatima al-Fihri, in the year A.D. 859.

Africa is home to the world's longest river, the Nile.

Africa is home to the Kigelia tree, also known as the **sausage tree,** because its fruit look like two-foot (60-cm)-long wieners!

Fez

Mediterranean Sea

Red Sea

Nile

TUNISIA
MOROCCO
Western Sahara (Morocco)
ALGERIA
LIBYA
EGYPT
MAURITANIA
MALI
NIGER
CHAD
SUDAN
ERITREA
DJIBOUTI
ETHIOPIA
SOMALIA
SOUTH SUDAN
CENTRAL AFRICAN REPUBLIC
CAMEROON
NIGERIA
BENIN
TOGO
GHANA
CÔTE D'IVOIRE (IVORY COAST)
BURKINA FASO
GUINEA
SIERRA LEONE
LIBERIA
GUINEA-BISSAU
THE GAMBIA
SENEGAL
CABO VERDE

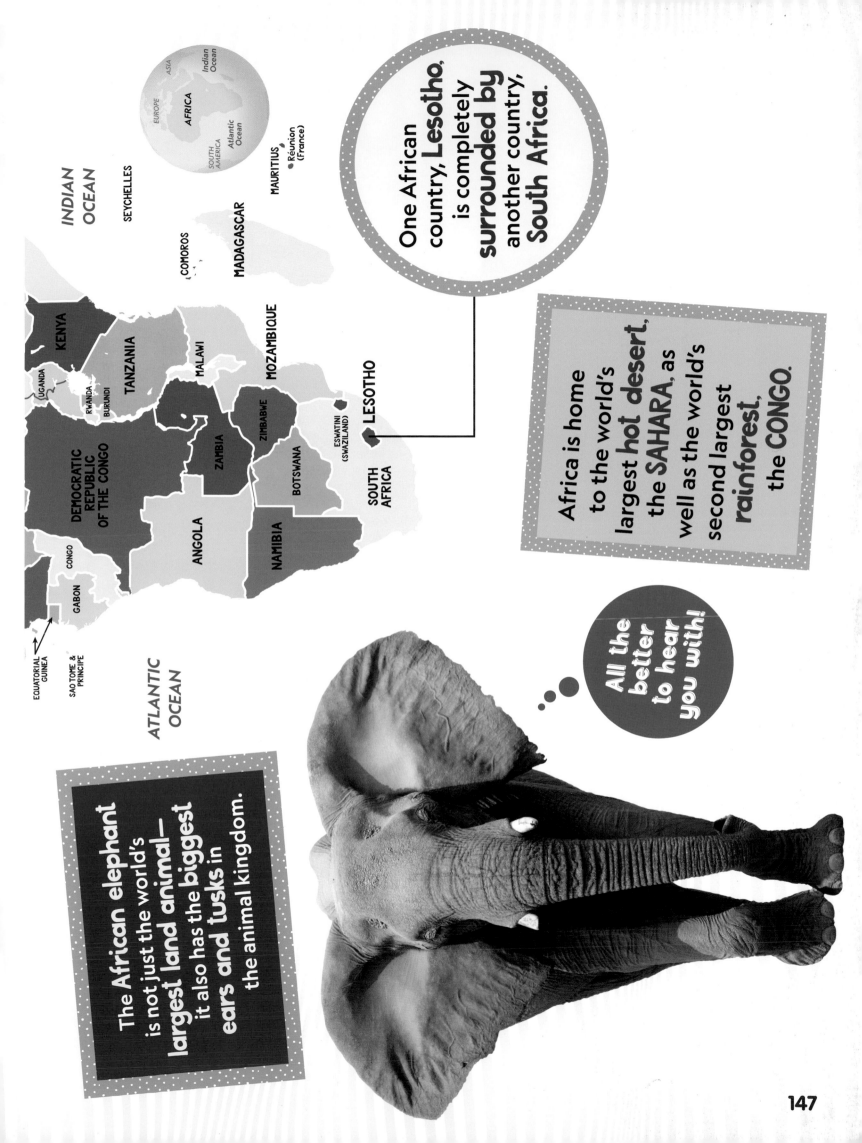

INDIAN OCEAN

SEYCHELLES

ASIA
EUROPE
AFRICA
Indian Ocean
Atlantic Ocean
SOUTH AMERICA

COMOROS

MADAGASCAR

MAURITIUS

• Réunion (France)

KENYA

UGANDA

TANZANIA

RWANDA
BURUNDI

MALAWI

MOZAMBIQUE

DEMOCRATIC REPUBLIC OF THE CONGO

ZIMBABWE

ZAMBIA

ESWATINI (SWAZILAND)

LESOTHO

CONGO

ANGOLA

BOTSWANA

NAMIBIA

SOUTH AFRICA

GABON

EQUATORIAL GUINEA

SAO TOME & PRINCIPE

ATLANTIC OCEAN

One African country, Lesotho, is completely **surrounded by** another country, **South Africa.**

Africa is home to the world's largest hot desert, the SAHARA, as well as the world's second largest rainforest, the CONGO.

All the better to hear you with!

The African elephant is not just the world's largest land animal— it also has the biggest ears and tusks in the animal kingdom.

147

WAY UP HIGH

Highest Mountain, Tallest Tree
Kilimanjaro, Tanzania

The highest point in the whole of Africa is the peak of Mount Kilimanjaro, a volcano in Tanzania. It's 19,340 feet (5,895 m) high, and the top is always covered in snow—even though the mountain is almost on the Equator! This is because air gets colder the higher you go. So, although the lower slopes are covered in tropical forests, above 16,000 feet (5,000 m), it's almost always below freezing. In 2016, a scientist exploring the mountain forests discovered another Kilimanjaro claim to fame: Africa's tallest tree—the Muyovu tree.

The Muyovu tree reaches **267 feet (81.5 m)** tall—as high as a **27-story building.**

Check out these moves!

Stilt Dancing
Atakpamé, Togo

In Atakpamé, a city in Togo, West Africa, you might see someone with eight-foot (2.5-m)-long legs strolling past! But don't panic—it's just a stilt dancer. Tchébé, the art of walking and dancing on stilts, is local to this area. It's an old tradition, but it's recently been revived as a modern art form. When learning, dancers start with short stilts, then gradually work their way up to stilts taller than themselves. The performers put on shows for both locals and tourists, wearing traditional costumes and body paint. As well as dancing in formation, they do tricks like catching hold of each other's stilts or hopping!

Bloukrans Bridge Bungee
Western Cape, South Africa

Scared of heights? Then you wouldn't want to even go near the terrifyingly tall Bloukrans Bridge in South Africa. It's Africa's highest bridge, with a single concrete span that carries cars 708 feet (216 m) above the tiny-looking Bloukrans River below. But wait ... it gets worse! Tourists come here not just to admire the bridge, but to leap right off it! It's home to one of the world's highest bridge-based bungee jumps. To get to the jumping platform in the middle, you have to clamber along a walkway under the main bridge. Needless to say, you don't try this at home!

THIS BUNGEE JUMP IS **SO SCARY** THAT **TWO OUT OF 10** PEOPLE WHO SIGN UP DON'T GO THROUGH WITH IT!

Giraffes
African Grasslands

There's no other animal like it—the yellow and brown-spotted, towering, long-necked giraffe, ambling across Africa's savannas. A giraffe's legs alone are taller than most humans, and its full height can reach 19 feet (5.8 m), making it the tallest animal on Earth. Its long neck helps the giraffe to reach food other animals can't, especially the leaves and buds of acacia trees, which they pluck with their rubbery tongues. Being tall also gives them a great view, to look out for predators such as lions and leopards. And males use their necks for fighting, whacking them against each other to win the position of top dog (or giraffe!) in the herd.

Curious CREATURES

Hairy Frog

Frogs are not hairy. But the hairy frog is—kind of! During the breeding season, the male frog grows strange tassel-like parts along his sides. They are actually made of skin, and they're thought to help the frog take in extra oxygen when he's underwater guarding his eggs. However, that's not even the weirdest thing about hairy frogs! They also have bones in their feet that can turn into claws. If the frog is in danger, its toe bones snap, then stick out through its skin, ready to fight off predators. This has earned it the nickname "the Wolverine frog"!

Satanic Leaf-Tailed Gecko

This small tree lizard from the island of Madagascar is a master of camouflage. It's not just its tail that looks like an old, dead leaf—so does every other part of its body! Its brilliant disguise helps it to hide from predators, and also to creep up on prey without being seen. To add to the effect, the gecko can flatten itself against a tree trunk. So far, so leafy, but why is it called "satanic"? It's because it has bright red eyes and two little horns, which give it a devilish look.

Mandrill

Imagine a giant monkey that's gone wild with some face paint, and you have ... a mandrill! This bizarre-looking beast from the jungles of West Africa is the world's biggest monkey species. Its strangely long face is bright blue and red, with a fluffy yellow beard to complete the look. And as if that's not enough, its butt has a matching color scheme! Male mandrills are bigger and have the brightest colors, as this helps to attract a female mate.

Camel Spider

Don't like spiders? Look away now! This is the spider of your nightmares. It grows up to six inches (15 cm) long, including its legs, and has sharp jaws that take up a third of its body length, and runs after people at 10 miles an hour (16 km/h). But wait! Camel spiders aren't actually spiders at all, and maybe they're not as scary as you think. They live in the deserts of northern Africa, and are a relative of spiders, called solpugids. Unlike spiders, they have no venom. They use their large jaws to munch prey, such as insects and small lizards, but rarely bite people. As for the chasing, camel spiders do follow people, but only because they're trying to avoid the hot sun by staying in your shadow!

Bush Baby

Could there be a cuter creature than this? With its enormous, innocent-looking eyes and snuggly fur, a bush baby, or galago, looks very much like a cuddly toy. Bush babies are nocturnal; they leap around in the trees at night catching insects and eating fruit. Their big round eyes help them to see in the dark, but they also use their super sensitive hearing and sense of smell to find food. You might think the name "bush baby" comes from the way they look, but it's actually because of their call. Echoing through the forest at night, it sounds just like the cry of a human baby!

Shoebill

Guess you can see how this bird got its name! One of Africa's strangest-looking creatures, the shoebill has a huge beak that looks like a shoe. Or maybe a whale, seeing as it's also known as the whale-headed stork (though it's not considered a stork anymore). It's a huge, fish-eating water bird, standing up to five feet (1.5 m) tall! You might not expect a bird like this to have a beautiful singing voice—and you'd be right. Instead, the shoebill makes a clattering noise with its beak, or a strange mooing sound like a cow.

BY the NUMBERS

PYRAMIDS AT GIZA

The Pyramids at Giza in Cairo, Egypt's capital, are among the most famous buildings in the world. The ancient Egyptians built the three largest pyramids as tombs for three pharaohs, Khufu, Khafre, and Menkaure. They were made by cutting and stacking layer upon layer of big, heavy stone blocks, probably by dragging them up ramps of earth. It was an incredible feat, especially so long ago, when there were no power tools, cranes, or bulldozers!

HEIGHT OF THE GREAT PYRAMID TODAY:

449.5 FEET (137 M)

AGE OF THE PYRAMIDS:

OVER 4,500 YEARS

WIDTH OF THE GREAT PYRAMID:

756 FEET (230 M)
—AS LONG AS TWO SOCCER FIELDS

HOW LONG THE GREAT PYRAMID STOOD AS THE WORLD'S TALLEST BUILDING:

3,871 YEARS

WEIGHT OF EACH STONE BLOCK:

AT LEAST **2.5** TONS (2.3 t)

—AS MUCH AS 35 PEOPLE, OR ONE SMALL ELEPHANT

NUMBER OF STONE BLOCKS IN THE GREAT PYRAMID:

2.3 MILLION

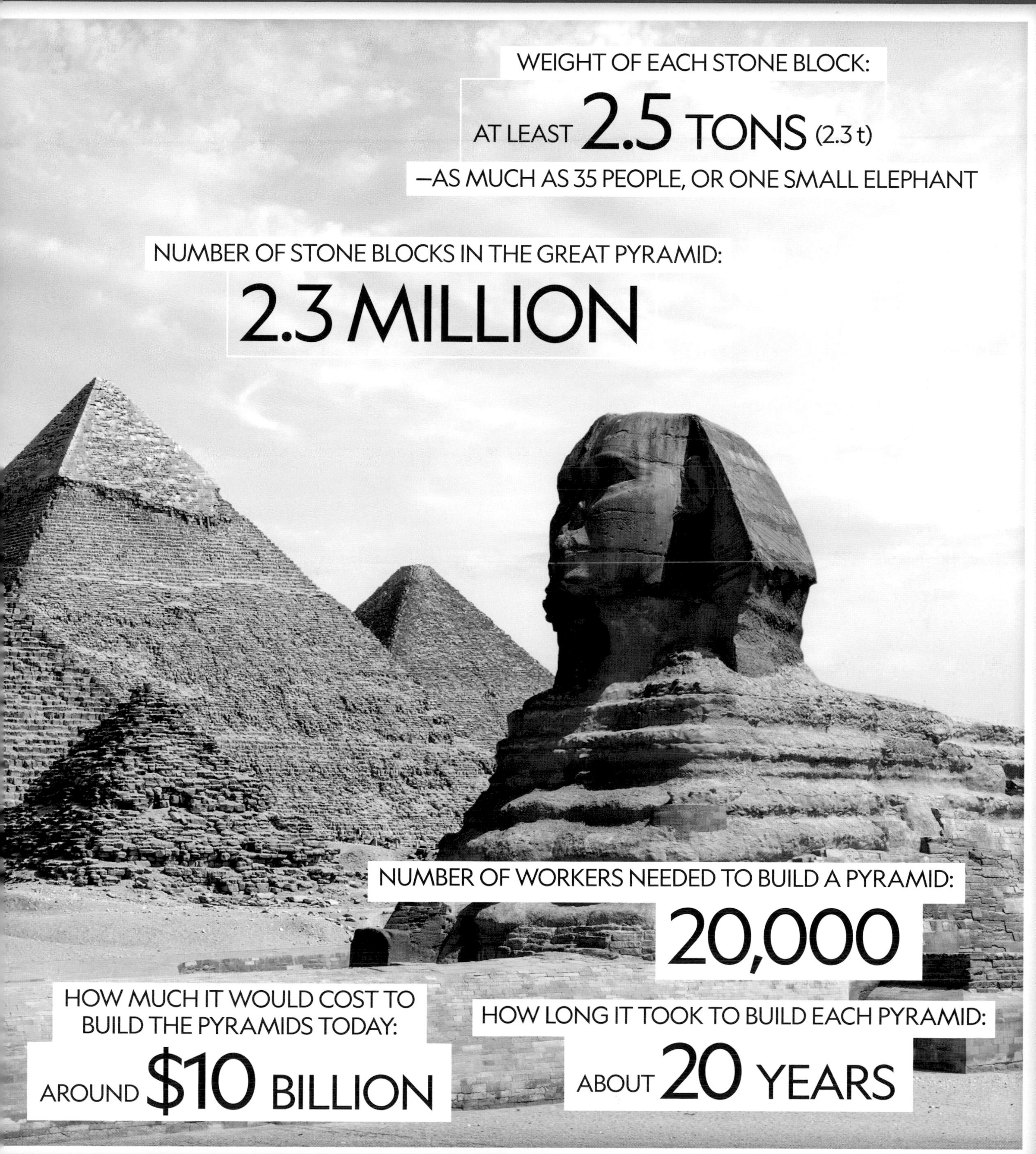

NUMBER OF WORKERS NEEDED TO BUILD A PYRAMID:

20,000

HOW MUCH IT WOULD COST TO
BUILD THE PYRAMIDS TODAY:

AROUND **$10** BILLION

HOW LONG IT TOOK TO BUILD EACH PYRAMID:

ABOUT **20** YEARS

EERIE AFRICA

Pirate Cemetery
Nosy Boraha, Madagascar

In the 1700s, Nosy Boraha, off the coast of Madagascar, was a real-life Pirate Island, used by raiders from around the world as a hideout! Cargo ships laden with gold, silver, gems, and spices passed nearby on the main trading route between Asia and Europe. That made the little island the perfect place to lie in wait for ships to attack, and to hide stolen loot. Sometimes, the pirates died on the island, and then their friends buried them in their own special cemetery. You can still visit it today and see the pirates' gravestones.

SOME OF THE CEMETERY GRAVESTONES ARE CARVED WITH SKULLS AND CROSSBONES.

Skeleton Coast
Namibia

The spookily named Skeleton Coast is in Namibia, where the dunes of the baking hot Namib Desert meet the cold and stormy Atlantic Ocean. It's a harsh, dangerous environment, and it really does have skeletons! Long ago, whale-hunting ships sailed here. You can find whale bones along the shore, as well as skeletons of long-dead desert animals. There are also the rusted remains of hundreds of ships, wrecked on the sandbanks and beaches by the powerful waves. And beneath the sand, there are human skeletons, too. In the past, any sailors who survived a shipwreck found themselves in the desert, far from help, with no fresh water, so were doomed to stay forever.

The **Khoisan people** of Namibia call the Skeleton Coast **"the land god made in anger."**

Weirdly Cute!
Hammer-Headed Bat

Hands off my dinner!

Imagine this freaky-faced bat flapping around you at night! Not only is the hammer-headed bat strange to look at, it's also a flying fox, or megabat. That means it's really big—a male's wingspan can measure 38 inches (97 cm) across—but it won't hurt you. Like most other megabats, this cuddly critter feeds on fruit! Only the male has a hammer-shaped face, while the female has a more fox-like snout. This is because the male has a large chamber in his face, which he uses to make incredibly loud honking noises to attract a mate. Instead of being scared, locals just get annoyed when the honking keeps them up at night!

Cool CONSTRUCTIONS!

Big Pineapple

SpongeBob SquarePants may live in a pineapple under the sea, but this real-life pineapple building is on land, in Bathurst, South Africa. It was built in the 1980s to celebrate the local pineapple-growing industry, which took off in the 1800s after farmers realized how well pineapples grew there. This pineapple isn't actually a house, however. Inside, its four floors contain a pineapple-themed museum and shop. Though there are other pineapple buildings in the world, this one is the tallest, so it holds the record for the biggest pineapple on Earth!

Crocodile House

Don't worry, this crocodile won't bite! It's actually a concrete house in Abidjan, in the West African country of the Ivory Coast, that was built by an artist named Moussa Kalo. After he died, his assistant moved in and added the finishing touches. There isn't a whole lot of room inside a crocodile, but at least it's bigger than life-size! It has a bedroom in the head and a toilet at the tail end, as well as a spacious courtyard outside.

Lemon Squeezer Church

Is it a rocket? Is it an upside-down flower? No—it's a lemon squeezer! Or at least that's the nickname given to the Church of St. Anthony in Maputo, Mozambique. Built in 1962, it's made of smooth sheets of concrete that look as if they've been folded up like origami. The shape is exactly the same on the inside as on the outside. There's just one big, circular room, with a zigzagging, folded ceiling, and a view all the way up the tall, cone-shaped spire, lit up by beautiful stained-glass windows.

Hotel With Wings

Would you like to stay in a hotel room that sticks out in midair? This amazing hotel is the Hotel du Lac in Tunis, the capital of Tunisia. The floors get longer and longer as you go up, with the top floor twice as long as the bottom floor. It was built in the early 1970s—and not long after that, the makers of the first *Star Wars* movie came to Tunisia to film in the desert. Some say they saw the hotel, and it inspired the shape of the Sandcrawler, a huge desert vehicle that appears in the movies. Sadly, the hotel is no longer used, so you couldn't stay in it even if you wanted to!

The Shoe

You've heard of the old woman who lived in a shoe. Well, this house proves it's possible! There are actually quite a few shoe-shaped houses in the world, but this one in Ohrigstad, South Africa, has to be one of the cutest. It was built by artist Ron van Zyl for his wife, and proved so popular with tourists that he added more attractions nearby, including a restaurant, a swimming pool, a shop, an underground cave, and guest cabins. Sadly, though, you can't stay overnight in the shoe itself, because it's used as an art gallery.

Mauritius is a tropical island nation in the Indian Ocean. If you fly over its southwestern point and look down, you'll see an amazing sight—what looks like a huge waterfall in the sea, plunging from the shallow water down into the ocean depths. But this is actually not a waterfall! The seabed does suddenly get deeper, just off the coast. What looks like water pouring over the edge is actually trails of sand, washed down the slope from the island's beautiful white beaches.

UNDERWATER WATERFALL

Mauritius

what you're seeing is sand trickling **THOUSANDS OF FEET** into an underwater crevasse.

REMARKABLE ROCKS

White Desert
Farafra, Egypt

In the middle of Egypt's Western Desert, which is part of the Sahara, is a smaller, much stranger desert. It's as white as snow, and covered in tall chalk-white rocks in all kinds of weird shapes. The formations have been compared to mushrooms, meringues, and even modern art. They are made by the wind blasting desert sand over rocks and wearing them away over thousands of years. They're said to look especially magical at sunset, and by moonlight—so tourists often come here for an overnight stay and sleep under the stars.

Mystery Footprint
Mpumalanga, South Africa

Near the village of Lothair in South Africa, there's a footprint stamped into a vertical wall of rock. A BIG footprint—four feet (1.2 m) long. It's known as the Giant's Footprint, but does that mean a giant walked this way long, long ago? Um ... no! The rock formed three billion years ago, and the only living things around then were single-celled microbes. Instead, experts say the shape appeared by chance as the rock wore away over time. People may have given it a sneaky helping hand by carving it to make it look more like a footprint, too!

To have feet as big as this footprint, you'd have to be about 27 feet (8 m) tall!

Balancing Rocks
Harare, Zimbabwe

These rocks in Zimbabwe look so carefully balanced, it seems like a deliberate design, but they're actually natural. They, and many other massive boulders, can be found piled up in teetering towers in a park in Harare, Zimbabwe's capital. The incredibly hard rocks formed there long ago, when volcanic lava pushed up from underground, then cooled and solidified. They ended up on top of softer rock, which crumbled and wore away over time, leaving the boulders behind. They're so well known in Zimbabwe, they feature on some of the country's paper money.

DATING SHOWS THAT THE STONE CIRCLES COULD BE UP TO 1,000 YEARS OLD.

Senegambian Stone Circles
Senegal and Gambia

If you love mysterious ancient stone circles, forget Stonehenge and head to West Africa! In a smallish region of Senegal and Gambia, you'll find not just one stone circle, but over a thousand of them—the biggest group of stone circles in the world. The stones in each circle are neatly carved and shaped into square or round blocks to match each other. No one knows who made them, and the locals have a variety of different stories. Some legends say ancient gods put them here when time began, or that the blocks are ancient humans who turned to stone. Others say they are the graves of kings or giants who lived long ago. Excavations have found skeletons buried in the circles, but the mystery of who built them remains.

PERSONALITY QUIZ

Which odd abode should you call home?

Take the quiz to find out!

1 **Does your dream home have a sea view?**

a. Yes, I'd love to live right next to the sea!

b. Not really. It's what's inside my home that counts.

c. No, I prefer grassy meadows.

d. No, but a lake would be nice.

2 **Where would you like your home to be?**

a. Somewhere remote, wild, and rocky

b. Surrounded by mountains

c. In the countryside, surrounded by wildlife

d. In a lovely forest setting

3 **Do you need lots of space?**

a. Not really—just somewhere to shelter from the weather!

b. No, as long as there are things to do nearby.

c. Small and quirky suits me best!

d. Of course—I want a home fit for royalty!

4 **Something with a bit of history, perhaps?**

a. Ooh yes—in fact, the older the better!

b. Just as long as the building has a story to tell, I'm happy.

c. That doesn't matter to me.

d. I'd like history AND mystery, please!

5 Is it important to you to impress the neighbors?

a. Nope. Don't want any neighbors.

b. Oh yes, I want works of art on show.

c. I want them to think my house is totally unique!

d. Never mind the neighbors—I want the whole world to be impressed!

6 Of course you have great style—but what kind of style?

a. Rustic, natural, and eco-friendly

b. Arty and original

c. Cozy, quirky, and folksy

d. Aristocratic and grand

7 What outfit would you wear to a costume party?

a. Fake fur cloak

b. A mop cap and an apron

c. Fairy costume

d. A crown fit for royalty

Mostly A's
Your ideal home is … Blombos Cave!
Admittedly, it's a bit of a fixer-upper. But this cool cave is right on the seafront in South Africa, and it's full of fascinating artifacts from pre-historic times. Perfect if you want to get away from it all!

Mostly B's
Your ideal home is … the Shoe!
This tiny, boot-shaped building will satisfy your desire for culture AND cuteness. Inside, it's filled with artwork—and there are attractions aplenty on your doorstep, too. Its definitely a shoe-in!

Mostly C's
Your ideal home is … a hollow baobab tree!
As long as you don't mind a rustic dwelling, a home in a baobab tree is chic, unique, and easy to look after. Wildlife lovers can enjoy a permanent safari on their "doorstep."

Mostly D's
Your ideal home is … Great Zimbabwe!
For you, only a royal residence will do! OK, it might have seen better days, but this is still one of the biggest, most important medieval buildings in Africa, in a stunning countryside setting.

INCREDIBLE EDIBLES

Ostrich Eggs
Southern Africa

Fancy an egg for breakfast? In South Africa, where there are a lot of ostrich farms, you can have an ostrich egg—but you'd better be hungry! Ostriches are the biggest birds in the world, and they lay the biggest eggs. An ostrich egg is about six inches (15 cm) long, and weighs roughly the same as 25 chicken eggs. If you want it hard-boiled, it will take an hour and a half to cook! However, this strength makes the shells very useful. The San people of the Kalahari Desert have used them as pots to store water in since ancient times, and they use smaller, broken pieces of shell to make beads.

You would need a hammer to crack open a hard-boiled ostrich egg!

Sensational Snails
West Africa

France is probably the country best known for its snail recipes, but they're a big favorite in West Africa, too. And when we say big, we mean giant! Giant African land snails can grow to be eight inches (20 cm) long, so you don't need that many to make a meal. In Nigeria, Ghana, and other West African countries, they are made into stew, or cooked with hot peppers to make a much-loved finger-food snack called peppered snails. Snails are super healthy, too, as they're low-fat and full of protein. And what do they taste like? Most people say a chewy, earthy mouthful of snail is most similar to eating a fried mushroom!

Ginormous Jackfruit
East Africa

These massive green boulders aren't boulders at all—they're fruit! Jackfruit are the biggest tree fruits in the world, growing up to two feet (60 cm) long and weighing up to 40 pounds (18 kg). They're native to India but were brought to East Africa by trading ships in the 1600s, and are now found all over Kenya, Tanzania, and Uganda. Inside the fruit's rock-hard bumpy skin are lumps of chewy yellow flesh, and lots of incredibly sticky juice. Jackfruit are now becoming popular with vegans around the world because they make a good meat substitute!

Insect Milk
South Africa

In many parts of the world, insects are an important food. In Africa, crunchy mopane worm caterpillars, fried crickets, and even stink bugs (don't worry, the stinky part is removed before eating) are all popular. But some people don't like the idea of eating bugs, so food scientists in South Africa have come up with an alternative: insect milk! No, insects don't produce milk like cows do, and you can't milk them. (Even if you could, it would take ages to collect a pint!) Instead, this milk substitute, called EntoMilk, is made from insect larvae. So far, you can only get it in South Africa, but maybe in the future, insect milk will be a dairy alternative around the world.

INSECT MILK IS HIGH IN PROTEIN AND CAN BE MADE INTO ICE CREAM.

PECULIAR FACTS ABOUT

The **BAOBAB TREE** grows in **dry grassland areas** and stores **water in its trunk,** like a cactus.

To avoid being eaten by desert animals, **LITHOPS PLANTS** are **CLEVERLY DISGUISED** as rocks!

When the creepy, gross-smelling *HYDNORA AFRICANA FLOWER* opens up, it looks like a fleshy red hand trying to grab you!

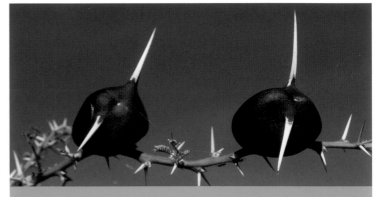

The **WHISTLING THORN** has large hollow thorns, which make a whistling noise when the wind blows past them.

AFRICAN PLANTS

THE **PLUMP, WATER-FILLED STEM OF THE BASEBALL PLANT** LOOKS LIKE A BASEBALL SITTING ON THE GROUND.

High on East Africa's Rwenzori and Virunga Mountains, **lobelia and heather plants,** which are small in other places, **GROW TO HUGE SIZES.**

THE **COCO DE MER** PALM TREE OF THE SEYCHELLES IS FAMOUS FOR ITS GIGANTIC, **BUTT-SHAPED NUT!**

SAND

There's not much snow in the Sahara, but you can still go snowboarding—or sandboarding, to be exact. Using either a snowboard or a special sandboard, riders zoom, carve, and jump down the gigantic sand dunes in Morocco's *ergs*. An erg, also called a dune sea or sand sea, is an area of loose sand in the desert, blown by the wind into a landscape of dunes. Some of these sand mountains can be 1,000 feet (300 m) high! And they're not just used for boarding—you could try off-roading in a four-wheeler, quad bike racing, or, the toughest challenge of all, running desert marathons.

Time to catch some waves—er—sand!

SURFING

The Sahara desert covers
3.5 MILLION SQUARE MILES
(9 million sq km).

WILD MADAGASCAR!

You should see me tap-dance!

Verreaux's Sifaka
Coastal Forests

If you see an animal that looks like a skinny, fluffy white monkey, dancing and skipping along on two legs, it's probably a Verreaux's sifaka (pronounced Ver-ohs suh-fah-kuh)! Sifakas are not monkeys, but lemurs, a related group of primates from Madagascar. They are brilliant at leaping from tree to tree, easily covering gaps of 30 feet (9 m). But if the distance is too far, they hop, skip, and jump along the ground with their arms in the air.

Madagascar Leaf-Nosed Snake
Lowland Forests

Also unique to Madagascar is this strange-looking snake, with its long, flat, pointed nose. No one really knows what it's for—it could help the snake disguise itself as a vine as it dangles from trees, or maybe it helps males and females of this species recognize each other. You can tell which is which, as the male has a single point on his snout, while the female's snout has a frilly tip.

Aye-Aye
Tropical Forests

Meet the aye-aye, probably the only animal in the world that's famous for its fingers! This scruffy-looking, nocturnal lemur creeps around between tree branches, tap-tap-tapping on the bark with its super-skinny middle finger. It can tell where tasty grubs are hiding by listening to the sound this makes. When it strikes lucky, it gnaws a hole, then uses its extra-long fourth finger, with a hooked claw on the tip, to pull out the prey.

I may be itsy-bitsy, but my web isn't!

Darwin's Bark Spider
Rainforest Rivers

Imagine canoeing happily along a river in Madagascar, when suddenly your face gets caught in the world's biggest spiderweb! It's the work of Darwin's bark spider, which spins webs across rivers by letting a long thread of silk float through the air to the opposite bank on the breeze. In the middle, it constructs a web up to 10 feet (3 m) across to catch water-loving insects such as dragonflies. Besides weaving the biggest webs, it has the strongest spider silk on Earth. But the spider itself is small—only about half an inch (1.5 cm) long.

Brookesia micra
Nosy Hara Island

This is the teeniest, tiniest chameleon in the world. When fully grown, *Brookesia micra* is just over an inch (25 mm) long. During the day, it hides in leaf litter on the ground, climbing trees at night to sleep in safety, and feeds on tiny fruit flies. It was discovered on Nosy Hara, a small island off the coast of Madagascar, in 2007. Not surprisingly, scientists hadn't spotted it up until then!

Weirdly Cute!

Giraffe-Necked Weevil

Giraffes don't live on the island of Madagascar. Instead, their mini-me lives there—the tiny, but incredibly long-necked giraffe weevil! This plant-eating beetle is found in leafy rainforest trees. Females use their long necks to help them roll up leaves to make safe holders for their eggs. Males have even longer necks—longer than their bodies—which they use to fight and push each other away in battles over females.

WEIRD WATER

Lake Natron
Arusha Region, Tanzania

If you visit Lake Natron, whatever you do, don't go for a swim! It's not because crocodiles will get you, but because the water is so full of salty minerals, you might not come out alive. Rivers and springs carry natural chemicals into the lake, including a salt called natron. Then, as the water evaporates, the chemicals get left behind. Some life can survive in the water—it often looks red because of the algae that live in it, which local flamingos feed on. Creatures that die in the lake end up preserved and encrusted with chemicals, making it look as if they've been spookily turned to stone.

The **ancient Egyptians** used the **salt natron** to **preserve mummies.**

Devil's Pool, Victoria Falls
Zambia and Zimbabwe

Swimming right up to the edge of the world's biggest waterfall might seem like a bad idea. But at Victoria Falls, between Zambia and Zimbabwe, you really can do this, thanks to a natural pool known as the Devil's Pool, near the edge of the falls. It has a rocky ledge that stops you slipping off, so you can swim up to the edge and peer over to see the water plunging more than 350 feet (108 m) into the gorge below. However, you can't just jump into the pool on your own. People who want to experience the thrill have to take a guided tour, with expert staff to make sure they're safe.

Danakil Depression
Ethiopia

A depression is an area that's lower than its surroundings—and Ethiopia's Danakil Depression is so low, it's more than 400 feet (120 m) below sea level. It's formed by three tectonic plates, the chunks of rock that make up Earth's crust, pulling away from each other—and it's packed with volcanic activity. Among the spouting geysers, bubbling hot springs, and acidic lakes, the land is covered with crusty white, yellow, and green minerals. Danakil also has some of the hottest average temperatures on the planet, so coming here feels like a trip to an incredibly hot, strange, and colorful alien world.

Boiling Lake Bogoria
Kenya

Kenya's Lake Bogoria has dozens of springs around the edges, some of them so hot you can actually see areas of water bubbling and boiling. Although the lake is quite hard to get to, tourists come here to eat lunch, and use the hot springs to boil eggs for their picnics (taking care not to fall in, of course!). Nearby there's a river where the hot spring water mixes with cooler water. This creates the perfect temperature of a warm bath, and it's safe to take a nice relaxing dip.

THERE CAN BE AS MANY AS TWO MILLION FLAMINGOS FEEDING IN LAKE BOGORIA AT ONCE.

ANCIENT MYSTERIES

Giraffe Carvings
Niger ➤

In the Sahara desert in Niger, carved into a big, flat, sloping rock, are two beautiful giraffes, a male and a smaller female. There are other rock carvings here too, but the giraffes are the biggest, with the male around 18 feet (5.5 m) tall, or life-size. They date from around 8,000 years ago, when the Sahara was a lush grassland, with rivers, trees, and many more animals than it has now, including giraffes. No one knows who made these artworks, or why. What's more, the giraffes appear to have leashes, or reins. Did the ancient people of the Sahara have tame or pet giraffes? It's a mystery!

Is there water in my ear?

Heracleion
Alexandria, Egypt

In 1933, a pilot flying over the bay of Alexandria, on the coast of Egypt, looked down and saw ruins under the water. Later, divers explored the seabed and found statues, columns, coins, sunken ships, and the remains of a temple. These ruins were remnants of the city of Heracleion, one of ancient Egypt's most important ports, which stood on islands in the bay, 2,500 years ago. At some point, the islands were washed away, and the buildings collapsed and sank into the sea. No one knows exactly when or how. It might have been a tsunami, earthquakes, or rising sea levels, or maybe all of the above! And there's probably much more of Heracleion waiting to be found, under the muddy seabed.

Mystery of Mount Lico
Mozambique

In 2018, a team of scientists and climbers set out on a daring mission: to climb Mount Lico, a tall mountain surrounded by vertical cliffs on every side. Why? To explore the rainforest on top. Thanks to the ancient volcano's sheer sides, the top of the mountain was unexplored. Its crater contained an ancient forest that had remained undisturbed for centuries. The explorers discovered a pristine habitat, with several previously unknown species. But they also found something weirder: some ancient, human-made pottery, half-buried in the ground. Someone had been here before, in ancient times—but who they were, and how they reached the top, is unknown.

A DRONE WAS USED TO TAKE IMAGES OF THE FOREST INSIDE THE CRATER, BEFORE THE TEAM CLIMBED INTO IT.

Helicopter Hieroglyphs
Abydos, Egypt

The ancient Egyptian temple of Seti I, like many Egyptian buildings, has carvings all over its inside walls. Among the more familiar hieroglyphs showing birds, suns, and plants, there are some that are a LOT more mysterious. These pictures look like a helicopter, a plane, and some kind of space rocket. They've led a lot of people to wonder if the ancient Egyptians had advanced flight technology that's now been lost—or were even visited by aliens! Archaeologists have a simpler explanation. They say the same piece of stone was carved over twice, creating the strange sci-fi symbols entirely by accident.

QUIZ WHIZ

Think you're a whiz at Weird But True?
Test your knowledge with these quirky questions!

1 **Why does Mount Kilimanjaro have snow on top?**

a. It's not snow, it's a rare white mineral called Kilimanjarite.

b. It's not snow, it's eagle poop.

c. Because its summit is so high, it's freezing cold.

d. It's put there by a snow machine so that people can go skiing.

2 **The incredibly noisy shrill thorntree cicada is as loud as:**

a. A rock concert

b. A road drill

c. A rocket launch

d. A blue whale

3 **How old is the Great Pyramid of Giza?**

a. 550 years old

b. 2,000 years old

c. 12,000 years old

d. 4,500 years old

4 The scary-looking camel spider of North Africa isn't actually a spider. It's a ...

a. Solpugid
b. Scorpion
c. Centipede
d. Sifaka

5 How does the male hammer-headed bat make a loud honking noise?

a. By honking inside an echoey tree hollow
b. By breaking wind loudly
c. By using an echo chamber in its face to amplify sound
d. By funneling its call through its leathery wings

6 How long does it take to hard-boil an ostrich egg?

a. 24 hours
b. 3 hours
c. 1.5 hours
d. 30 minutes

7 The Church of St. Anthony in Maputo, Mozambique, has a nickname. What is it?

a. The Cheese Grater
b. The Lemon Squeezer
c. The Garlic Crusher
d. The Frying Pan

8 What do lithops plants look like?

a. Hands
b. Sausages
c. Stones
d. Butts

6

ASTOUNDING ASIA

Watery wonders, terrific temples, colorful constructions, and more!

Where the weird things are.

These macaques live FARTHER NORTH than any other primate (aside from humans).

The name Pokémon is a mash-up of the words "POCKET" and "MONSTER."

WEIRD in the WORLD

Check out some of the **INCREDIBLE, UNIQUE,** and totally **JAW-DROPPING ANIMALS** and **PLACES** across **ASIA.**

In Seoul, South Korea, you can visit a ghostly abandoned theme park to witness the crumbling rides.

Roughly **60 percent** of the world's total population lives in Asia.

Asia has the longest coastline of any continent.

ARCTIC OCEAN

PACIFIC OCEAN

JAPAN

NORTH KOREA

Seoul

SOUTH KOREA

RUSSIA

MONGOLIA

KAZAKHSTAN

KYRGYZSTAN

TAJIKISTAN

UZBEKISTAN

TURKMENISTAN

AFGHANISTAN

IRAN

KUWAIT

SAUDI ARABIA

IRAQ

AZERBAIJAN

ARMENIA

GEORGIA

TURKEY

SYRIA

LEBANON

ISRAEL

JORDAN

EGYPT

Mediterranean Sea

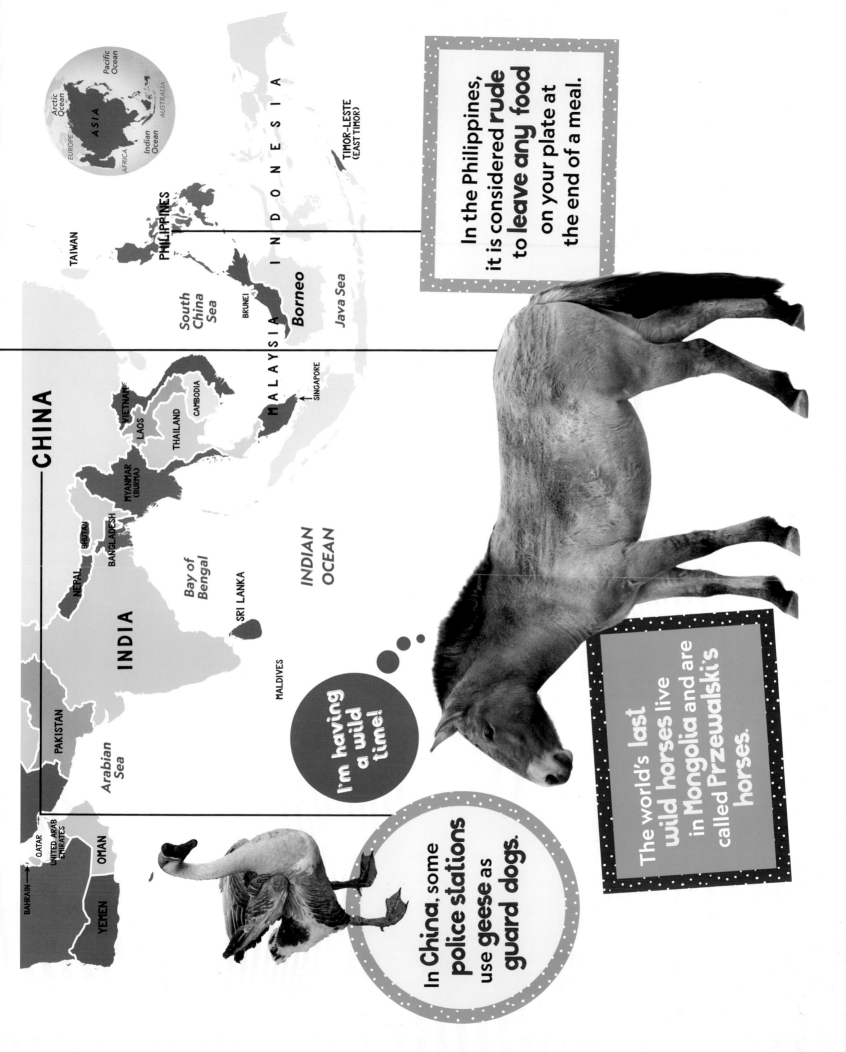

ASIA

Arctic Ocean

EUROPE

Pacific Ocean

AFRICA

AUSTRALIA

Indian Ocean

CHINA

TAIWAN

PHILIPPINES

INDONESIA

TIMOR-LESTE
(EAST TIMOR)

South China Sea

BRUNEI

Borneo

Java Sea

MALAYSIA

SINGAPORE

VIETNAM

LAOS

CAMBODIA

THAILAND

MYANMAR
(BURMA)

NEPAL

BHUTAN

BANGLADESH

Bay of Bengal

SRI LANKA

INDIA

INDIAN OCEAN

MALDIVES

PAKISTAN

Arabian Sea

QATAR

UNITED ARAB EMIRATES

BAHRAIN

OMAN

YEMEN

In the Philippines, it is considered **rude to leave any food** on your plate at the end of a meal.

I'm having a wild time!

The world's last **wild horses** live in Mongolia and are called Przewalski's horses.

In China, some **police stations** use geese as **guard dogs.**

183

ANIMAL MAGIC

Muju Firefly Festival
South Korea

Light shows at festivals may be pretty common, but this one is far from average. At the Muju Firefly Festival the skies are illuminated by tiny bugs. That's right—fireflies, and there's an entire eco-friendly festival dedicated to them. Each year, thousands of visitors flock to Muju in South Korea for music, storytelling, reenactments of traditional weddings, and more. But the real fun starts after dark, when the fireflies light up the night sky. Muju is a perfect natural habitat for the fireflies; because fireflies only inhabit super-clean places, these critters represent Muju's unspoiled environment.

Pigeon Towers
Iran

While many people around the world think pigeons are a big nuisance, 16th- and 17th-century Iranians knew a good thing when they saw it. So, they built these honeycomb-like towers for more than just decoration: These beautiful structures housed thousands of pigeons. Why? So that their poop could be harvested and used as fertilizer for growing watermelons and cucumbers. Iran's Pigeon Towers were six stories high and 45 to 75 feet (14–23 m) in diameter. There are still some pigeon towers in operation today, but most fell into disrepair when artificial fertilizer replaced the natural stuff.

The **towers** could house around **14,000 birds.**

Kissing Dinosaurs
Mongolia-China Border

A pair of 60-foot (19-m)-high kissing dinosaurs is the last thing you'd expect to see when cruising along a barren highway. Each dinosaur statue is a whopping 112 feet (34 m) wide! Due to its remoteness, this statue rarely has visitors. So why did this romantic dino duo wind up in what seems like the middle of nowhere? The smooching brontosauruses stretch over the highway on the Sino-Mongolian border in northern China, near the remote town of Erlian (also known as Erenhot), where numerous fossils have been found. Paleontologists believe that the area was once a prehistoric paradise where many dinosaur species thrived. So this head-turner of a statue was part of plans to bring tourists to the area.

COLOR POP!

LED Color Canopy
Yas Island, United Arab Emirates

If you're looking for a hotel that shines bright long after sundown, come this way! There are many reasons why W Abu Dhabi on Yas Island is extraordinary. For starters, the futuristic hotel is the first in the world to be built over a Formula One race track! But the fun doesn't stop there. At night, the hotel hosts spectacular LED light shows. The hotel is draped in a 711-foot (217-m) multi-panel light canopy known as the Grid Shell. This canopy plays spectacular color-changing sequences that give the effect of a moving beam of light. It is one of the biggest LED lighting systems on the whole planet.

Danxia Landforms
Gansu Province, China

Have you never seen multicolored mountains? Well, take a trip to China's Zhangye Danxia Landform Geological Park and you will have a chance to do just that. The natural wonder has boardwalks and viewing platforms for visitors to take in the awesome site. These famous Rainbow Mountains are all shades of red, blue, yellow, and orange. It's hard to believe they haven't been painted! So how did these mountains get their stripes? The shape and vivid colors of the Danxia landforms are a result of weathering as well as tectonic plates shifting over millions of years. Over millennia, the sandstone and minerals have eroded into fascinating textures, shapes, and patterns, creating a landscape that's out of this world.

Village of Color
Kampung, Indonesia

Painted every shade from pastel yellows to vibrant pinks, this village is wall-to-wall color—nothing escaped the paintbrush! Welcome to Kampung Warna Warni Jodipan, or the Village of Color. Today, it might be one of the brightest villages on the planet, but not so long ago, this was a typical-looking Indonesian village. So why did it get a magnificent makeover? Kampung was painted these vivid colors by artists, students, and residents as part of a project to improve the area and bring tourists in. And it worked! Turning this traditional village into a work of art has attracted visitors eager to snap photos and share selfies.

Pink Palace
Jaipur, India

If you want a palace that looks like it's come straight out of a storybook, then look no further than the magnificent Pink Palace in Jaipur. The palace's 953 honeycombed windows allow for a gentle breeze to move through it—a welcome relief in the hot climate. The intricate latticework on the windows was also designed so that royal women could watch over the life going on outside of the palace without being seen. This ornate masterpiece is five stories high and built from sandstone, which gives the palace its pink hue. In fact, the city of Jaipur itself is known as the Pink City because so many of its buildings are rose-colored.

THE PALACE'S HINDI NAME IS **HAWA MAHAL,** MEANING "PALACE OF THE WINDS."

187

Weird but true!

The **PINHEAD-SIZE** Asian watermeal weighs about the same as **TWO GRAINS** of table salt (1/190,000 of an ounce) and grows the **WORLD'S SMALLEST FRUIT.**

While **A LOT** of plants might **EAT BUGS,** *Nepenthes rajah* also **EATS RATS!**

WHEN IT'S IN BLOOM, THE **AMORPHOPHALLUS TITANUM** SMELLS SO BAD THAT IT HAS BEEN NICKNAMED THE "CORPSE FLOWER."

ASIAN FLORA

Singapore's tallest solar-powered **"SUPER-TREES"** are 160 feet (50 m) high. They **light up,** and are packed with more than **150,000 living plants.**

DUBAI'S MIRACLE GARDEN CONTAINS **MILLIONS** OF **FLOWERS** AND **PLANTS,** PRUNED INTO INCREDIBLE SHAPES, INCLUDING **CASTLES, TORTOISES,** AND **MICKEY MOUSE.**

The rare **DRAGON'S BLOOD TREE** is found only on the island of **SOCOTRA** in the **INDIAN OCEAN,** and **OOZES BRIGHT RED SAP** when cut in to, almost like it's **BLEEDING.**

The rafflesia plant has **NO ROOTS, STEM, OR LEAVES,** but each flower **can be up to 3.3 FEET (1 M)** in diameter **and weigh up to a HEFTY 24 pounds (11 kg).**

COOL CRITTERS

Giant Technicolor Squirrels
India

These orange-black-and-purple creatures are magnificent Malabar giant squirrels. The rainbow rodents can grow up to three feet (1 m) long from head to tail and weigh four pounds (2 kg). They are skilled leapers (much like their smaller squirrel relatives!) and can jump an impressive 20 feet (6 m) between trees in their forest home. While many squirrel species keep their supplies of nuts and seeds underground, Malabar giant squirrels store their food up high in trees. You might think that their striking coloring makes these squirrels stand out, but actually it helps them camouflage in the sunny and shady patches created by the forest canopy.

Mossy frogs sometimes play dead when they are frightened.

They'll never find me!

Mossy Frog
Vietnam

It's not hard to see how this bumpy-skinned green critter got its name. The mossy frog's textured markings make it look just like a patch of moss! Besides being able to hide in the undergrowth easily, these little frogs have another cool trick. They can make it sound as though they're 10 to 13 feet (3–4 m) away from where they really are, sending predators off in the wrong direction.

Binturong
Thailand

What do you notice about the binturong? Maybe you see its bearlike body, or cat-like face. This cute animal is sometimes called a "bearcat"—although they're not actually related to bears or cats at all. Stranger still, they smell like popcorn! Buttery popcorn, to be precise. They move around, marking branches as their territory using scent glands under their tail. These rare mammals live in Southeast Asia's tropical rainforests and are rarely seen by humans.

THE BINTURONG HAS A LONG TAIL THAT CAN GRIP ON TO BRANCHES TO HELP IT CLIMB.

Weirdly Cute!

Draco Lizard

When you think of cute animals, a flying lizard may not be top of your list! Prepare to change all of that when you meet the Draco lizard, or flying dragon. Found in the tropical rainforests of Southeast Asia, they only grow up to about eight inches (20 cm), including their tail. These flying lizards have some awesome adaptations that help them find food and dodge danger. Their extendable ribs have folds of skin between them, which open out into colorful wings. They use them to catch the wind and glide between trees, using their slender tails to steer like a pro and avoid going close to the ground.

191

BY the NUMBERS

DEAD SEA

The Dead Sea is a landlocked salt lake between Israel and Jordan. Why is it called the Dead Sea? Because the high salt levels in the water mean almost no life can survive there, apart from some types of bacteria. The surface of the Dead Sea is the lowest point on Earth at 1,380 feet (420 m) below sea level.

THE DEAD SEA IS ABOUT
30 MILES (48 KM) LONG.

THE LAKE IS MADE UP OF
30% SALT.

IT IS
6 TIMES
SALTIER THAN THE OCEAN. IT IS THE **FIFTH SALTIEST** BODY OF WATER ON THE PLANET.

124°F (51°C) IS THE **MAXIMUM TEMP** IT REACHES IN SUMMER.

2.5 INCHES (6.5 CM) **OF RAIN A YEAR**

THE LEVEL OF THE LAKE **DROPS** BY ABOUT **3 FEET** (1 M) EACH YEAR.

THE DEAD SEA IS OVER **1,000** FEET (306 M) **DEEP.**

ROCKIN' RESTROOMS

Modern Toilet Restaurant
Taipei, Taiwan

Forget your regular dining furniture and crockery—here diners eat out of toilet-shaped bowls while sitting on toilet-shaped seats! Yes, you heard right. The creators started out by selling ice cream in toilet-shaped containers and grew a loyal fan base from there. In 2014, they opened up the Modern Toilet Restaurant. The owner, Wang Zi-Wei, was inspired by a Japanese cartoon character who liked playing with poop!

Poopoo Land
Seoul, South Korea

Poopoo Land is a museum celebrating what you flush down the toilet! You can explore everything from flatulence to the science of poop—all while getting the chance to pose for selfies on toilet seats and more! At the end, visitors wander through a digestion maze with obstacle courses, and boogie to tunes in the Poo Party Zone before exiting speedily down a steep slide. After all that fun, visitors can refuel at a café packed with, you guessed it, toilet-themed food and drink.

Toilet Bowl Waterfall
Foshan, China

Some might say this sculpture is total washout, but there's a lot to love about it! China's Shiwan Park is home to many ceramic sculptures, including this epic toilet bowl waterfall. It took two months for Chinese artist Shu Yong and his team to install this wall of 10,000 repurposed ceramic toilets, sinks, and urinals. No, we're not yanking your chain! The fabulous fountain stretches 330 feet (100 m) long and 16 feet (5 m) high, and it can be flushed to create the effect of a calming waterfall.

TOILET PAPER IS A POPULAR HOUSEWARMING GIFT IN SOUTH KOREA.

Has anyone got any toilet paper?

Most Remote Toilet in the World
Altai Mountains, Siberia

Only explorers daring enough to venture 8,530 feet (2,600 m) up in the Altai Mountains can find the world's most remote toilet. The precarious-looking restroom is part of Siberia's highest weather station, Kara-Tyurek. This lonely latrine is not for the faint of heart—as you can see, it stands teetering over a cliff edge and is about as remote as you can get. The nearest village is 60 miles (100 km) away, which means toilet paper deliveries come by helicopter!

WEIRD WONDERS ▶ CHINA'S

Panjin Beach is home to **OVER 260** bird species, including the endangered crown crane and black-beaked gull.

RED BEACH

Panjin, China

As beaches go, this one in Panjin is pretty extraordinary. Forget sand or pebbles, China's red beach is carpeted with a plant called seepweed that turns vibrant crimson each autumn. It's part of one of the world's largest wetlands, found along the Liaohe River Delta. The area is also home to lots of endangered wildlife and has been protected since 1988. Most of it is closed to tourists, but a 6,500-foot (1,980-m)-long wooden boardwalk jutting out into the sea allows visitors to bird-watch and enjoy the spectacular red hues.

JUST JAPAN

Gotokuji Temple
Tokyo, Japan

This cat is called the *maneki-neko,* which means "beckoning cat." This famous feline has become a symbol for Japan, and today it is recognized around the world—mostly as the "Lucky Cat" figurine. But why is there a sea of them at this Buddhist temple in Setagaya? It's believed to be the birthplace of the maneki-neko. The legend goes that a lord named Naotaka Li was caught in a storm. Luckily, a cat waving its paw led him to shelter inside this temple. The lord was so grateful that he gave gifts of rice and land to the temple in thanks, and even chose it as his final resting place. Today, hundreds of maneki-neko are left to honor the legendary feline.

Pikachu Outbreak Festival
Yokohama, Japan

How should people finish up a day of exploring Yokohama? With a parade of dancing Pikachus, of course! Get ready for the cutest event in Japan's calendar—Pikachu Outbreak! For one week, the streets of Yokohama are filled with Pikachus of all shapes and sizes for this annual festival. Whole neighborhoods are decorated in Pikachu memorabilia, and some stores even offer discounts to people dressed as the yellow Pokémon. But the main action happens after dark. There are light shows, parades, and dancing Pikachus aplenty. Pokémon fan or not, have your cameras at the ready—if you go, you'll want photos.

During the festival, as many as 2,000 Pikachus can be spotted in the streets.

What's **Weird** About This**?**

That's weird!

Have you ever heard of a forest that can make its own music? This is the Sagano Bamboo Forest on the edge of Kyoto in Japan, and the home of the Tenryu-ji Temple, a UNESCO World Heritage site. When the long bamboo stalks sway in the wind they create a swishing *zawa-zawa* noise—a sound considered so important by the Japanese government that it has become a national protected soundscape. Visitors come to this six-square-mile (16-sq-km) site to experience the peaceful tranquility of this forest. As well as the relaxing sounds, the way that the sunlight filters through the leaves gives the forest a serene green glow.

PERSONALITY QUIZ

Which Quirky Creature Are You?

Take this quiz and keep track of your answers on a separate piece of paper to find out!

1 Pick your dream holiday:

a. Urban adventure; I love experiencing different cultures.

b. Anything and anywhere, as long as I'm with my friends.

c. Safari; it's all about the animals.

2 Which of the below best describes you?

a. Chilled out

b. Funny

c. Wise

4 Which is your favorite animated film?

a. *The Aristocats*

b. *The Jungle Book*

c. *Dumbo*

Mostly A's

You're the … maneki-neko cat

Just like the maneki-neko, you're a quick thinker and always know how to get people out of a sticky situation. Your friends would describe you as calm and kind—the ideal person to have around in a crisis! You also love relaxing at home.

3 On the weekend, you're most likely to …

a. Be at home relaxing

b. Spend time with friends

c. Spend time doing family things

5 Your dream job would be ...

a. Pilot, because you have a head for heights

b. Comedian, because you love entertaining people

c. Nurse, because you are patient and love helping people

6 Your friends turn to you for ...

a. Advice; you always have a solution to every problem.

b. Laughs; you know how to cheer people up.

c. Support; you're a great listener.

7 What is your favorite subject at school?

a. P.E.; you love being active.

b. Languages, so you can talk to everyone you meet, wherever you are.

c. History; learning about the past is fascinating.

8 Your perfect pet would be ...

a. Rabbit—soft and fluffy to cuddle up to

b. Puppy—playful, fun, and full of energy

c. Tortoise—gentle and slow-paced

Mostly B's
You're the ... Japanese macaque!
Confident, funny, and mischievous—you're a macaque! You are super sociable and love spending time with your friends. You're fun to be around and always know how to cheer people up—making people laugh is what you do best of all!

Mostly C's
You're the ... elephant!
Like these beloved gentle giants, you are calm and wise. Friends rely on you to listen to their problems and everybody can see how kind you are. You are incredibly patient and will do anything to help others.

Breathtaking BUILDS!

Robot Building
Bangkok, Thailand

It may look like it's escaped from a sci-fi movie, but this sleepy-looking robot is actually a bank. The 20-story-high building was completed in 1987 for the Bank of Asia. The design was meant to highlight the way technology was taking over the banking world. The striking building was created by architect Sumet Jumsai, who was inspired by his son's toy robot.

> I'm a lean, mean workplace machine!

Bottle House of Ganja
Ganja, Azerbaijan

As the name suggests, this amazing house is decorated with glass bottles—48,000 in total! Bottles of various shapes and sizes, along with colorful stones, make up a giant mosaic on the outside of this private house. But the Bottle House is far more than just decorative. It was built by the Jafarov family as a shrine to their brother, Yusif, who was lost in World War II. The house features a portrait of Yusif, along with words and patterns that tell the story of this family. The best time to see this masterpiece is when the sun is shining through the colorful glass!

Highest ATM in the World
Gilgit Baltistan, Pakistan

Way up in Khunjerab Pass sits the highest-altitude ATM in the world. Found at the dizzying height of 15,396 feet (4,693 m) above sea level—you'd need a head for heights to get cash out here! So why did the National Bank of Pakistan choose this unlikely location for an ATM? The bank wanted to make an ATM powered by solar panels and wind turbines. The record-breaking ATM opened to the public in 2016.

Largest Statue in the World
Gujarat, India

Towering over the surrounding landscape and bridge, the Statue of Unity by sculptor Ram V. Sutar is the largest in the world. The magnificent monument stands at almost 600 feet (182 m) tall—that's almost double the height of the Statue of Liberty. The steel and bronze statue was built to honor India's first deputy prime minister, Sardar Vallabhbhai Patel, known as the Iron Man of India. He died in 1950 and was an important figure in uniting India's states into one independent country.

Hanging Temple of Hengshan
Shanxi Province, China

Talk about precarious—this fifth-century temple is built into the side of an almost vertical cliff. It was built around 1,500 years ago by a Chinese Buddhist monk named Liao Ran. The Hanging Temple, or Xuankong Si, sits 190 feet (58 m) above the riverbed and is made up of a series of bridges and corridors with a total of 40 rooms. Originally it was held in place with just wooden beams in the rock, but thankfully it has been made stronger over the years.

Sun Cruise Resort and Yacht
Jeongdongjin, South Korea

This hotel takes the idea of keeping things "shipshape" to a whole new level. Welcome to the world's first cruise liner shaped hotel. That's right, this liner stays put on a cliff over Jeongdongjin beach in South Korea. So if you dream of the glitz and glamour of a cruise ship vacation, but without the sea sickness, this could be the answer. With porthole windows and the sound of lapping waves playing over the sound system, guests feel like they're really cruising the sea.

BY the NUMBERS

TURBO TRAIN

Shanghai Maglev in China is the world's fastest passenger train. How does it move so fast? Well, it floats ... kind of! It's called a magnetic levitation train, which means the train is propelled by using electromagnets. They create magnetic fields to push or pull the train along guideways rather than tracks . Shanghai Maglev runs from Shanghai's Pudong International Airport to the Longyang metro station on the outskirts of Shanghai.

OPENED:
2004

NUMBER OF LINES: **1**

NUMBER OF STATIONS: **2**

DISTANCE:
19 MILES (30 KM)

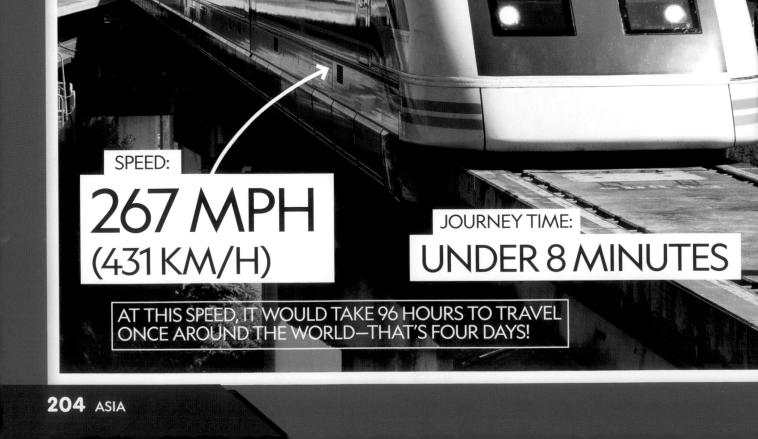

SPEED:
267 MPH
(431 KM/H)

JOURNEY TIME:
UNDER 8 MINUTES

AT THIS SPEED, IT WOULD TAKE 96 HOURS TO TRAVEL ONCE AROUND THE WORLD—THAT'S FOUR DAYS!

What's **Weird** About This **?**

Changi Airport slides take the "bored" out of boarding. Who said that airports had to be a yawn-fest? Singapore Changi Airport's super slide is practical and playful! Passengers can glide to their gates on the 39-foot (12-m)-high slide—that's almost four stories! It opened in 2010 and is Singapore's tallest slide and the tallest airport slide anywhere in the world. But one slide wasn't enough, so Changi Airport unveiled a new slide called the Chandelier in 2018. This one comes with poles and climbing nets.

WATERY WONDERS

Yuncheng Salt Lake
Yuncheng, China

During the summer, Yuncheng Salt Lake looks like an enormous paint palette. The natural wonder was formed over 500 million years ago and is around 46 square miles (120 sq km), making it the third largest inland salt lake in the world. It's estimated that locals have harvested its salt for as long as 4,000 years. So what turns this lake into a rainbow? It's all down to an algae called *Dunaliella salina*. This mostly appears green, but it can change color when it reacts with salt and light.

LOW TEMPERATURES IN WINTER TURN THE SALT LAKE INTO AN EXPANSE OF WHITE CRYSTALS.

Weirdly Cute! Japanese Macaques

It's no wonder these snow monkeys love bathing in the hot springs—100°F (37°C) water no doubt makes a welcome break from the below-freezing temperatures they live in. Japan's Jigokudani Monkey Park is home to a troop of 160 Japanese macaques who soak in the natural hot springs, often dozing as they enjoy the heat of the water. The park was set up as a conservation area in 1964 with a pool built especially for the monkeys. Here, the monkeys are free to live as wild animals, so it's a place where you can observe the creatures in their natural environment. Curiously, this monkey troop is the only one known to bathe like this.

Suoi Tien Park

Ho Chi Minh City, Vietnam

Part of a vast Buddhist theme park, this water park looks like no other. The pools are over-looked by the huge head of an ancient emperor and are surrounded by mythical creatures from Vietnamese folklore, which means you can speed out of the mouth of a dragon while riding on a large floaty toy! The mythical theme extends to the staff, who are often dressed as golden monkeys, ready to take photos with visitors and entertain them. Unlike other water parks though, there is also a scary attraction that explores the Buddhist version of hell—visitors agree that the Palace of Unicorns is not suitable for children—better stick to the waterslides!

Visitors can feed crocodiles raw meat on the end of wooden poles!

NATURE VS. ARCHITECTURE

The Root Bridges of Cherrapunji
Cherrapunji, India

During monsoon season, the valleys and gorges of Meghalaya are one of the wettest places on the planet. Its fast-flowing rivers become impossible to cross, cutting off whole villages. Luckily, the Khasi tribes who live here have found a solution. The Indian rubber trees which grow in the forest have incredibly strong roots, which can be nurtured into living bridges, known locally as *jing kieng jri*. While manufactured materials can weaken with age, the roots become stronger. The Khasi plant trees on each side of the river and build a frame to connect them using bamboo. Over time, the roots are woven through the bamboo to make a crossing strong enough to hold more than 35 people at a time.

It took **six years** to construct the amazing **artificial island.**

Palm Jumeirah
Dubai, United Arab Emirates

Palm Jumeirah, an artificial island in Dubai, was built to solve overcrowding. The palm tree-shaped island is more than three miles (5 km) in diameter and adds almost 50 miles (80 km) to Dubai's coastline, making it one of the biggest artificial islands in the world. As you can imagine, there's a lot to think about when building an island—like how to make sure it doesn't get washed away, or sink. In order to construct Palm Jumeirah, more than three billion cubic feet (85 million cu m) of sand were dredged up from the Persian Gulf and sprayed into place using special equipment. To stop the island from drifting, millions of tons of rock were used to create its sturdy foundations.

WEIRD WONDERS

Visit the temple where the trees have taken over!

TEMPLE OF TREES

Siem Reap, Cambodia

When you look at Ta Prohm, it's hard to tell where the building ends and tree roots begin. This ancient Buddhist temple in Angkor was built in 1186, but it was abandoned and left to become entwined with the roots and branches of jungle trees. Over the centuries, the sacred site has continued to evolve and grow alongside nature—making the site all the more magical. The temple is a collection of courtyards, walkways, and towers, packed with carved stone blocks.

ECCENTRIC ELEPHANTS

Elephant Stairs
Lahore, Pakistan

You might be wondering what this grand entranceway has to do with elephants. Well, these stairs were actually built especially for them! Dating back to the 11th century, Lahore Fort is found within the walled city. It was partly built by Emperor Akbar, who reigned between 1556 and 1605. The fort has two entrances, one of which contains the Elephant Stairs, known locally as the Hathi Paer. The stairs lead to the royal quarters and were built so that elephants could carry royalty right up to the doorway. They were designed to allow elephants to climb safely, with wide, shallow steps for their jumbo feet.

THE FORT'S STAIRS ARE LARGE ENOUGH TO HOLD SEVERAL ELEPHANTS AT ONCE.

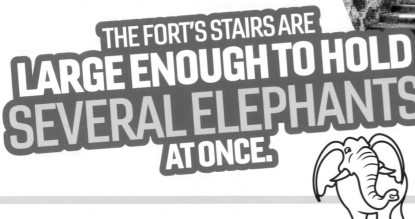

Elephant Building
Bangkok, Thailand

Since 1997, the Elephant Building, or Chang Building, has loomed over Bangkok's business district. The jumbo-size high-rise is the largest elephant-shaped structure in the world. It's made up of three connecting towers—two for the elephant's legs, and the third for its mighty trunk. The building's 32 floors reach 335 feet (102 m) high, with big windows for eyes and multi-story balconies for ears. There is a specific reason why it was chosen as the shape for this building. The elephant is Thailand's national animal and an important symbol for the country. So although not everybody thinks the tusked tower is beautiful, many locals are fond of it.

Elephant Foot Yam

Southeast Asia

If tropical plants make you think of sweet-scented flowers—think again! The foul-smelling elephant foot yam is not for the fainthearted. Yes, as well as looking pretty odd, this intriguing plant smells like rotting flesh to attract the flies and beetles that pollinate it. Despite its deathly aroma, elephant foot yams are edible. If you come face-to-face with one of these botanical beasts, you'll sure know about it!

Its stem can grow a staggering 6.5 feet (2 m) tall when it's pollinated!

Elephanta Caves

Mumbai, India

Gharapuri Island, or Elephanta Island, in Mumbai Harbor is home to a huge human-made cave that was once a Hindu place of worship. The island's name comes from a large stone elephant found nearby by the first European visitors to the site in the early 16th century. Inside the cave are stone carvings of the Hindu god Shiva; the carvings are some of the finest works of early Indian art. The cave was carved out of solid stone in the mid-sixth century, though the island has other smaller caves, rock art, and archaeological remains from as far back as the second century B.C.

BIZARRE BODY PARTS

Giant Glass Slipper Church
Budai, Taiwan

This ultra-modern glass structure, known as the High Heel Church, doesn't exactly blend in with its surroundings! The Cinderella-inspired construction is 55 feet (16 m) high and over 36 feet (10 m) wide, and it stands proudly in a fishing village called Budai in Taiwan. Although it's called a "church," this neon blue structure is only used for wedding ceremonies and photo shoots. It cost $686,000 to build and was completed in 2016, when it entered the Guinness World Records as the largest building shaped like a shoe.

The slipper is constructed out of **320 tinted glass panels** fitted into a metal frame.

Kick back and enjoy the game!

Sepak Takraw
Southeast Asia

Welcome to the world of *sepak takraw*, otherwise known as kick ball—a high-energy game combining martial arts, football, and volleyball. The acrobatic ancient sport dates back to the 15th century. *Sepak* is Malay for "kick," and *takraw* is the Thai word for the ball that was traditionally used. The game is played a bit like volleyball—only you can't use your hands or arms! Instead, three players on two opposing teams (known as *regu*) use their feet, legs, chest, and head to keep the ball off the ground and aim it over the five-foot (1.5-m)-high net. This means players need to be very nimble and have lots of energy—the best players are like acrobats.

Eye of the Sky

Guizhou Province, China

Check out the largest radio telescope in the world ... the FAST! At 1,640 feet (500 m) in diameter, the FAST is the world's largest single-dish radio telescope. Its full name is the Five-hundred-meter Aperture Spherical radio Telescope, and its nickname is Tianyan, which means "Eye of the Sky." Since 2016, it has been monitoring the skies on the lookout for undiscovered stars, new galaxies, and alien life. It took more than 20 years of planning and five years to build—not surprising when you discover that it contains 4,450 giant triangular aluminum panels.

"EYE OF THE SKY" IS THE MOST SENSITIVE LISTENING DEVICE IN THE WORLD!

Golden Bridge

Hoa Phu, Vietnam

When it comes to crossing this bridge in Vietnam, you're in safe hands ... literally! In the hills of Vietnam, you can cross the spectacular Cau Vang (Golden Bridge) and enjoy spectacular views of the Annamese Mountains. The breathtaking construction is 500 feet (152 m) long and stands 4,600 feet (1,402 m) above sea level. But unlike your average bridge, this one is held up by two humongous stone hands. It is said that these mighty mitts represent the hands of a mountain god. Despite their size, the moss-covered hands seem to belong to the landscape, and the bridge's curving path appears to flow with the shape of the mountains.

QUIZ WHIZ

Think you're a whiz at Weird But True?

Test your knowledge with these quick questions!

1 What sound does South Korea's Sun Cruise Resort and Yacht play to guests?

a. Orchestral music
b. The sound of lapping waves
c. Clapping and cheering
d. Bird song

3 Where would you find the highest ATM in the world?

a. Pakistan
b. Abu Dhabi
c. Indonesia
d. Japan

2 Yokohama in Japan holds a festival to celebrate which character each year?

a. Mickey Mouse
b. Pikachu
c. Minnie Mouse
d. Harry Potter

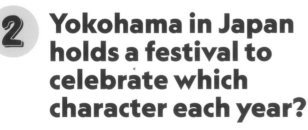

NBP ATM

THE WORLD'S HIGHEST ATM

WORLD'S HIGHEST ATM IN PAKISTAN

4 What piece of clothing is the glass church in Taiwan?

a. Hat
b. Jumper
c. Coat
d. High-heeled shoe

5 Which animal had stairs built especially for them in Lahore Fort, Pakistan?

a. Elephant
b. Dog
c. Giraffe
d. Monkey

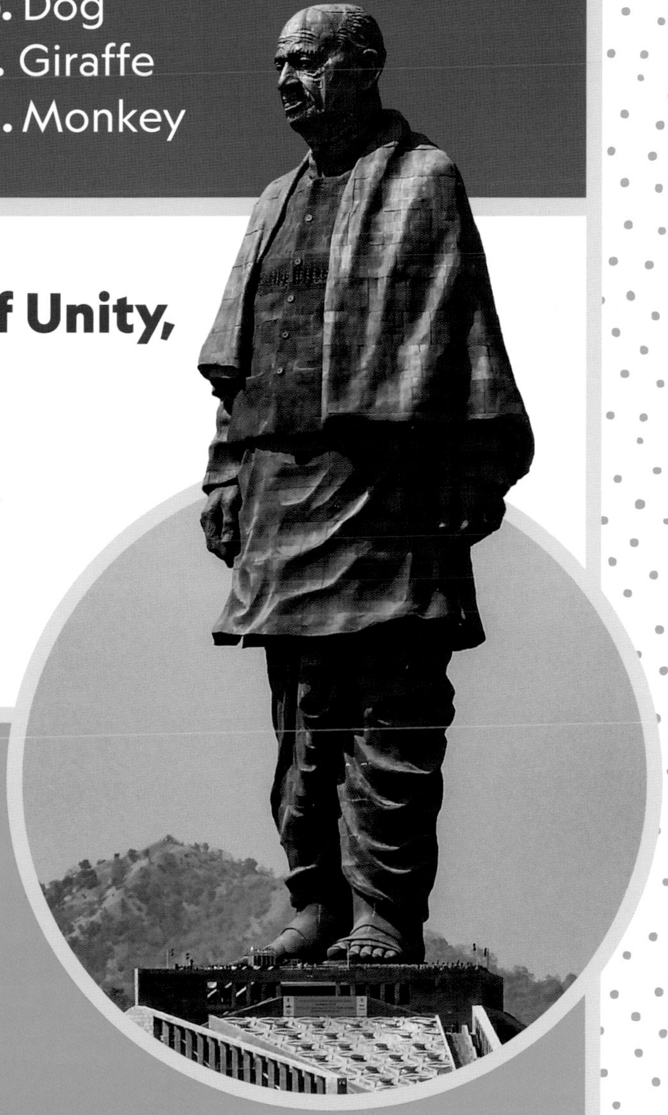

6 Where can you find the Statue of Unity, the largest statue in the world?

a. China
b. Japan
c. Vietnam
d. India

7 The Bank of Asia building in Bangkok is shaped like a ...

a. Flower
b. Robot
c. Car
d. Whale

8 What's the name of this plant?

a. Dragon's blood tree
b. Nepenthes rajah
c. Corpse flower
d. Great Banyan Tree

Answers: 1. b, 2. b, 3. a, 4. d, 5. a, 6. d, 7. b, 8. c

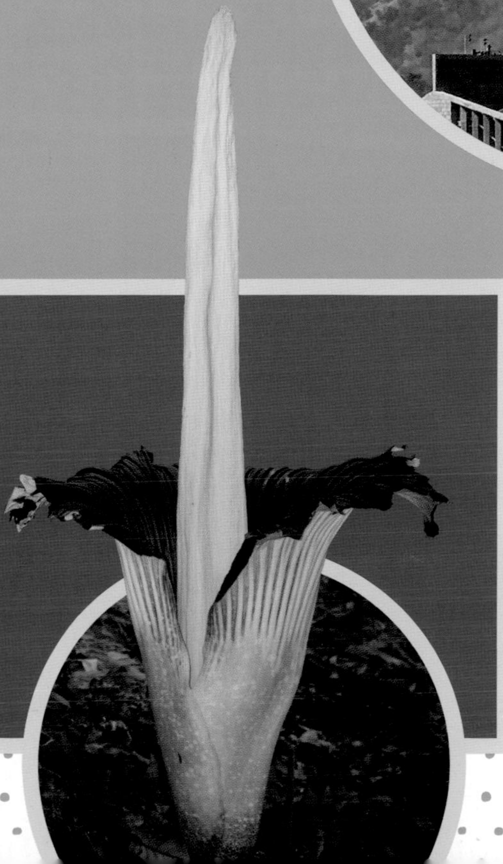

Weirder than fiction

OUTSTANDING OCEANIA

Where can you find the world's biggest butterfly and the smallest wallaby? How about the steepest street and the largest coins? They're all waiting for you in Oceania!

Gnomesville in Ferguson Valley, Australia, is home to at least 7,000 of the little folk!

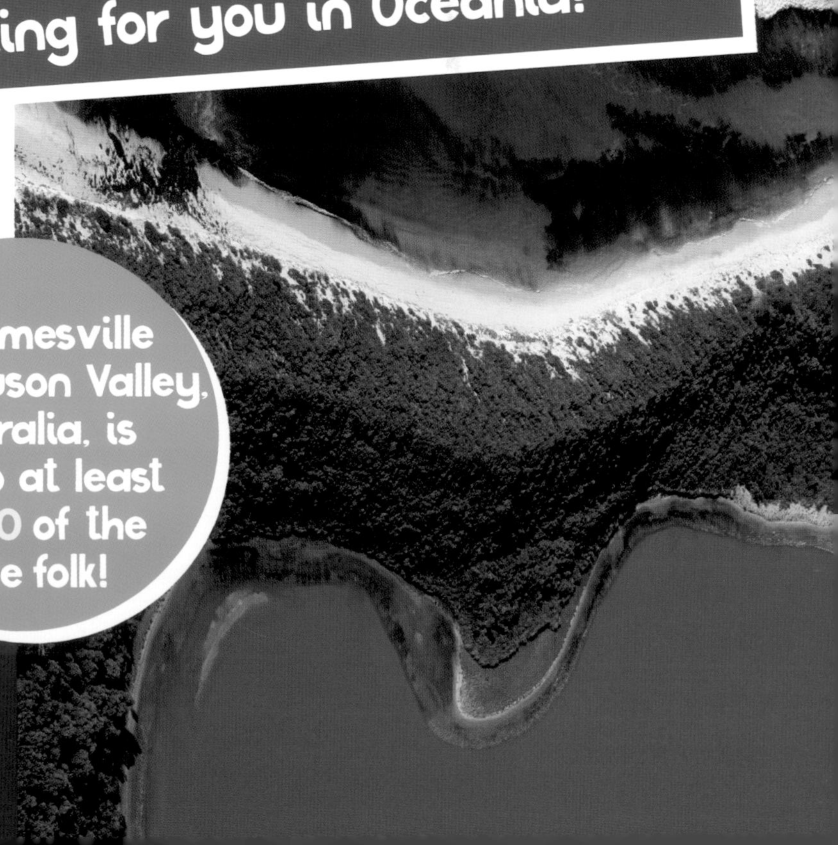

WELCOME

Rainbow eucalyptus trees can grow to an incredible 250 FEET (76 m) tall!

OCEANIA is the **SMALLEST** of the seven continents, and only Antarctica is home to fewer people. But that doesn't mean it isn't packed with **INCREDIBLE ANIMALS, LUDICROUS LANDSCAPES,** and **BIZARRE BUILDINGS!**

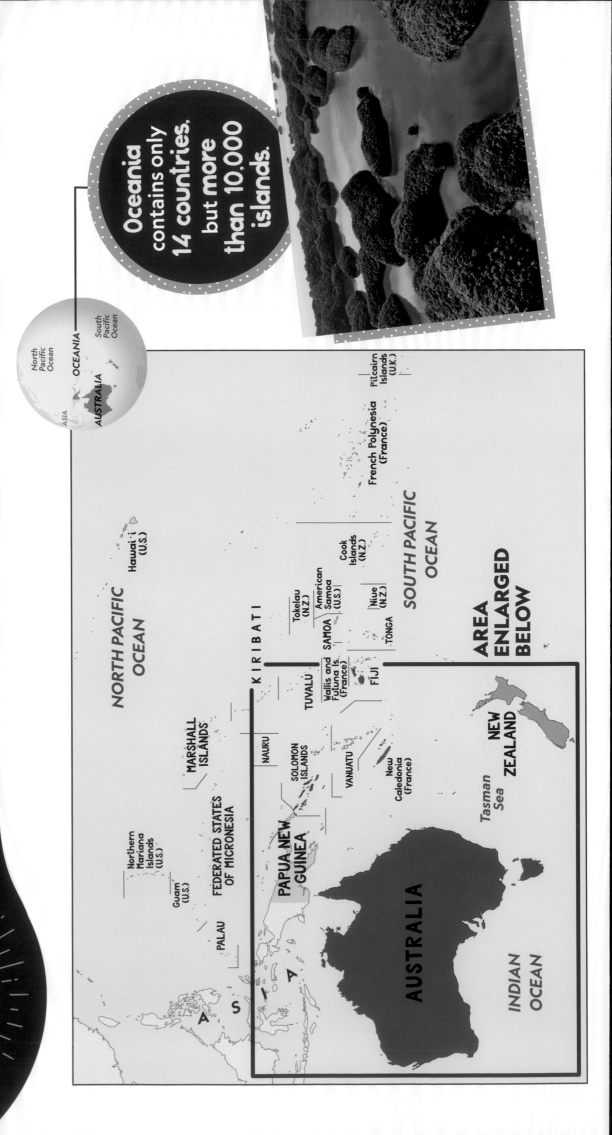

Oceania contains only 14 countries, but more than 10,000 islands.

North Pacific Ocean

OCEANIA

ASIA

AUSTRALIA

South Pacific Ocean

Hawai'i (U.S.)

NORTH PACIFIC OCEAN

Tokelau (N.Z.)

American Samoa (U.S.)

SAMOA

Niue (N.Z.)

TONGA

Cook Islands (N.Z.)

French Polynesia (France)

Pitcairn Islands (U.K.)

KIRIBATI

TUVALU

Wallis and Futuna Is. (France)

FIJI

SOUTH PACIFIC OCEAN

MARSHALL ISLANDS

NAURU

SOLOMON ISLANDS

VANUATU

New Caledonia (France)

AREA ENLARGED BELOW

Northern Mariana Islands (U.S.)

FEDERATED STATES OF MICRONESIA

PAPUA NEW GUINEA

NEW ZEALAND

Tasman Sea

Guam (U.S.)

PALAU

ASIA

AUSTRALIA

INDIAN OCEAN

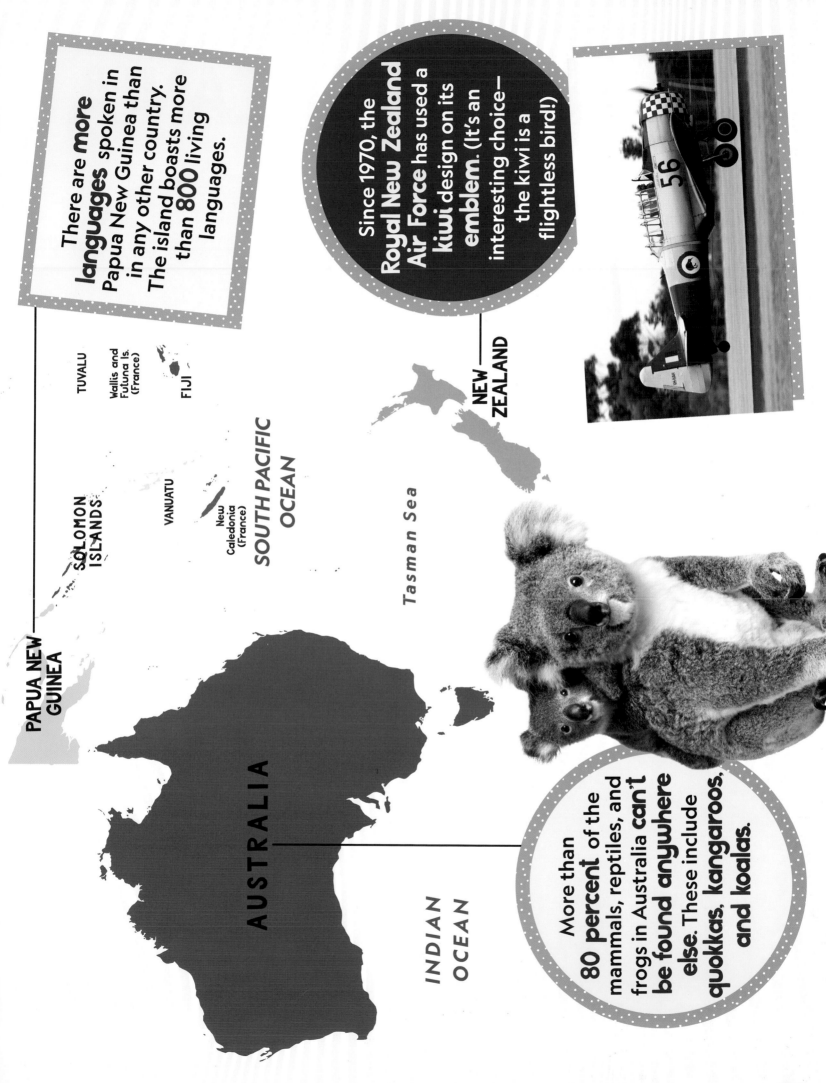

There are more **languages** spoken in Papua New Guinea than in any other country. The island boasts more than **800** living languages.

Since 1970, the **Royal New Zealand Air Force** has used a **kiwi** design on its **emblem.** (It's an interesting choice— the kiwi is a flightless bird!)

NEW ZEALAND

PAPUA NEW GUINEA

TUVALU

Wallis and Futuna Is. (France)

FIJI

SOLOMON ISLANDS

VANUATU

New Caledonia (France)

SOUTH PACIFIC OCEAN

Tasman Sea

AUSTRALIA

INDIAN OCEAN

More than **80 percent** of the mammals, reptiles, and frogs in Australia **can't be found anywhere else.** These include **quokkas, kangaroos, and koalas.**

219

ISLANDS OF OCEANIA

Ball's Pyramid
Pacific Ocean

Rising out of the Pacific Ocean, Ball's Pyramid is the remains of a shield volcano. It was originally part of Zealandia—a "lost continent" that is now almost entirely underwater. At 1,844 feet (562 m) tall, the pyramid is higher than the Empire State Building, and the world's tallest volcanic stack. The isolated rock is a favorite among climbers, who need a permit to visit. But they aren't as alone as they think out there. In 2001, scientists found a colony of 24 Lord Howe Island stick insects living 330 feet (100 m) above sea level. This creature, thought to be extinct since 1920, is as long as an adult human hand. Also known as the tree lobster or land lobster, it's the world's rarest and most endangered insect.

THERE ARE AT LEAST 6,000 STONE COINS DOTTED AROUND THE YAP ISLANDS.

Stone Coins
Yap, Micronesia

Traders on the Yap Islands in Micronesia once used giant stone coins up to 13 feet (4 m) in diameter for currency. One piece could weigh up to 4.4 tons (4 t)—that's heavier than a hippo. The coins, called *rai,* were made from limestone, even though there is no natural source of limestone on Yap. Instead it came from Palau, 300 miles (482 km) away. The limestone was transported to Yap by canoe, and was originally carved into fish shapes. Eventually, though, the circular shape became more popular. The rai were the main currency on Yap until the 20th century, and they are still used today for important events, such as land deals and marriages.

Coconuts
Solomon Islands

Coconuts are big business in the Solomon Islands—hundreds of thousands of tons of them are harvested there every year. As well as providing yummy fruit and coconut water, the trees are chopped up to build huts and bridges, and the roots are used in medicine and to make dye for clothes. Now they are even powering diesel engines as fuel! The oil is extracted from the coconut meat by grating, drying, and pressing it. It's cheaper than other fuels, which are expensive to transport to the Pacific Islands, and less harmful to the environment. More good news is that other vegetable oils have also been found to be effective in vehicles—maybe we'll see car(rot) fuel next!

Baby echidnas are called puggles.

Monotremes
Australia and Papua New Guinea

Most mammals give birth to live young, but monotremes obviously didn't get the memo! These animals, found only in Oceania, lay eggs instead. There are only five species of monotreme alive today. Four of those are varieties of echidnas (like the one pictured), also known as spiny anteaters. A female echidna carries its egg around in a pouch on its belly until it hatches. Predators quickly learn not to mess with an echidna—if it is under attack, it uses its claws to speedily dig a hole to hide in. Only its sharp spikes stick out, which don't provide much of a mouthful! The fifth kind of monotreme is the bizarre-looking duck-billed platypus, which is only found in eastern Australia.

SURPRISING FACTS ABOUT

Over 200 architects competed to design the **Sydney Opera House,** and **Jørn Utzon's** design was chosen as the **winner.**

MORE THAN **10.9 MILLION** people **visit** the SYDNEY OPERA HOUSE every year.

The **original budget** to build the Opera House was **$7 million** Australian dollars. It ended up costing **$102 million**—that's more than **$74 million** in U.S. dollars today.

In **2015**, genius physicist **STEPHEN HAWKING** appeared live onstage as a **HOLOGRAM.**

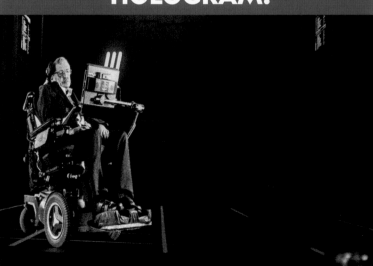

In 1960, American actor and singer **PAUL ROBESON** became the first person to perform at the Sydney Opera House when he climbed the scaffolding and sang to the construction workers!

THE SYDNEY OPERA HOUSE

The building is **cooled using seawater** taken directly from the harbor.

After a **chicken** fell on a **cellist** during an opera in the 1980s, a **net was installed** above the orchestra pit in one theater!

The **ROOF** is covered in more than **ONE MILLION** tiles.

When the **Sydney Symphony Orchestra** plays there, the **temperature** in the **Concert Hall** must be kept at **72.5°F (22.5°C)** to keep the instruments in tune.

It took **14 YEARS** to **CONSTRUCT** the building— **10 MORE YEARS** than expected.

The **GRAND ORGAN** in the Concert Hall has **10,154 PIPES,** making it the **LARGEST MECHANICAL ORGAN** in the **WORLD.**

LAKE HILLIER

Middle Island, Western Australia

WEIRD WONDERS

It's not time for an eye exam—that really is a pink lake!

This piece of pink perfection is **1,970 FEET** (600 M) long and **820 FEET** (250 M) at its widest point.

Like lovely-looking lakes? You've probably never seen one quite like this before! Most easily viewed overhead by helicopter, Lake Hillier looks like a gigantic wad of bubble gum has been splatted across the land. No one knows for sure what's causing the remarkable color. Discovered in 1802, Hillier is a salt lake, and for a few years, salt was mined from it. It's possible that a reaction between the salt and sodium bicarbonate, which can be used in baking and is found naturally in the lake's water, might be responsible for the pink tint. The most popular theory, though, is that it's down to microorganisms in the water. Lake Hillier contains micro-algae called *Dunaliella salina*, which loves salt and creates a red pigment. The salt crusts that have formed around the shoreline also contain red bacteria. Whatever the cause, the water is not harmful to touch, but drinking is a no-no because of all that salt. Best stick to strawberry milkshakes!

It's time to think pink!

WATERY WEIRDNESS

Carbrook Golf Course Sharks

Carbrook, Queensland, Australia

Golfers usually only have to deal with long grass and sand-filled bunkers. But Carbrook Golf Course takes the prize for the most lethal obstacle. The 15th hole has a lake full of bull sharks! It all began in the mid-1990s, when the nearby Logan River burst its banks. After the floodwater receded, several sharks were left behind in the course's lake. The numbers have grown since, so it seems that the sharks have been breeding. Bull sharks can grow to a length of 11.5 feet (3.5 m) and can be aggressive toward humans. A sizable number of players have sliced their shots into the lake, but no one has been foolish enough to attempt to retrieve their ball.

WARNING
NO SWIMMING

Bull sharks will eat just about anything—even other sharks!

Waitomo Glowworm Caves

Waitomo, North Island, New Zealand

Picture yourself drifting on a raft on an underground river. As the light from outside fades, all you have are candles to illuminate the way. As your journey continues, somehow you see more clearly. You look up and gasp in wonder at the glowing lights covering the cave ceiling. That's what happened to Maori chief Tane Tinorau and Englishman Fred Mace in 1887, when they used a small raft to go exploring. The light was provided by thousands of glowworms called *Arachnocampa luminosa*, which are only found in New Zealand. The fascinated men made more trips to the caves, which also contain albino ants and giant crickets, as well as limestone formations.

Jellyfish Lake
Palau, Micronesia

Would you go for a swim if you could see a jellyfish in the water? What if there were 10 ... or 100? Would you think twice if there were 1,000? Jellyfish Lake, as the name suggests, contains quite a few. In 2005, there were around 30 million golden jellyfish in there—but it didn't deter people from taking a dip! That's because their stingers are weak, so they're not a threat to humans. The lake is home to moon jellyfish, too, and they won't harm you in the water either. In fact, it's the jellyfish who need looking after—their numbers change a lot from year to year and sometimes the lake is closed to encourage them to reproduce.

IN THE 1990s, SCIENTISTS SENT MOON JELLYFISH TO SPACE TO STUDY THE EFFECTS OF WEIGHTLESSNESS.

Rere Rockslide
Ngatapa, New Zealand

Slides are fun. Playing in the water is fun. Put the two together, and you know you're in for a good time! The Rere Rockslide is a 200-foot (61-m)-long rock formation. It descends at an angle of 30 degrees into a large pool. The combination of water constantly flowing from the Wharekopae River and slippery, mossy rocks ensures that any journey from the top to the bottom is a swift one! The experience is more comfortable using a flotation device. Visitors use anything from inner tubes and inflatable chairs to bodyboards and yoga mats! A popular destination for adventurers, it's like a free theme park ride.

HEADS, SHOULDERS, KNEES, AND TOES

Quasi Sculpture
Wellington, New Zealand

New Zealand artist Ronnie van Hout is well known for his sculptures that combine household objects with human body parts. He describes his 16.4-foot (5-m)-tall work "Quasi," which was made from scanning bits of his own body, as a partial self-portrait. A stern face stares out from the back of a hand, which stands upright on two fingers. The sculpture's name was inspired by Quasimodo in *The Hunchback of Notre Dame.* The tragic bell-ringer in that famous book was shunned because of his appearance, and opinion is split on his bizarre-looking namesake. Some locals have called him weird, but others think he's funny and a hero!

Cassowary
New Guinea and Australia

If you've ever wished you could fly, spare a thought for the poor cassowary. It does have wings, but they are tiny and their feathers aren't adapted for flight. That means the cassowary must rely on its feet for getting around. But those feet aren't only used for locomotion—they're deadly weapons, too! If they think their territory is being invaded, they'll fight to defend it. A cassowary can be seven feet (2.1 m) tall, and has strong, muscular legs—it can run faster than a human, so it's difficult to escape from one. It will also kick out powerfully if threatened. Luckily, these big birds are shy and aren't keen on fighting. If you're lucky enough to see one, just keep your distance—it pays to be cassowary-wary!

The **claw** on a **cassowary's** inner toe can be **five inches** (13 cm) long and cuts like a **dagger!**

BY the NUMBERS

HEAD STONES

It's difficult to shake the feeling you're being watched on Easter Island! That's because it's famous for its hundreds of huge stone statues. Most of these gigantic sculptures called *moai* depict a head and torso with no legs, although lots of them are buried in the ground up to their shoulders. Nearly all the statues face inland, perhaps watching over the villages to keep them safe.

887 STATUES
ARE DOTTED AROUND EASTER ISLAND.

A.D. **1050** TO **1680**
IS WHEN MOST OF THE STONE STATUES WERE CARVED.

72 FEET (21.9 M)
IS THE HEIGHT OF THE TALLEST MOAI. CALLED EL GIGANTE (THE GIANT), IT WAS LEFT UNFINISHED NEAR A QUARRY.

ABOUT **25%**
OF THE STATUES WERE PLACED AROUND THE ISLAND, BUT 75% WERE NEVER MOVED OR WERE ABANDONED DURING TRANSPORTATION.

33 FEET (10.1 M)
IS THE HEIGHT OF PARO—THAT'S THE NAME OF THE TALLEST COMPLETED MOAI. IT WEIGHS 82.7 TONS (75 T).

7 MOAI AT A SITE CALLED AHU AKIVI
STAND IN A LINE FACING THE SEA, PERHAPS INTENDED TO HELP SAILORS NAVIGATE TO THE ISLAND.

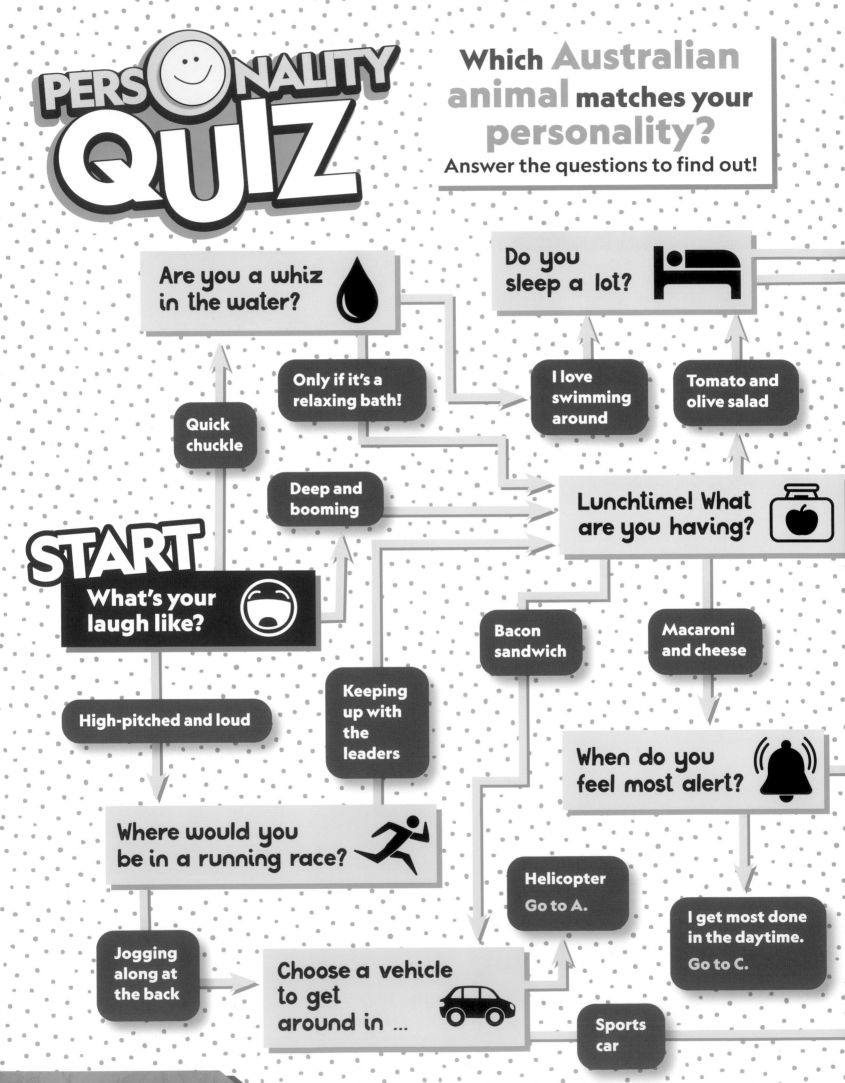

PERSONALITY QUIZ

Which Australian animal matches your personality?

Answer the questions to find out!

Are you a whiz in the water?

Only if it's a relaxing bath!

Quick chuckle

Deep and booming

Do you sleep a lot?

I love swimming around

Tomato and olive salad

START
What's your laugh like?

High-pitched and loud

Keeping up with the leaders

Lunchtime! What are you having?

Bacon sandwich

Macaroni and cheese

Where would you be in a running race?

When do you feel most alert?

Helicopter
Go to A.

Jogging along at the back

Choose a vehicle to get around in ...

I get most done in the daytime.
Go to C.

Sports car

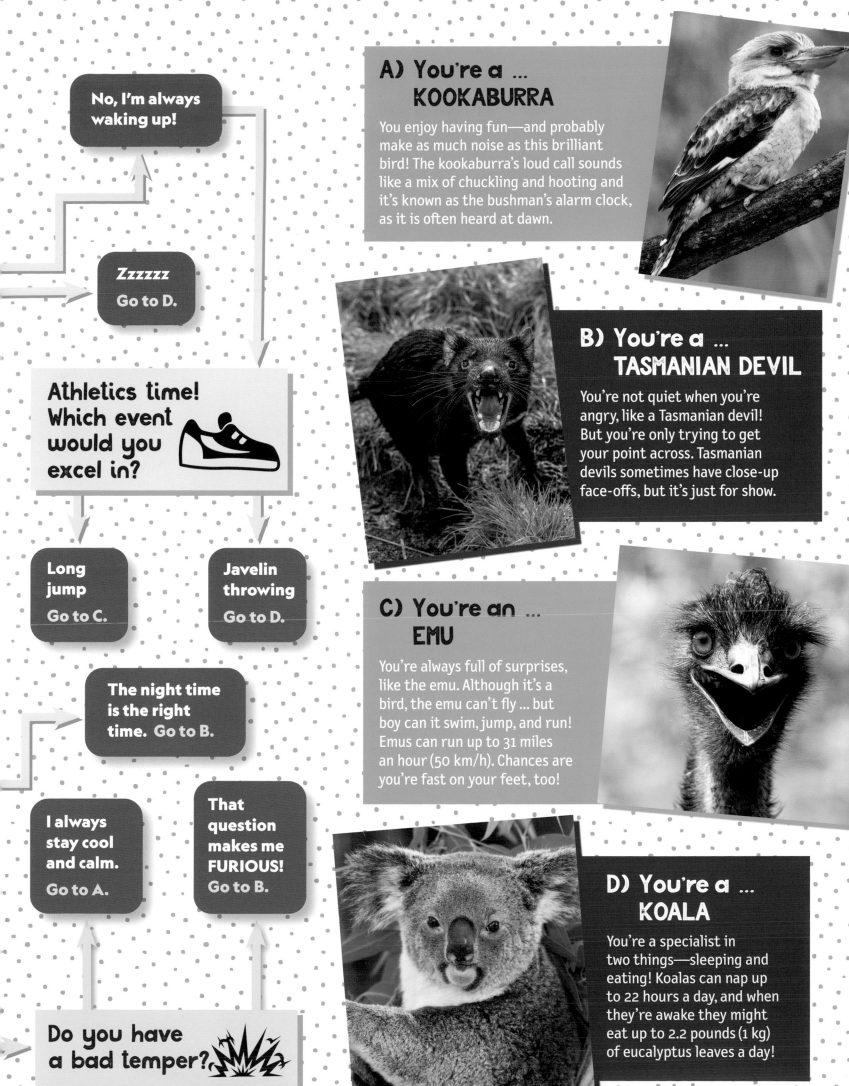

No, I'm always waking up!

Zzzzzz
Go to D.

Athletics time! Which event would you excel in?

Long jump
Go to C.

Javelin throwing
Go to D.

The night time is the right time. Go to B.

I always stay cool and calm.
Go to A.

That question makes me FURIOUS!
Go to B.

Do you have a bad temper?

A) You're a ... KOOKABURRA

You enjoy having fun—and probably make as much noise as this brilliant bird! The kookaburra's loud call sounds like a mix of chuckling and hooting and it's known as the bushman's alarm clock, as it is often heard at dawn.

B) You're a ... TASMANIAN DEVIL

You're not quiet when you're angry, like a Tasmanian devil! But you're only trying to get your point across. Tasmanian devils sometimes have close-up face-offs, but it's just for show.

C) You're an ... EMU

You're always full of surprises, like the emu. Although it's a bird, the emu can't fly ... but boy can it swim, jump, and run! Emus can run up to 31 miles an hour (50 km/h). Chances are you're fast on your feet, too!

D) You're a ... KOALA

You're a specialist in two things—sleeping and eating! Koalas can nap up to 22 hours a day, and when they're awake they might eat up to 2.2 pounds (1 kg) of eucalyptus leaves a day!

WHAT'S THE POINT?

Jean-Marie Tjibaou Cultural Centre
Nouméa, New Caledonia

Listen up! Rising up out of the dense vegetation by the coastline of Boulari Bay are 10 amazing curved columns that were built so that winds from the ocean would vibrate the structure and make it sound like singing. Opened in 1998, this beautifully designed project was built to celebrate the culture of the Kanak people, Native inhabitants of New Caledonia. Inside the buildings are a museum, library, galleries, dance studios, a botanical garden, and much more. All in all, it's a cultural center that's music to your ears!

The slime that oozes from devil's fingers smells like rotting flesh!

Devil's Fingers
Australia and New Zealand

Devil's fingers might not be the most appealing name—but it's not as off-putting as its alternative title of "octopus stinkhorn"! Whatever you call it, everyone can agree this is one foul fungus. Devil's fingers starts as a gooey egg around one inch (3 cm) in diameter, partially buried in the ground. Four to six red tentacles, each between two and three inches (5–8 cm), burst out from the egg. They ooze greenish black slime and look straight out of a sci-fi flick! The slime attracts flies, which carry away the spores to help spread the fungus—and they're doing a good job. Originally found in Australia and New Zealand, devil's fingers began appearing around the world in the early 20th century.

Thorny Devil
Australia

Making a meal of the thorny devil is a tough task for hungry predators. This desert lizard has a number of self-defense strategies that make it a challenge to chomp! Those sharp spikes covering its body obviously make this critter hard to swallow. But the lizard's cleverest trick involves a false head, which appears when it lowers its real head. Predators are fooled into attacking the fake, keeping the real one safe. Another thorny devil ploy is to fill its chest with air to make itself look more of a threat. It uses camouflage, too, changing color to blend in with its surroundings. And if all else fails, it can run away—these lizards have been known to reach a speedy 37 miles an hour (60 km/h), which is as fast as a racehorse.

THORNY DEVILS CAN EAT 3,000 ANTS IN A DAY.

DISTINCTIVE DWELLINGS

Bulls

North Island, New Zealand

The small farming town of Bulls on New Zealand's west coast really lives up to its name. A taste of what's in store is revealed by the welcome sign, which proclaims "Herd of Bulls? A Town Like No Udder." If it's bovine puns you're after, you've hit the jackpot! Hungry visitors should stampede over to the Delect-A-Bull café or the Lick-A-Bull ice cream parlor. There's also the Read-A-Bull library and the town hall, known by locals as Social-A-Bull! And if there's any trouble you can head on over to the police station, Const-A-Bull, identified by a mural of bulls in police uniforms. But possibly the biggest joke is that naming the town had zilch to do with animals! It was named after English settler James Bull, who owned the first general store there.

Bulls has a fitting twin city on the Isle of Wight, U.K., called Cowes.

Police
CONST-A-BULL

Parking
PARK-A-BULL   A-BULL

Central House Movers
MOOVE-A-BULL 200kms

Mothered Goose Cafe
DELECT-A-BULL

Bulls Town Hall
SOCIAL-A-BULL

Brittons House Movers
TRANSPORT-A-BULL 900kms

Bulls Library
READ-A-BULL

Himalayan Bull
Indian Restaurant & Takeaway
90 High Street

wis your Agent
A-BULL

Bulls RSA
ReSpect-A-BULL

Storage Pro Dalziel Street
STORE-A-BULL

Bulls 4 Square
RESTOCK-A-BULL

Cafe & Farm Park
A-BULL

COWES
Isle of Wight UK

Korowai Tree Houses

Papua, Indonesia

The Korowai tribe in Papua live in tree houses, most of which are 20 to 39 feet (6–12 m) off the ground. Some of the buildings are as high as 131 feet (40 m) up in the air! Constructing one involves finding a sturdy tree and removing the top. The building materials all come from the jungle. The frame is made from branches, bound together with rattan palms, and the roof is made from large leaves. A ladder carved from a tree trunk hangs from the bottom of the house for access. The treetop homes sit high above seasonal floodwaters to protect the inhabitants from biting insects at ground level. Over the last few years, many Korowai have moved to live in villages, so this generation may be the last to call the aerial accommodations home.

Queen Alexandra's Birdwing
Papua New Guinea

When an insect has such an extravagant name, you'd expect it to impress. Queen Alexandra's birdwing doesn't disappoint—it's the largest butterfly in the world! It doesn't start its life so huge, though. A female Queen Alexandra's birdwing can lay more then 240 eggs during its lifetime—and each egg is just .16 inch (.41 cm) in diameter. The egg hatches into a caterpillar, which becomes a chrysalis around the size of a human thumb. When the beautiful butterfly emerges, the females can have wingspans measuring 11 inches (28 cm). This incredible insect is only found in Papua New Guinea and sadly is an endangered species. It does have a clever survival technique during its caterpillar stage—the vines it eats make the caterpillar poisonous to predators.

THESE BUTTERFLIES HAVE WINGSPANS THAT ARE ALMOST BIG ENOUGH TO COVER A MAN'S CHEST.

Weirdly Cute!
Dwarf Wallaby

You might think there isn't much left of the natural world to explore, but you'd be wrong. Scientists believe there are at least one million species on the planet that we don't know about yet. In 2008, an expedition to the remote peaks of New Guinea's Foja Mountains discovered at least 12 of them! These included a blossom bat, a tree frog with a long nose, a tree mouse, and this furry, little dwarf wallaby. Wallabies belong to the same family as kangaroos, but are usually smaller. This new species is only 18 inches (46 cm) long and weighs 3.5 pounds (1.6 kg), making it the size of a rabbit—and the smallest of all the wallabies. Most small wallabies are active during the night, but this pint-size species prefers to be busy during the day.

WEIRD WONDERS

Rainbow eucalyptus trees reach heights of

250 FEET (76 M)

(nearly the height of the Statue of Liberty).

It might look like someone has been busy with a paintbrush, but these multicolored trees are absolutely natural! This is the only species of eucalyptus that grows in the rainforest, thriving in wet, tropical environments in Papua New Guinea as well as Indonesia and the Philippines. The rainbow eucalyptus's orange-tinted bark sheds in strips, revealing a bright green layer. Over time, the bark matures and the green changes to red, then orange, purple, and finally brown. And because the bark is shed at different times, one tree can display all these colors at once. Botanists have tried to grow rainbow eucalyptus trees in gardens around the world, but the colors are never as vibrant as they appear in their natural habitat. The trees' thin layers of bark can be used to make pulpwood, which bizarrely, is the main ingredient in white paper!

RAINBOW EUCALYPTUS

Papua New Guinea

AUSSIE ODDITIES

Gnomesville
Ferguson Valley, Australia

An area of land near a roundabout in southwest Australia is gnome—sorry, home—to a huge collection of tiny statuettes. Gnomesville began in 1995 when the roundabout was being built. First one gnome appeared. (Although it's unclear whether it was watching over the work or protesting against it.) Soon, more little folk arrived, distracting drivers from the road. So the statuettes were moved nearby. The collection began to attract visitors who brought their own gnomes to help the tiny town grow, and it wasn't long before gnomes started to arrive from all around the world. The number grows every year. Well, gnome wasn't built in a day, was it?

Gnomesville is home to at least 7,000 fun figurines.

Garlic Festivals
Tasmania, Australia

The cold winters and cool climate make garlic a perfect crop to grow in Tasmania. Tasmanians love this pungent plant so much they have devoted not one, but two festivals to it. The Koonya Garlic Festival, usually held in February, features cooking master classes, garlic-flavored food, and the all-important growers' competition. Judges consider the appearance, size, and, yes, the taste of the entries, so a breath mint is probably in order once the winner has been decided! And anyone who misses that food fiesta needn't despair—just head north to Selbourne for the Tasmanian Garlic and Tomato Festival in March, where you can get your fill of both tasty treats.

Pink Slugs
Mount Kaputar, Australia

This magnificent mollusk is only found at the top of Mount Kaputar in New South Wales. The mountaintop is a unique ecozone formed by a volcanic eruption that happened 17 million years ago, and there are at least 20 species of slugs and snails that aren't found anywhere else in the world. These amazing pink slugs are eight inches (20 cm) long. They live in beds of snow gum eucalyptus leaves, where their color helps to camouflage them from predators. However, the pink slugs emerge in the hundreds after it rains to feed on tree moss—and they definitely stand out from their surroundings then! A lot of poisonous animals are brightly colored to warn predators. Although the pink slug isn't toxic, its amazing color might discourage hungry hunters.

Quokkas
Rottnest Island, Australia

Found on islands off the coast of Western Australia, the quokka has been nicknamed the "happiest animal in the world" because of its big grin. When Dutch explorer Willem de Vlamingh first saw them in 1696, he thought they were giant rats! He named their island "Rotte nest," meaning "rat nest" in Dutch. Today, Rottnest Island is the best place to see this cute marsupial. Of about 14,000 wild quokkas, between 10,000 and 12,000 of them live here. Though small—about the size of a cat—they are not afraid of humans and will often allow people to get close. They became famous worldwide when they started appearing in selfies with visitors to the island, including celebrities, though this practice is now discouraged.

TENNIS ACE ROGER FEDERER HAS SNAPPED HIMSELF WITH A QUOKKA!

QUIZ WHIZ

There's only so much weirdness a brain can take—but how much can you remember about amazing Oceania?

1 **What does the slime on devil's fingers smell like?**
   a. Burning wood
   b. Cooked cabbage
   c. Rotting flesh
   d. Sweaty socks

2 **Who was the first singer to perform at the Sydney Opera House?**
   a. Frank Sinatra
   b. Dame Kiri Te Kanawa
   c. Kylie Minogue
   d. Paul Robeson

3 What is the world's rarest insect?

a. Glowworm
b. Lord Howe Island stick insect
c. Queen Alexandra's birdwing
d. Rust fly

4 What color is Lake Hillier?

a. Blue
b. Green
c. Pink
d. Yellow

5 Which of these colors isn't usually seen on a rainbow eucalyptus?

a. Green
b. Orange
c. Purple
d. Silver

6 What is the police station in Bulls called?

a. Arrest-A-Bull
b. Const-A-Bull
c. Lock-A-Bull
d. Solv-A-Bull

7 What creatures are in the lake by the 15th hole at Carbrook Golf Course?

a. Alligators
b. Bull sharks
c. Giant squid
d. Jellyfish

8 What is the world's smallest wallaby called?

a. Dwarf wallaby
b. Foja wallaby
c. Micro wallaby
d. Wobbly wallaby

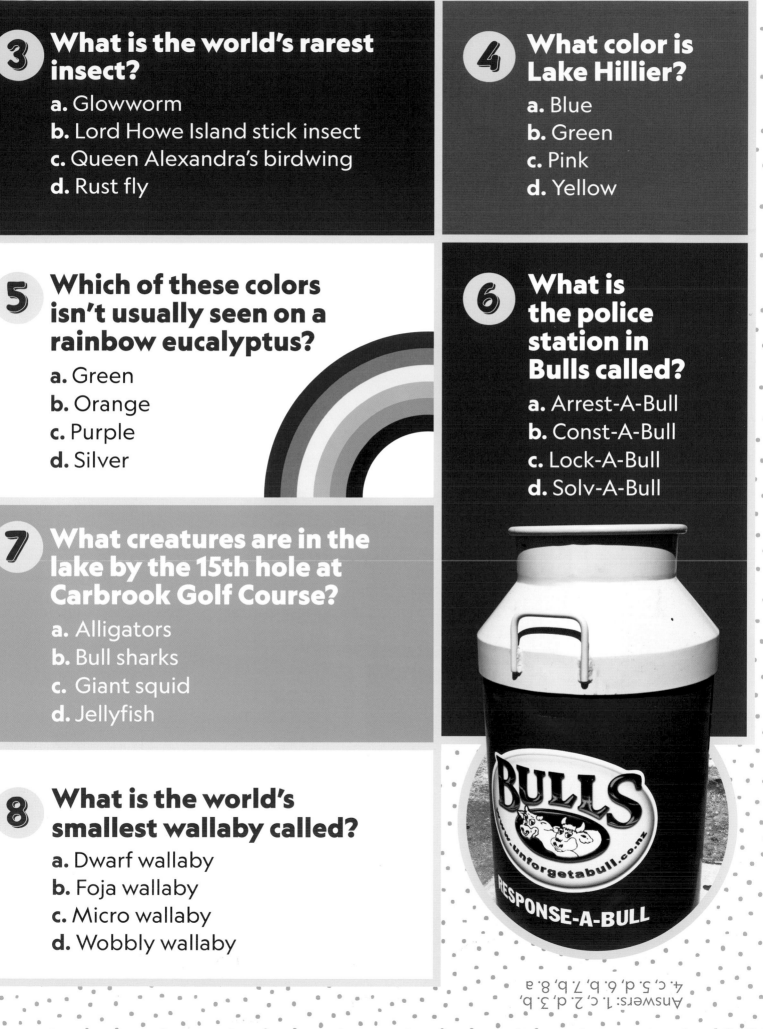

Answers: 1.c, 2.d, 3.b, 4.c, 5.d, 6.b, 7.b, 8.a

243

In some places, Antarctic ice is up to THREE MILES (5 km) thick!

Calm, cool, and weird!

CHAPTER
8

AMAZING ANTARCTICA

Singing ice, sea spiders, elephant seals, and more!

Sea spider fossils have been found that are OVER 400 MILLION YEARS OLD!

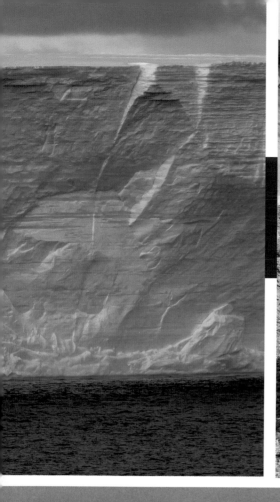

In Antarctic waters, penguins like to snack on JELLYFISH.

WEIRD in the WORLD

Check out some of the **WACKIEST, COOLEST,** and **DOWNRIGHT WEIRDEST PLACES** and **ANIMALS** across **ANTARCTICA!**

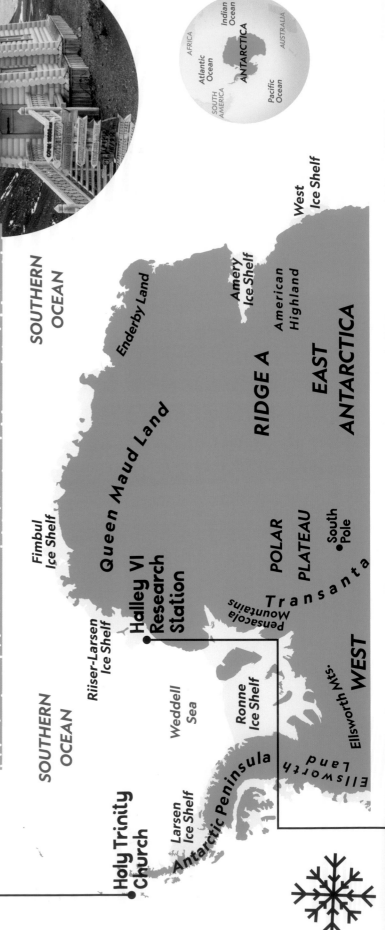

Holy Trinity Church is a Russian Orthodox church on King George Island. The little wooden church was built in **Russia** and shipped to this extreme location, near **Russia's Antarctic station.**

SOUTHERN OCEAN

Enderby Land

Amery Ice Shelf

American Highland

RIDGE A

EAST ANTARCTICA

Queen Maud Land

Fimbul Ice Shelf

POLAR PLATEAU

South Pole

Transanta

Pensacola Mountains

Riiser-Larsen Ice Shelf

Halley VI Research Station

Weddell Sea

Ronne Ice Shelf

Ellsworth Mts.

WEST

Ellsworth Land

Antarctic Peninsula

Larsen Ice Shelf

Holy Trinity Church

SOUTHERN OCEAN

West Ice Shelf

AFRICA

Indian Ocean

Atlantic Ocean

SOUTH AMERICA

ANTARCTICA

AUSTRALIA

Pacific Ocean

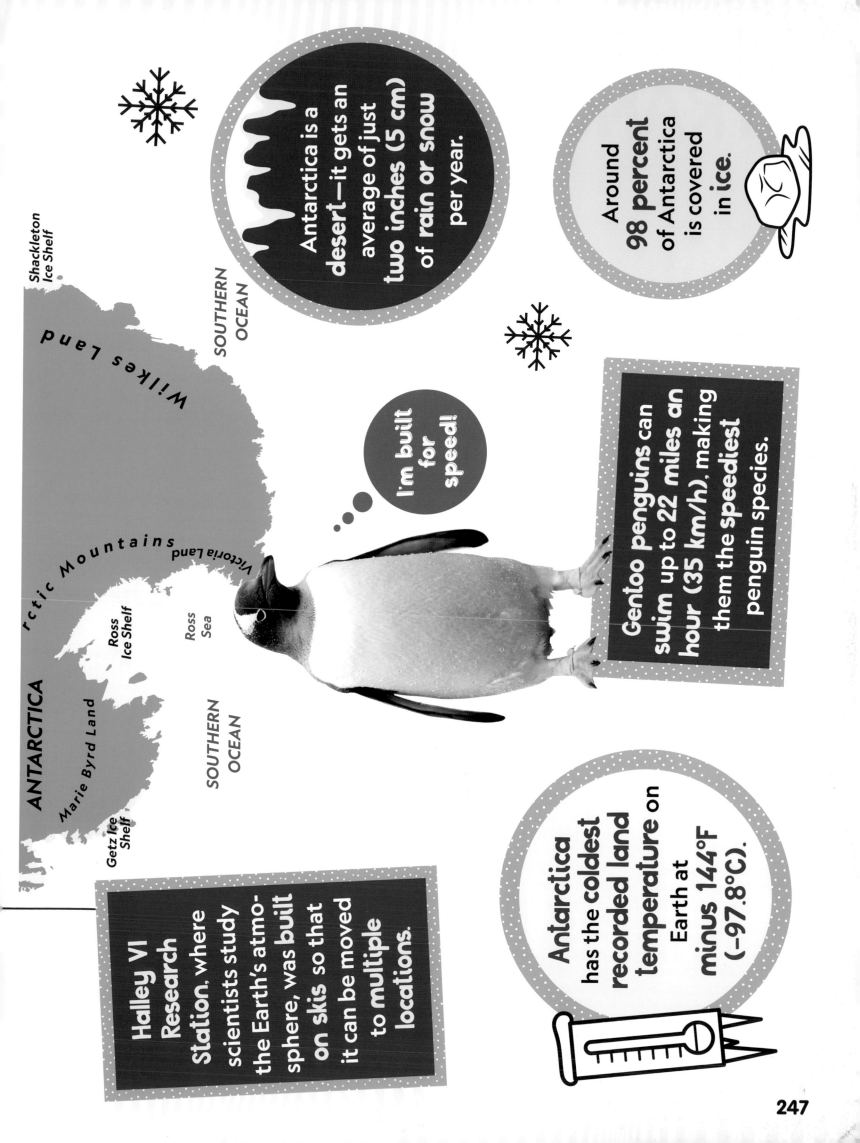

Shackleton
Ice Shelf

SOUTHERN
OCEAN

Wilkes Land

Antarctica is a desert—it gets an average of just two inches (5 cm) of rain or snow per year.

Around 98 percent of Antarctica is covered in ice.

ANTARCTICA

rctic Mountains

Victoria Land

Marie Byrd Land

Ross
Ice Shelf

Ross
Sea

SOUTHERN
OCEAN

Getz Ice
Shelf

I'm built for speed!

Gentoo penguins can swim up to 22 miles an hour (35 km/h), making them the speediest penguin species.

Halley VI Research Station, where scientists study the Earth's atmo-sphere, was built on skis so that it can be moved to multiple locations.

Antarctica has the coldest recorded land temperature on Earth at minus 144°F (–97.8°C).

247

STRANGE LANDSCAPES

Blood Falls
Lake Bonney, McMurdo Dry Valleys

Fear not—this waterfall isn't actually flowing with blood! When geologists discovered Taylor Glacier's rusty red wonder in 1911, they believed that algae turned the water red. But the color really comes from high levels of salt and iron in the underground rivers that lie beneath the glacier. As the iron-rich liquid bubbles up and comes into contact with oxygen in the air, the salts in it turn red. The liquid's chemical makeup is also the reason these falls don't freeze over completely—even when the air temperature is as low as minus 4°F (-20°C).

The **water** that supplies the falls is unique—it contains almost **no oxygen!**

Marie Byrd Land
West Antarctica

Welcome to the largest area of uninhabited land on Earth. In 1929, explorer Richard E. Byrd named it after his wife. His expedition there wasn't easy—the conditions were so hostile that the crew couldn't even set up camp. The barren, mountainous area averages 2,600 to 6,500 feet (790–1,980 m) above sea level, with many peaks over 11,000 feet (3,350 m) high, making it inhospitable and very hard to reach. This is probably the reason that no nation has claimed the land. In 1959, scientists opened a research base there. People still work at the base today, but only during the milder months of the year. So, during the winter, the area is completely uninhabited.

McMurdo Dry Valleys
Transantarctic Mountains

NASA described this land as the place on Earth that is most similar to Mars. This hostile landscape may seem like it belongs on a distant planet, but it's actually Antarctica's McMurdo Dry Valleys. While most of Antarctica is covered in ice and snow, this area has no ice covering at all, as rain is very rare. Deserts are extreme environments at the best of times, but this is one is especially harsh. The roughly 1,850 square miles (4,800 sq km) of alien-looking terrain is incredibly windy and cold. The valleys are kept ice-free (apart from a few patches) by scouring winds that blow away most falling snow before it even gets a chance to land!

MUMMIFIED SEALS HAVE BEEN FOUND IN THE DRY VALLEYS, MANY MILES FROM THE SEA.

COOL FACTS ABOUT THE HALLEY VI

weird but true!

The station is built on a **426-FOOT (130-M)-THICK FLOATING ICE SHELF** in the Weddell Sea.

At Halley, you need to **keep a radio on you at all times** so that people **always know where you are.** Whenever someone leaves the station, they must fill in a **logbook.**

For **105 days a year,** it's **DARK** for **24 hours a day.**

EIGHT MODULES make up the RESEARCH FACILITY.

Up to **70 STAFF** work at **Halley** over the **SUMMER.**

RESEARCH STATION

Everyone at the base keeps **backup batteries** for their **headlamps** in an inside pocket to **keep them warm!**

Halley researchers **FREQUENTLY** spot **EMPEROR PENGUINS, MINKE WHALES,** and **WEDDELL SEALS** near the station.

Everyone has a **P (PERSONAL) BAG** with a sleeping system that includes a **THICK WOODEN BOARD** to insulate, a **FOAM ROLL MAT**, a **THICK SHEEPSKIN RUG**, a down **SLEEPING BAG,** and **LINERS** for the sleeping bag.

Besides breakfast, lunch, and dinner, people at the research station have tea breaks called **SMOKO.**

RESEARCHERS EAT LOTS OF **CHOCOLATE BARS** FOR ENERGY—THEY HAVE TO BE STUFFED IN A POCKET TO KEEP THEM FROM TURNING ROCK HARD IN THE **COLD.**

TEMPERATURES AROUND THE BASE DROP AS **LOW AS MINUS 4° TO MINUS 67°F (-20° TO -55°C)** IN WINTER.

UNUSUAL UNDERWATER CREATURES

Sea Cucumbers

Sea cucumbers have an awesome tactic when predators approach. They simply fling their toxic internal organs at the attacker and regrow new ones—easy as that! Some are actually green, like their edible namesakes, but they can be black, white, or brightly colored—some even glow in the dark. Sea cucumbers can live in very shallow waters to the deepest seafloor. Their tubelike feet help them to move, and they feed with tentacles.

Sea cucumbers range in size from smaller than a fingernail to as long as a python!

Rotifers

Without a microscope, it would be almost impossible to see one of these—scientists think that around 100 rotifers could fit into one drop of water! Rotifers are zooplankton—tiny marine animals—usually between .004 and .02 inch (0.1–0.5 mm) in size. "Rotifer" means "wheel bearer," after the circle of hairlike structures around their mouth. These "hairs"—known as cilia—ripple one after the other, like a rotating wheel helping rotifer to move around and to eat. Bdelloid rotifers can survive being dried out completely and then rehydrated—a handy adaptation for life in Antarctica!

Antarctic Sea Spiders

Although related to their land-based cousins, Antarctic sea spiders are not actually spiders. They live at the bottom of the ocean, where they devour tiny animals, bacteria, and organic matter in the sediment. Their shells are often encrusted with barnacles and algae, which can make it harder for them to breathe and can slow them down, too. Some species can grow as big as 12 inches (30 cm) across, including their legs—as big as a dinner plate! Despite this, their bodies are actually small, so their guts are found in their long, spindly legs instead. In addition to their eight legs, they also have special hooks that are used for grooming and moving their eggs.

FEATHER STARS TAKE BETWEEN THREE AND SIX MONTHS TO REGROW MISSING BODY PARTS.

Feather Stars

These pretty, plantlike creatures from the deep have been around for 200 million years! Some feather stars swim, and others crawl along the seafloor using their arms, which they can regrow when damaged or injured. Once fully regrown, there is no sign of an injury ever occurring. In fact, they can regrow most body parts as long as the disk in the center of their body, called the centradorsal, is not too damaged. Many different organisms, such as tiny shrimps, make their homes on these magical-looking living structures. The feather stars provide these animals with food (which gets stuck in the feathery arms) and shelter.

NATURE'S GIANTS

Belgica antarctica ⌁⟶

It's hard to believe, but this tiny, wingless midge is the largest animal that lives only on land in Antarctica. Measuring up to a whopping 0.2 inch (6 mm) long, these Antarctic "giants" have special abilities to help them survive the two years they spend developing as larvae. During that time they can withstand temperatures as low as 5°F (-15°C)! They then enjoy a mere 10 days as an adult insect who has to lay eggs before dying. Brutal!

Sometimes albatrosses **eat so much** that they **can't fly!**

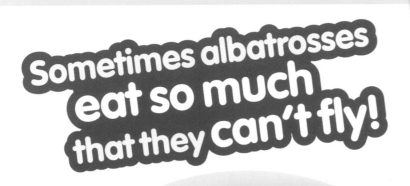

Wandering Albatross

These impressive birds have the largest wingspan of any living bird on the planet—up to 11 feet (3 m), or the same as the length of a small car. It's not just the size of their wings that is record-breaking. The wandering albatross can travel an incredible 620 miles (1,000 km) in just one day while out at sea. They can live for 60 years or more and weigh between 13 and 26 pounds (6–12 kg) when fully grown. It's no surprise that these feathered beasts have a huge appetite and will eat just about anything they can get their beaks around.

BY the NUMBERS

Antarctica is one of the coldest places on the planet, but that doesn't deter the emperor penguin. These ultimate survivors spend their entire lives on the ice and in the frigid water. Take a look inside the supercool life of an emperor penguin.

WEIGHT:

UP TO **88** POUNDS

(40 KG)

DIVE DEPTH:

1,850 FEET (564 M)

DISTANCE A FEMALE WILL TRAVEL TO FIND FOOD:

ABOUT **50** MILES

(80 KM)

TIME EMPEROR PENGUINS CAN STAY UNDERWATER:

20 MINUTES

SWIMMING SPEED:

46 MPH (74 KM/H)

ICE AND FIRE

Erebus Volcanic Ice Caves

Ross Island

Incredible ice formations were found around the summit of Mount Erebus, in a system of hidden caves! If these twinkling ice caves weren't surprising enough already, they're also toasty warm! It all has to do with the volcanic activity. Heat from volcano rises through cracks, melting areas of snow and ice. This liquid then refreezes as it comes into contact with the cold atmosphere and forms caves. Scientists have discovered the DNA of mosses, fungi, and roundworms in the caves. This suggests that some plants and animals may have once lived in volcanically heated ground near the volcano summit.

Temperatures inside the caves can reach 77°F (25°C).

Antarctic Fire Department

Ross Island

Even a continent covered in ice needs a fire service! Antarctica Fire Department (AFD) is the fire and rescue service for McMurdo Station (United States Antarctic Program), Amundsen-Scott Station (New Zealand's research station), and United States Air Force airfields. These busy places have lots of machinery, plus large stores of toxic chemicals, and that means lots of potential risk. When a fire does start, the extreme dry, cold, and windy climate means that flames spread quickly, and water—a basic necessity to fight most fires—soon freezes solid. To combat this, the fire engines have pumps to keep the water continually moving.

Lava Lake
Mount Erebus

On Ross Island, you will find the southernmost active volcano on Earth. This is the place where fire and ice meet! Lava has flowed from Mount Erebus, but unlike many volcanoes, its slopes are covered in snow and ice. This frozen volcano was discovered in 1841 on an expedition led by Sir James Clark Ross. It started to form 1.3 million years ago and now stands at 12,450 feet (3,800 m) high. The extreme climate ranges from minus 4°F (-20°C) in summer to as low as minus 58°F (-50°C) in winter. While most volcanoes are dormant (nonactive) most of the time, this one is always bubbling and sometimes even hurls exploding lava bombs! The lava lake may bring up magma from miles beneath Earth's surface.

THE VOLCANO'S LAVA LAKE REACHES TEMPERATURES OF AROUND 1700°F (927°C).

Ocean ODDITIES !

I'm as good as gold!

Scale Worm

Say hello to the Antarctic scale worm, or *Eulagisca gigantea*. They can grow up to eight inches (20 cm) long, and their backs are covered in scales—hence their name. It is believed that their golden bristles, or fringing, helps them to move along the ocean floor, swim, and defend themselves. Don't let that fabulous gold fringing lure you in—they also have a jaw full of spiky teeth, suggesting they are predators or scavengers!

Minke Whale

Minke whales are common in Antarctica, but that doesn't mean they're easy to spot! These streamlined creatures speed through water so quickly that it's difficult for scientists to track what they get up to under the ocean. Compared to other whales, this species is quite small. Minkes are under 10 tons (9 t) and half the length of humpback whales, which weigh around 40 tons (36 t). They mostly travel alone or in small groups, but you wouldn't guess that from the noise minkes make—their vocalizations can be up to 152 decibels. That's as loud as a jet plane taking off!

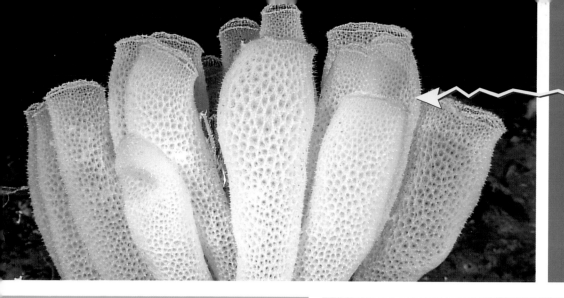

Glass Sponge

Found deep down on the seafloor, the glass sponge is a living creature with a skeleton made out of silica—the sand used to make glass. Although they are fragile, the sponges' silica has a needlelike sharpness, so watch out!

Elephant Seal

Elephant seals can grow up to 20 feet (6 m) and weigh as much as 4.5 tons (4 t)—that's as heavy as two rhinoceroses! And it's not just their size that makes them elephant-like. The species is actually named after the nose of male elephant seals, which looks a bit like a trunk. They use their bulbous trunks to make loud and threatening noises to ward off other males.

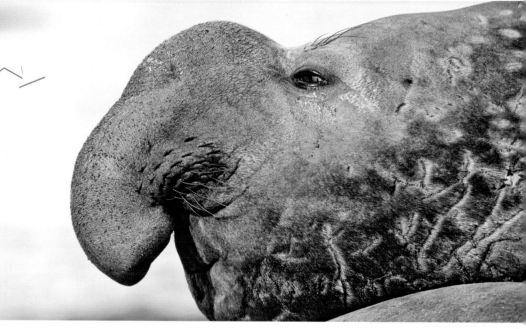

Tardigrade

Nicknamed the "water bear" or "moss piglet," tardigrades like the one in this microscopic image may be miniature, but boy are they mighty! They can live in the most extreme environments and survive both near-zero temperatures and boiling water.

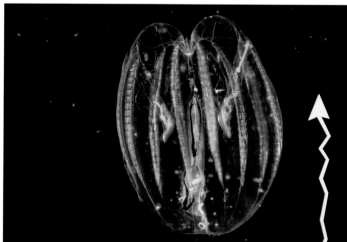

Floating Antarctic Comb Jelly

The comb jelly is named after the rows of hair-like structures, known as cilia, along their body. Rainbows of color appear when light travels through these combs. As well as making beautiful rainbows, their combs help the creatures to move through the water.

259

UNEXPECTED ANTARCTICA

Mummified Penguins
East Antarctica's Long Peninsula

In 2016, the bodies of hundreds of mummified penguins were discovered after snow and ice melted away to reveal them, perfectly preserved. Scientists believe that mummification happens in Antarctica as a result of the dry, cold climate—these conditions even preserve penguin's bones and feathers. But, even in Antarctica, it's unusual to find so many mummies in one place. Researchers suspect that the hundreds of penguins died gradually as a result of two periods of extreme rain and snow that occurred around 750 and 200 years ago.

A fossilized tree stump that is 280 million years old was found in Antarctica.

Antarctica's Ancient Forests

It's hard to imagine, but Antarctica was once covered in forest. Yes, millions of years ago, before the continent experienced what is known as "the deep freeze," Antarctica was home to rainforests and lush greenery. Go back as far as 100 million years and Antarctica would have been alive with dinosaurs and many species of pre-historic plants. Discoveries of fossilized logs are helping scientists to better understand the ancient climate and its plants, and to learn more about the conditions they needed to survive in, such as months of darkness at a time, before months of daylight.

What's **Weird** About This **?**

The ice that covers Antarctica's Ross Ice Shelf sings! Unfortunately, humans can't actually hear the eerie, low humming sound it makes. Researchers discovered this fascinating fact by using seismometers, which are microphones for the ground, to study the snow and ice. They recorded the sound for two years and found that the hum is caused by wind blowing over the surface of the ice. Interestingly, they also discovered that the sound changes slightly depending on the weather conditions. For example, if wind moves the snow around and changes the shape of the snow dunes, or if areas of the ice melt, the sound's pitch changes. This means that scientists can track the ice's singing to monitor how stable the ice is, and whether it's in danger of cracking or collapsing.

QUIZ WHIZ

Think you're a whiz at Weird But True?
Test your knowledge with these quirky questions!

2 Hundreds of animals were found mummified in East Antarctica. What animals were they?

a. Penguins
b. Polar bears
c. Seals
d. Whales

1 What does the ice covering Antarctica's Ross Ice Shelf do that's unusual?

a. Dance
b. Bake
c. Sing
d. Count

3 Which description is NOT true of a wandering albatross?

a. They have the largest wingspan of any living bird.
b. They can live for 60 years or more.
c. They can travel 620 miles (1,000 km) in a single day.
d. They are as big as three cars.

5 How long does it take a feather star to grow a new arm?

a. three to six days
b. three to six weeks
c. three to six months
d. three to six years

4 Where will you find Mount Erebus?

a. Joss Island
b. Ross Island
c. Moss Island
d. Loss Island

6 What planet has the McMurdo Dry Valleys been compared to?

a. Mars
b. Jupiter
c. Saturn
d. Neptune

7 What is this creature?

a. Scale worm
b. Tardigrade
c. Floating Antarctic comb jelly
d. Glass sponge

8 How long can an emperor penguin stay underwater?

a. 25 minutes
b. 30 minutes
c. 35 minutes
d. 20 minutes

Answers: 1. c, 2. a, 3. d, 4. b, 5. c, 6. a, 7. b, 8. d

The best of both weirds!

CHAPTER 9

SENSATIONAL SEA AND SPACE

Strange creatures, mysterious marvels, brain-bending numbers, and weirdness that's out of this world!

Scientists estimate that there are at least **200 TRILLION GALAXIES** in the universe.

Each dolphin has a UNIQUE WHISTLE, which is used to IDENTIFY IT, like a name.

The longest ever space walk lasted for EIGHT HOURS AND 56 MINUTES.

Travel beyond the human domain, into the

DARKEST DEPTHS of the OCEAN and the
DISTANT REACHES of OUTER SPACE...

That's weird!

Challenger Deep, the deepest part of the ocean, is deeper than the height of Mount Everest.

The Pacific Ocean is so wide that if you view it from space, you can hardly see any land.

PACIFIC OCEAN

Challenger Deep

A S I A

Mount Everest

ARCTIC OCEAN

EUROPE

AFRICA

ATLANTIC OCEAN

NORTH AMERICA

PACIFIC OCEAN

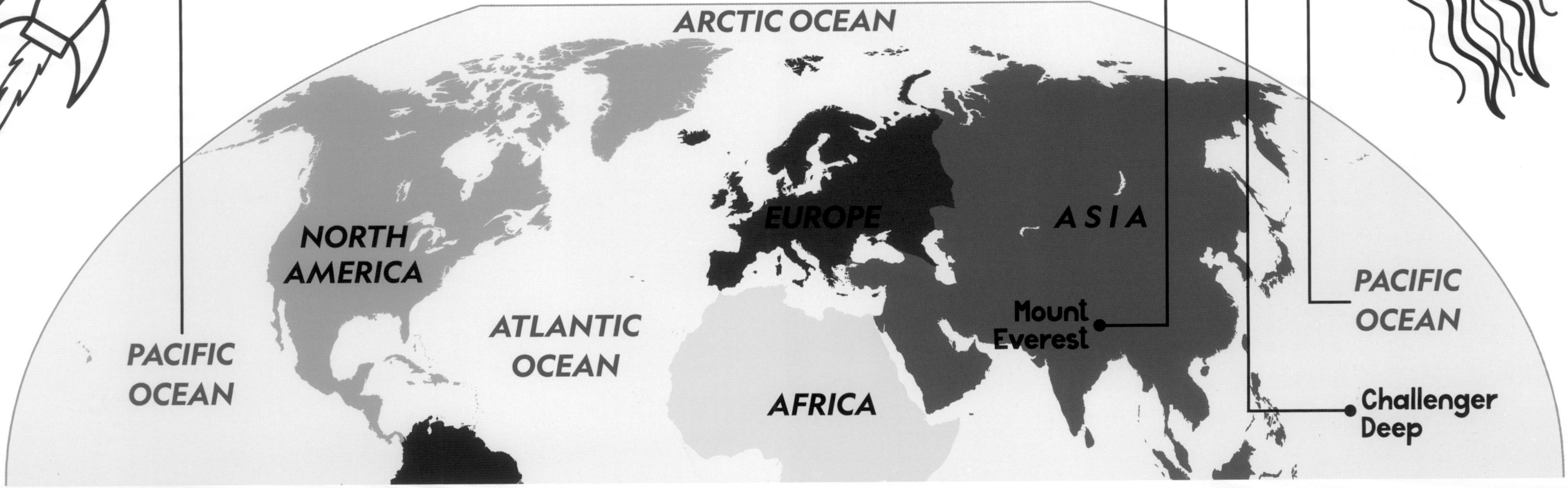

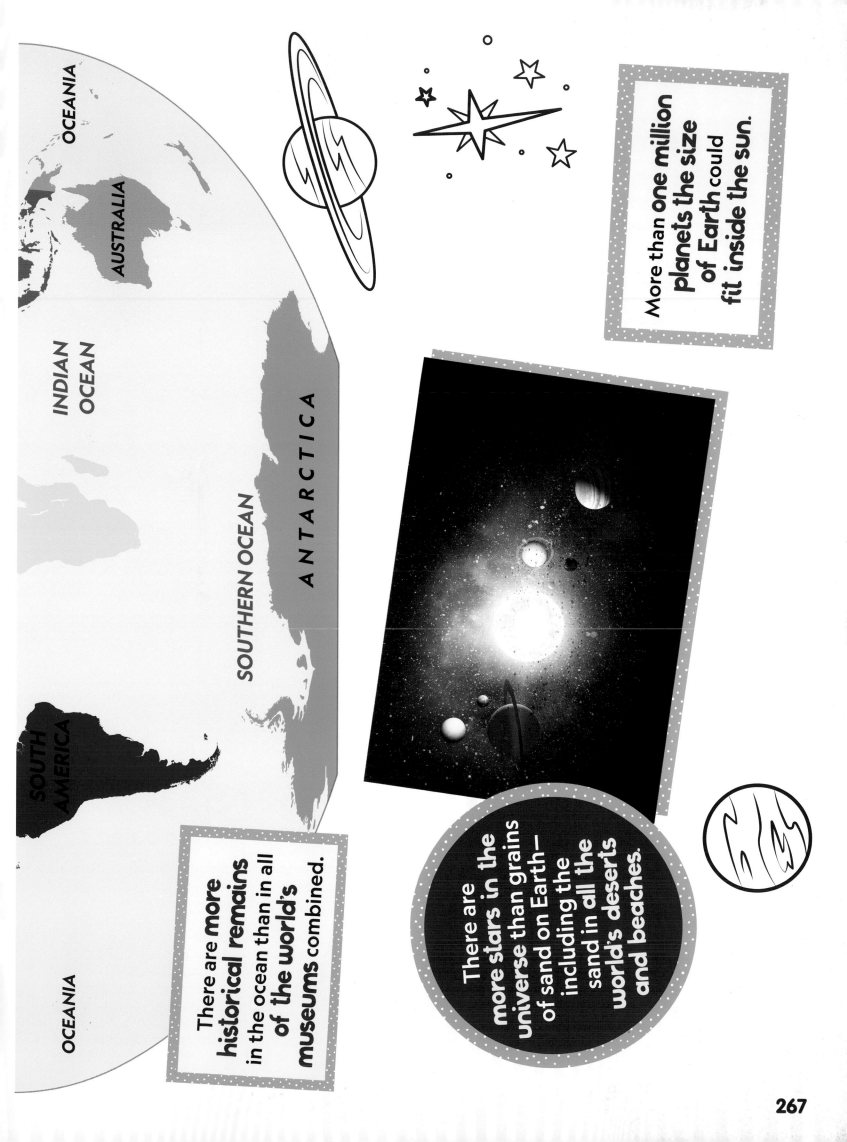

OCEANIA

AUSTRALIA

INDIAN
OCEAN

SOUTHERN OCEAN

ANTARCTICA

SOUTH
AMERICA

OCEANIA

More than one million planets the size of Earth could fit inside the sun.

There are more historical remains in the ocean than in all of the world's museums combined.

There are more stars in the universe than grains of sand on Earth—including the sand in all the world's deserts and beaches.

UNDERWATER WEIRDNESS

Pufferfish Circles

Pacific Ocean, Japan

When divers first found strange circular patterns on the seabed near Japan, they were stumped. The circles have rings of ridges around them, so neat and detailed, they look like something a human artist might make. Eventually, however, the real artist was spotted at work—and it was a fish! It turns out that the male of a species of pufferfish makes the patterns. He creates the ridged circles by swimming in and out around the circle, shaping the sand as he goes. The resulting pattern is actually a nest, which the male makes to impress a female pufferfish. If she likes it, she'll lay her eggs in the middle, and the male then guards them until they hatch.

A pufferfish's intricate **circular patterns** are up to **6.5 feet (2 m) across.**

Giant Pyrosome

Warm Seas and Oceans

Imagine you're on a dive in the ocean. You see a glowing, 50-foot (15-m)-long, tube-shaped creature with a gaping mouth at one end, big enough to swallow you up. Yikes! But this isn't a snake or a sea monster, and it won't eat you. In fact, it's not even an animal. It's a colony, or group, of thousands of much smaller animals called zooids. They are joined together and float around in the sea, feeding on plankton. Each zooid can glow with light, giving the whole tube its name, "pyrosome," meaning "fire body."

Underwater Post Office

Vanuatu

The island nation of Vanuatu in the Pacific Ocean is one of the best places in the world to go scuba diving. You can swim over beautiful coral reefs, watch ocean wildlife, explore shipwrecks—and send a postcard! Yes, Vanuatu has the world's first underwater post office, which opened in 2003. Located 160 feet (50 m) from the shore and 10 feet (3 m) below the surface, it's quite small, but it is a real post office, and the mail gets collected every day. But don't postcards get soggy underwater? Yes, they do. That's why shops in Vanuatu sell waterproof postcards!

WEST MATA WAS ONE OF THE VERY FIRST UNDERWATER ERUPTIONS TO BE CAUGHT ON CAMERA.

Undersea Volcano

Tonga Trench, Pacific Ocean

This is a picture of volcano West Mata erupting at the bottom of the Pacific Ocean, between Fiji, Tonga, and Samoa. Just like a volcano on land, it churns out red-hot molten rock, or lava. But instead of flowing down the volcano's sides, the lava hits the cold water immediately. This causes it to suddenly cool and solidify, turning the lava into lumps of volcanic rock that cover the seabed. Though we rarely see them, there are more volcanic eruptions under the sea than on land—which makes sense, as Earth has a lot more sea than land.

269

DOWN TO THE DEPTHS

Deepest Human Dive
Mariana Trench, Pacific Ocean

The deepest any human has ever been is 35,843 feet (10,9275 m)—almost to the bottom of Challenger Deep in the Mariana Trench. The record was set in 2019 by American explorer Victor Vescovo. He made the trip alone in a deep-sea submersible—a type of small submarine strong enough to resist the deep ocean water pressure. Right at the bottom, he spotted shrimplike sea creatures, and sadly, a plastic bag.

Vescovo has also climbed the **highest peaks** of all the world's continents.

Deepest-Diving Whales
Worldwide

Lots of sea creatures live deep down in the ocean, including giant squid, megamouth sharks, sea cucumbers, and many species of fish. But they have an advantage: They can all breathe underwater. The deepest-diving animal that breathes air (not including humans in submersibles) is a whale—Cuvier's beaked whale. On their way to hunt deep sea squid, some of these small, shy whales can reach depths of 9,816 feet (2,992 m) and stay under for more than three hours!

BY the NUMBERS

THE DEEP SEA

How deep does the ocean go? In most places, the seabed slopes gently away from the coast, forming the continental shelf, which then falls steeply away into the deeper ocean. The very deepest point in the whole of the ocean is called Challenger Deep, in the Mariana Trench near the island of Guam in the Pacific Ocean. This area is SO deep, it takes several hours to get there in a submarine, it's pitch black, and if you weren't protected inside a submarine, the water pressure there would squash you in a split second.

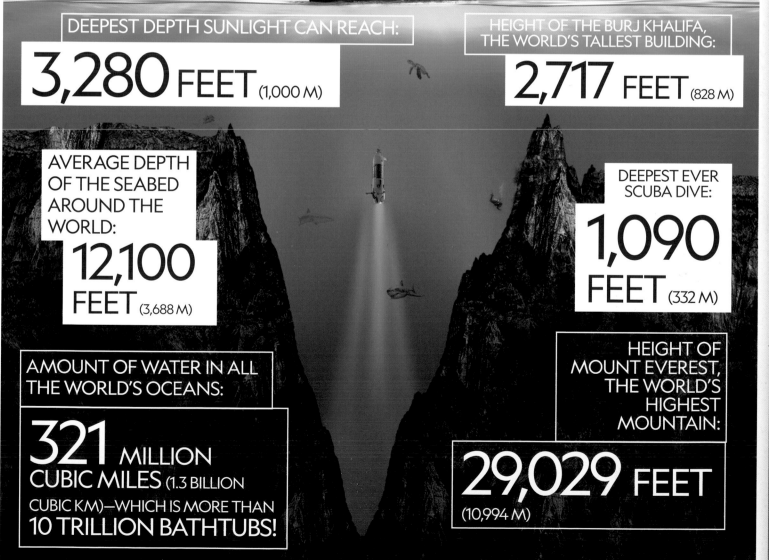

DEEPEST DEPTH SUNLIGHT CAN REACH:

3,280 FEET (1,000 M)

HEIGHT OF THE BURJ KHALIFA, THE WORLD'S TALLEST BUILDING:

2,717 FEET (828 M)

AVERAGE DEPTH OF THE SEABED AROUND THE WORLD:

12,100 FEET (3,688 M)

DEEPEST EVER SCUBA DIVE:

1,090 FEET (332 M)

AMOUNT OF WATER IN ALL THE WORLD'S OCEANS:

321 MILLION CUBIC MILES (1.3 BILLION CUBIC KM)—WHICH IS MORE THAN **10 TRILLION BATHTUBS!**

HEIGHT OF MOUNT EVEREST, THE WORLD'S HIGHEST MOUNTAIN:

29,029 FEET (10,994 M)

MONSTERS OF THE DEEP

Vampire Squid
Deep Waters Around the World

Does it have scary fangs and a taste for blood? No. The vampire squid got its name because it has a red cape and lives in the dark! Photographed by the team at the Monterey Bay Aquarium Research Institute (MBARI), this harmless creature lives in the deep sea where oxygen is low and predators are few. It's related to squids and octopuses, and feeds using two skinny tentacles to catch bits of food that drift down from the ocean surface. Its eight arms are connected by sheets of skin, resembling a cloak. When in danger, the squid can turn its "cape" inside out and hide inside, displaying the large spines on the insides of its arms to ward off attack.

Sometimes I think the other fish just look right through me.

Barreleye Fish
Warm and Tropical Oceans

Hovering silently in the murky ocean depths is a fish with a dome-shaped, see-through head, and two tube-shaped green eyes that rotate to point forward, or straight up. It's not made-up—this really is a fish, named the barreleye, and it's one of the weirdest animals in the world. Where it lives, there's only a little light filtering down from above. So it's thought the barreleye looks upward to spot the silhouettes of prey, such as smaller fish, as they pass overhead. Then, according to researchers at MBARI, the fish rotates its eyes forward to see its meal while it chows down. But why the transparent dome? The barreleye sometimes swims through jellyfish tentacles to steal the food they've caught—and the dome protects its eyes from stings!

Gulper Eel
Warm and Tropical Oceans

The clue's in the name ... this amazing eel of the deep is probably the best gulper on the planet! It has huge, long, hinged jawbones that fold up under its head, making it look pretty normal. Then, suddenly, it can open them out to stretch its mouth into a massive gaping chasm. It can also stretch its stomach, allowing it to swallow fish even bigger than itself. More often, though, it uses its mouth like a fishing net, to scoop up shoals of shrimps. The gulper eel is as rare as it is incredible: In more than 30 years of deep sea research, MBARI researchers have only spotted the creatures seven times.

THE GULPER EEL CAN INFLATE ITSELF WITH WATER TO LOOK BIGGER AND SCARIER!

Weirdly Cute!

Sea Pig

Just as land pigs snuffle around in the mud, sea pigs snuffle their way along the deep seabed in search of food. And like a real pig, a sea pig is plump, pinkish, and pretty cute! But that is where the likeness ends. A sea pig is actually a type of sea cucumber. And confusingly, a sea cucumber is not a cucumber, but a small animal related to starfish. They use their tentacles to "walk" and feel their way around, and they feed on the rotting bodies of other creatures that have died and sunk to the seabed. According to MBARI, sea pigs are some of the most common critters on the sea floor, making then quite the clean up crew! And if that's not weird enough for you, get this: They breathe through their butts!

WEIRD WONDERS

Just how big is this wave? You'll see how enormous it is when you spot the tiny surfer zooming along it! At Nazaré in Portugal, waves break at heights of up to 100 feet (33 m). And where you find the world's biggest breakers, you find the world's best surfers. Professionals like Rodrigo Koxa, Maya Gabeira, and Sebastian Steudtner have surfed waves between 70 and 90 feet (21–27 m) here, and they keep breaking records. As waves roll in toward Nazaré from the Atlantic, they overlap and increase in size, then pile up and break as they reach the edge of a deep underwater canyon. Crowds gather at a clifftop fort above the water—the perfect spot for wave-watching.

WORLD'S BIGGEST WAVES

Nazaré, Portugal

This massive wave swell occurs regularly and is nicknamed "BIG MAMA" by surfers.

LIFE UNDERWATER

Aquarius Reef
Florida, U.S.A.

Underwater bases are normally found in spy movies—but did you know they really exist? The most famous is Aquarius Reef, near the Florida coast. It sits on the seabed under about 60 feet (18 m) of water, next to a coral reef filled with wildlife. Since being built in 1986, the base's exterior has grown a covering of living coral and sea creatures, too. Visiting scientists usually stay for around two weeks at a time to study ocean life. But the base also hosts trainee astronauts, who practice doing tasks underwater (because it feels a bit like floating in microgravity) and sharing tiny living quarters.

Up to six people can live and work in Aquarius Reef at once.

Jules' Undersea Lodge
Florida, U.S.A.

The Aquarius Reef Base is usually closed to the public, but there is an alternative for underwater enthusiasts: Jules' Undersea Lodge, which is also in Florida, in a lagoon in Key Largo. It used to be a research base, but now it's an underwater hotel with two bedrooms, a living area and even hot showers. You have to dive to get in, though. It was here, in 2014, that two professors, Bruce Cantrell and Jessica Fain, broke the world record for the longest time spent living underwater: just over 73 days! They didn't sit around doing nothing, though—instead they hosted online biology lessons from the lodge.

Conshelf
Red Sea, Sudan

Jacques Cousteau was one of the greatest underwater explorers of all time. From the 1940s to the 1990s, he did underwater experiments, made films about the undersea world, helped to invent scuba diving equipment, and created three underwater habitats for humans to live and work in. The second one, Conshelf II, built in 1963, was the most sci-fi in style. It had a star-shaped living pod, a deeper mini pod, and an undersea garage, housing a mini-submarine known as the diving saucer. Five men lived in Conshelf II for 30 days, along with a parrot! Cousteau dreamed of much larger underwater villages, which sadly didn't happen. But divers still explore the coral-encrusted remnants of Conshelf II to this day.

THE UNDERWATER HOTEL'S BEDROOM IS SUBMERGED 16 FEET (4.9 M) BELOW SEA LEVEL.

Underwater Hotel
Maldives

Perhaps you'd prefer to sleep in style underwater, in a luxury, high-end hotel with no diving required? In that case, head to the Rangali Island resort in the Maldives, an island nation in the Indian Ocean. Its Muraka (meaning "coral") villa is mostly above the sea surface, but has an underwater bedroom and bathroom, reached via a spiral staircase and an elevator. The suite has thick, superstrong, clear acrylic walls and a curved roof, so you can watch reef sharks, turtles and octopuses as you sit in bed. Or maybe they're watching you— who knows?

277

Bizarre BEHAVIOR

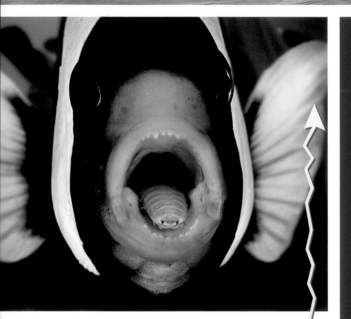

Take to the Air

You've probably heard of flying fish, but did you know just how good they are at flying? Launching themselves out of the sea at high speed and then spreading out their fins like wings, they can zoom along at 40 miles an hour (65 km/h) and travel up to 650 feet (200 m) in a single flight. The longest ever flying fish flight on record was 45 seconds. That's three times longer than the longest chicken flight, at only 13 seconds!

Blowing Bubbles

By puffing a big bubble of air out of its blowhole underwater, a dolphin can make a spinning bubble ring that hovers in the water. Then the dolphin chases the ring, bats it around with its flippers, pokes it with its snout, or, if it's big enough, swims right through it. Playing is a sign of intelligence, and dolphins are known for being very smart creatures. They've been seen playing with bubble rings in aquariums and in the wild, and one dolphin can learn to make rings by watching another.

Uninvited Guest

The tongue-eating louse is a parasite—a creature that survives on or inside another living thing. It swims in through the fish's gills, attaches itself to the base of its tongue, and bites through the blood vessels. The real tongue dies and falls off, and is replaced by the louse! The fish now has a living louse for a tongue, feeding on its blood. Luckily, this doesn't kill the fish or stop it from eating.

I love playing dress-up!

Master of Disguise

The mimic octopus of Indonesia can do impressions of other animals—and not just one or two, but around 12 of them! Like other octopuses, it can change the color and texture of its skin. But it can also change its shape, disguising itself as venomous or dangerous sea creatures to keep predators away. It imitates the deadly lionfish by arranging its tentacles like spiky fins, and becomes a sea snake by hiding most of its body and sticking out two tentacles in a long line. To mimic a flounder, which lies on the seabed, it arranges is body and tentacles into a flattened fish shape.

Fright or Fight?

When you first spot a sarcastic fringehead, you might think it's just a little grumpy. But this freaky fish has much more in store. Male fringeheads often fight over the best hiding places. To try to scare and shove each other away, they have massive mouths, which they snap open, kind of like popping open an umbrella. Suddenly, the fish's face looks like an alien bat-monster, complete with red-and-yellow lips, bristling teeth, and rubbery, winglike black cheeks. But don't be too alarmed—the whole fish is only 10 inches (25 cm) long.

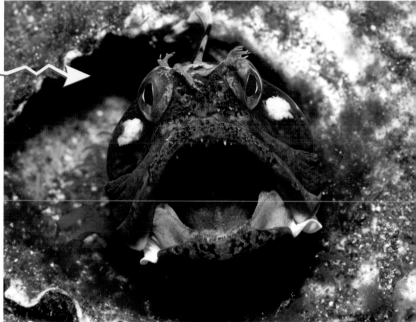

Coconut Carriers

One sign of smartness is tool use—using an object to help you do a particular task. Humans do it, and so do a few clever animals, such as chimps, dolphins, and crows. But scientists were amazed when they found some octopuses do it, too, as they are invertebrates, and more closely related to slugs and snails than to humans and chimps. The coconut octopus, from the western Pacific Ocean, carries two coconut shells with it when it moves around sandy areas with nowhere to shelter. If danger threatens, it hides inside!

BY the NUMBERS

INCREDIBLE SPACE STATS

You might think it's a long way to your grandparents' house, or a country across the world. But these distances, and in fact the whole of planet Earth, are absolutely tiny compared to the distances in outer space! The distances between planets, stars, and galaxies are so enormous, it's hard to imagine them. But maybe these mind-bending facts and figures can help.

SPEED OF EARTH'S ORBIT AROUND THE SUN:

67,000 MPH
(108,000 km/h)—that's more than **100 TIMES** faster than an airliner.

DISTANCE FROM EARTH'S SURFACE TO THE KÁRMÁN LINE, WHERE THE ATMOSPHERE MEETS SPACE:

62 MILES (100 KM)

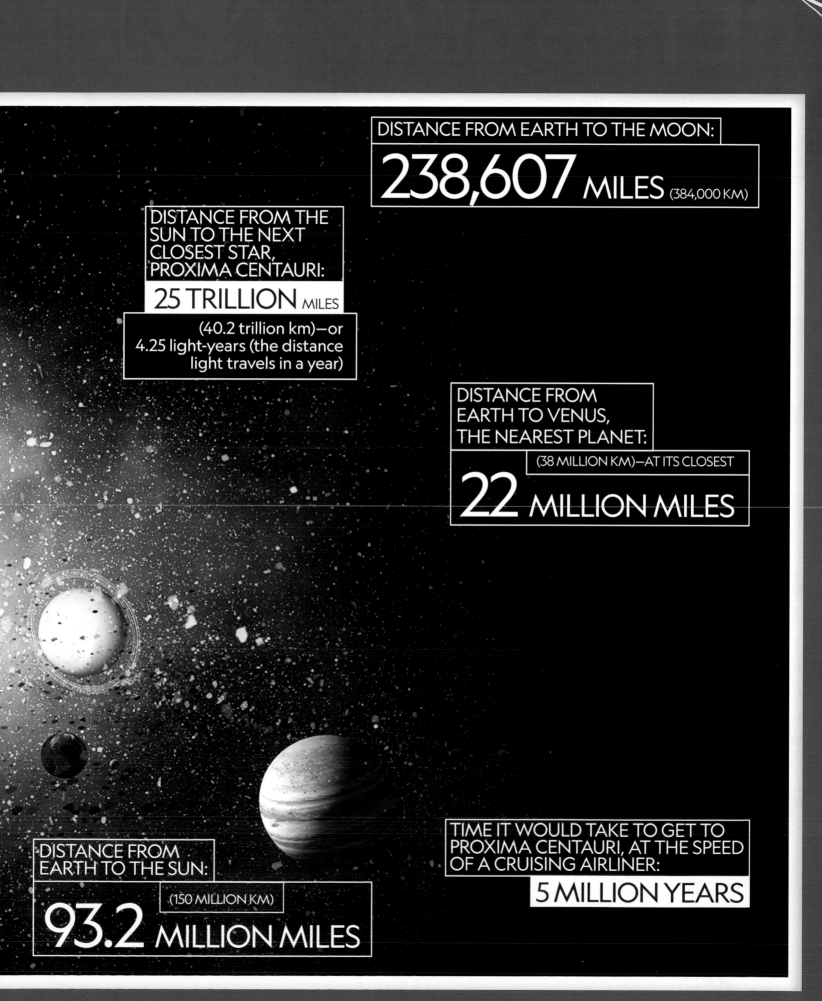

DISTANCE FROM EARTH TO THE MOON:

238,607 MILES (384,000 KM)

DISTANCE FROM THE SUN TO THE NEXT CLOSEST STAR, PROXIMA CENTAURI:

25 TRILLION MILES

(40.2 trillion km)—or 4.25 light-years (the distance light travels in a year)

DISTANCE FROM EARTH TO VENUS, THE NEAREST PLANET:

(38 MILLION KM)—AT ITS CLOSEST

22 MILLION MILES

DISTANCE FROM EARTH TO THE SUN:

(150 MILLION KM)

93.2 MILLION MILES

TIME IT WOULD TAKE TO GET TO PROXIMA CENTAURI, AT THE SPEED OF A CRUISING AIRLINER:

5 MILLION YEARS

GET INTO GEAR

Future Suits

NASA Laboratories, U.S.A.

When Bruce McCandless took his famous space walk, he had to wear a huge, bulky space suit, pumped full of gas to create pressure. This re-creates the air pressure we're used to on Earth—we can't survive without it! But for the future, scientists and designers are working on sleeker, more usable space suits, like the one in this picture. Instead of being pumped up with gas, they use strong elastic fabric to provide the pressure, making it much easier to move around and do things. They look cooler, too!

Two-thirds of **Vomit Comet** passengers **experience some amount** of nausea!

Vomit Comet

Re-creating Microgravity

Would you sign up for a ride on a plane nicknamed the "Vomit Comet"? It might not sound too good, but you'd probably love it! "Vomit Comet" is a nickname for a reduced-gravity aircraft—a plane that re-creates the feeling of being weightless in space. Since the 1950s, it's been used to train astronauts for the low gravity they will experience in space. To do this, the plane flies up high, then nosedives and starts to fall. The plane and the people inside fall at the same speed, so gravity seems to disappear. They can float around, push off from the sides of the cabin, and do somersaults in the air, just like you can in space. And what about the "vomit" part? That's because the experience makes some people feel like throwing up!

What's **Weird** About This **?**

I'm on top of the world!

This famous photo, taken in 1984, shows U.S. astronaut Bruce McCandless floating in space, completely alone. Unlike most space walks, on this one McCandless was not tethered to anything. He was just floating free in the vastness of the universe. Luckily, though, he wasn't actually lost. The photo was taken from the nearby space shuttle spacecraft, and McCandless was making his space walk using a special jet pack. It allowed him to control his direction, so he could return safely after flying 320 feet (98 m) away from the shuttle.

SPACE ROBOTS

Robonaut 2

Exploring space is extra difficult because, like the sea, humans can't survive in it without help. We need space suits and breathing equipment, and have to bring food and water supplies along, too. So it makes sense that NASA has a robot crew member who needs none of these things! Meet Robonaut 2, the latest version of this humanoid robot assistant. On board the International Space Station (ISS), it can clean, flip switches, and solve problems using artificial intelligence. In the future, robots like this will also be able to do risky space walks. And to help it get along with its human team, Robonaut has been programmed to high-five when it completes a task!

Shall I load the dishwasher next?

Canadarm2

This is a very different type of robot, which doesn't resemble a human at all. It's a huge, 60-foot (18-m)-long robot arm, attached to the outside of the International Space Station. It's not for waving at other spacecraft: This arm is busy doing all kinds of important tasks, such as moving supplies around the outside of the ISS, attaching new parts and modules, and locking onto visiting spacecraft when they deliver astronauts or food supplies. It can even detach and "walk" itself around the whole space station, holding on to different base points, like a huge, one-legged spider.

The **arm** is **made of parts** that can be replaced by **astronauts in space.**

Robot Rovers

When it comes to exploring other planets, robots lead the way—especially on Mars! The first human trips to Mars are being planned, but robots have been going there since the 1990s. And the smartest, most high-tech robot to have made the trip is the supercool Curiosity rover. This car-size, wheeled robot was sent to Mars in 2011 and landed in 2012. It roams around the surface, taking photos, collecting rocks and soil, and even doing experiments on them with its onboard scientific instruments to search for signs of life. Joined by a new rover, Perseverance, Curiosity will also find out more about conditions on Mars, which will help humans survive there, when we finally make it!

PERSEVERANCE IS DESIGNED TO TEST OUT NEW TECHNOLOGY FOR FUTURE ROBOTIC AND HUMAN TRIPS TO MARS.

Weirdly Cute!

Kirobo

How cute is this mini space robot? Named Kirobo, Japanese for "Hope Robot," he's only 13 inches (34 cm) long, and one of the friendliest robots you could meet. Kirobo was actually designed to be a friend—a chatty companion who can recognize your face and keep you company. He went to the International Space Station in 2013 as a companion for Japanese astronaut Koichi Wakata. It was part of an experiment to see how good robots are at helping with loneliness and befriending people—and the answer is, pretty good! In fact, more and more robots are being used this way on Earth as well as in space.

Far, Far AWAY!

Pillars of Creation

A nebula is a huge cloud of gas and dust in space. In some nebulae, new stars form, causing them to glow brightly. Nebulae are often named after their weird and wonderful shapes, which can resemble familiar objects. The beautiful "Pillars of Creation" are a small part of the Eagle Nebula. Tower-shaped masses of gas are filled with newborn stars. This famous nebula image was captured by the Hubble Space Telescope in 1995.

Black Eye Galaxy

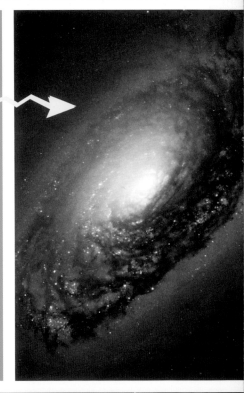

When new galaxies are discovered, astronomers give them a number-based name such as "NGC 4826," but also a nickname, usually chosen for what they look like. And here's one example! This galaxy, 17 million light-years away, has a band of dust that absorbs light, making it a galaxy with a dark side. It's known as the Black Eye Galaxy, or sometimes the Evil Eye Galaxy.

Sombrero Galaxy

It's a fabulous hat with a tiny middle and a brim 49,000 light-years wide—the galaxy named after a sombrero! Like many galaxies, including our own Milky Way, this one is spiral-shaped. But from Earth we see it sideways-on, and the bands of dust around the edge give it a solid-looking rim—so astronomers named it after a hat!

Eye to the Sky

In 1924, astronomer Edwin Hubble looked through the Hooker Telescope in California, U.S.A., and made a mind-blowing discovery. Until then, scientists had thought the Milky Way was the only galaxy in the universe. Hubble found it wasn't. The universe was much bigger than we had thought, and it was full of many other strange and wonderful galaxies. In 1990, a new telescope named after him—the Hubble Space Telescope—was launched into orbit. Since then, it's brought us amazing new images of faraway galaxies and nebulae, or gas clouds, and their weird shapes and patterns.

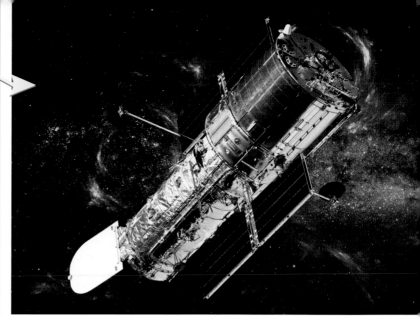

Neigh-bula!

In a colorful nebula, deep in the constellation of Orion, is a beautiful horse ... or is it more like a seahorse? Either way, the Horsehead Nebula is many space watchers' favorite nebula, thanks to the amazing horse head silhouette in the middle of a huge glowing dust explosion.

Spirograph Nebula

You can see how this nebula got its name: Its crisscrossing lines look like the patterns you can make with a spiral drawing toy. This kind of gas cloud forms when a star like our sun gets old, grows bigger, then shed its outer layers into space. But no one knows how it ended up with these mathematical-looking patterns—it's a mystery!

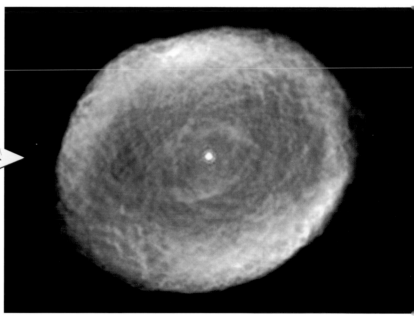

Galaxy Crash

This stunning galaxy, Centaurus A, seems to have several parts, resembling a giant jellyfish crashing through a galaxy-size pancake. That's because it's actually made up of two galaxies that have crashed together. This can happen when one galaxy's powerful gravity pulls on another galaxy nearby.

MYSTERIES OF THE UNIVERSE

Black Holes
Space Suckers!

Black holes are probably the weirdest things in the entire universe. A black hole forms after a big star gets old and collapses in on itself. Everything in the star is squished down into a tiny, super dense space. Its powerful gravity sucks in everything around it. More and more stuff gets packed down smaller and smaller, until it's all contained in one tiny point in space, called a singularity. Black holes have such powerful gravity that nothing can escape, not even light, once it gets close enough to be pulled in. (That's why black holes are black!) But don't panic—if you're not nearby, you won't get sucked in.

The **official name** of Tabby's star is **KIC 8462852.**

Tabby's Star
Flickering On and Off

In 2015, astronomer Tabby Boyajian spotted an odd light pattern coming from a faraway star, 1,470 light-years from Earth. It dimmed, then shone brightly again, in a regular cycle. It was so unusual, some space scientists said it might be a giant alien structure, built to orbit around the star and collect energy from it. Since people were talking about the star so much, they nicknamed it "Tabby's Star" after Boyajian. Since then, hundreds of astronomers have studied the star closely. They now think the light pattern could actually be caused by a massive dust cloud, but no one is sure.

Diamond Rain

Treasure of the Ice Giants

Diamonds are rare and valuable—on Earth, that is. They're formed under intense heat and pressure, such as when an asteroid crashes into Earth, or when rocks get squeezed deep under a volcano. Under this pressure, the element carbon takes on a new shape: the ultra-hard, sparkly diamond crystal. But it turns out that the distant ice giant planets, Uranus and Neptune, have a lot more diamonds than us! That's because their atmospheres contain methane, which contains carbon. These planets are also very big, and their powerful gravity creates a lot of pressure and heat, which crushes the carbon. Scientists think this process forms tiny diamonds, which then fall down toward the center of the planets.

THE WORD "DIAMOND" COMES FROM THE GREEK WORD *ADAMAS*, MEANING "INDESTRUCTIBLE."

SUPER-STELLAR FACTS ABOUT

As the **ISS ZOOMS** around **EARTH** every **92 minutes**, the **SUN** comes **up and goes down** about **16 times a day.**

ASTRONAUTS have to **DRINK OUT OF POUCHES WITH STRAWS** so their juice or coffee doesn't fly around everywhere!

Astronauts' **PEE** goes into a **cleaning system** and is **turned back** into **DRINKING WATER!**

On the **International Space Station, SALT AND PEPPER** come in **LIQUID FORM,** so they **don't float** off and **clog up the air vents.**

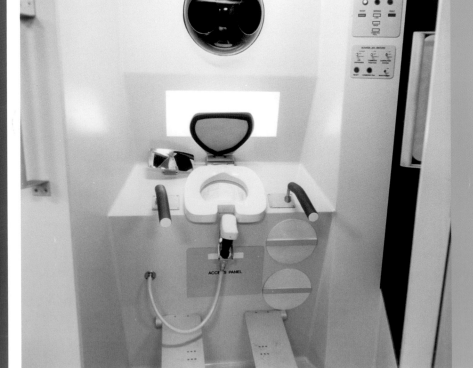

Space toilets use **SUCTION FUNNELS** to suck everything safely away.

LIFE IN SPACE

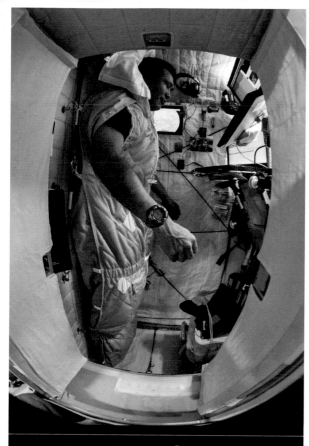

There's **no "down"** in space, so astronauts **can't lie down to SLEEP—** instead, they **strap themselves** and their **sleeping bag to a wall.**

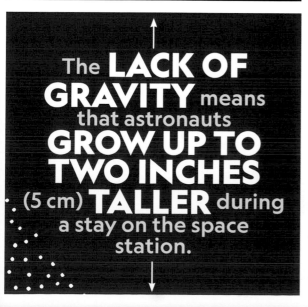

The **LACK OF GRAVITY** means that astronauts **GROW UP TO TWO INCHES** (5 cm) **TALLER** during a stay on the space station.

When they **return to Earth,** astronauts can **BARELY WALK** because their **bones** have gotten so **WEAK without gravity.**

OBJECTS AND TOOLS have to be **FIXED DOWN** with Velcro and duct tape so they **DON'T FLOAT AWAY.**

In 1974, each **NASA SPACE SUIT** cost between **$15 AND 22 MILLION—** that's about **$150 MILLION TODAY!**

QUIZ WHIZ

All clued up now on **weird facts** about the **sea** and **space?** The question is, can you remember them all?

1 **What patterns do male pufferfish make on the seabed?**

  a. Lightning bolts
  b. Patterns that look like pufferfish
  c. Circles with ridged edges
  d. Stars and flowers

2 **What is the deepest part of the ocean called?**

  a. Continental Deep
  b. Challenger Deep
  c. Creepy Deep
  d. Cousteau Deep

3 **Which animal lived on the Conshelf II underwater base?**

  a. A vampire squid
  b. A cat
  c. A sea pig
  d. A parrot

4 **What is a sea cucumber?**

a. A type of animal
b. A type of submarine
c. A type of marine plant
d. A type of inflatable boat

5 **What was the space robot Kirobo designed to do?**

a. Keep astronauts company
b. Transport heavy loads
c. Go on space walks
d. Do robot dances in space

6 **What are the Pillars of Creation?**

a. Four giant pillars that hold up Earth
b. Towerlike shapes in a nebula in outer space
c. Space probes sent to explore the solar system
d. Weird rock formations

7 **Which of these jobs is not carried out by Mars rover Curiosity?**

a. Collecting rock and soil samples
b. Taking photos
c. Planting seeds
d. Doing experiments

8 **What happens to pee on the International Space Station?**

a. It's fed to bacteria.
b. It's fired into space.
c. It's turned into drinking water.
d. It's stored in bags.

INDEX

INDEX

INDEX

INDEX

PHOTO CREDITS

All icons by Dynamo Ltd unless otherwise noted below.

AD=Adobe Stock; AL=Alamy Stock Photo; GI=Getty Images; IS=iStockphoto; SS=Shutterstock

FRONT COVER: (astronaut), Capitano Productions Film/SS; (pterodactyl), kamomeen/SS; (hot-air balloons), Mircea Costina/SS; (bird artwork), mattasbestos/SS; (sifaka), Eric Isselée/SS; (mummy), The British Museum/Trustees of the British Museum; (landmark artwork), avian/SS; **SPINE:** sifaka, Eric Isselée/SS; **BACK COVER:** (frog), Nature in Stock/AL; (statue), Richard Moat Photos/AL

FRONT MATTER: 1, Eric Isselée/SS; 4, Eric Isselée/SS; 5 (UP), Altefeuerwache Mannheim gGmbH/PEETA; 5 (LO), Alamy/Minden Pictures; 6 (UP), Eric Isselée/AD; 6 (LO), BlueOrangeStudio/AL; 7 (UP), SasinParaksa/AD 7 (LO LE), Danita Delimont Stock/AWL Images; 7 (LO RT), JPL-Caltech/MSSS/NASA; 8 (UP), nito/SS; 8 (LO LE), Farinoza/AD; 8 (LO RT), JS Callahan/tropicalpix/AL; 8 (roller coaster), Iconic Bestiary/SS; 9 (UP), Brooke Brisbine; 9 (LO), mbolina/AD; 10, BearFotos/SS; 11 (UP), Visual Generation/SS; 11 (CTR), Photozi/AD; 11 (LO), Neirfy/SS; **CHAPTER 1:** 12 (UP), VYCHEGZHANINA IS/GI; 12 (CTR), Eric Isselée/SS; 12 (LO LE), smereka/SS; 12 (LO RT), Steven Kovacs/Biosphoto; 13 (UP LE), OlegD/AD; 13 (UP RT), domnicky/IS/GI; 13 (LO LE), Newscom/AL; 13 (LO RT), GAGAnuma/SS; 14 (UP), Michael Nola/Robert Harding; 14 (CTR), Jacek Fulawka/SS; 14 (LO LE), Megan Betteridge/SS; 14 (LO RT), pets in frames/SS; 14 (calendar), linear_design/SS; 15 (UP LE), temele/IS/GI; 15 (UP CTR), Studio Light and Shade/IS/GI; 15 (UP RT), cunaplus/AD; 15 (LO LE), D_Darmawan/SS; 15 (LO RT), Roman Samborskyi/AL; 15 (ninjas), REVector/SS; 16, smereka/SS; 16 (Earth), Blan-k/SS; 16 (food scraps), AVIcon/SS; 16 (trash can), Cube29/SS; 17 (UP), Van Oord Dredging and Marine Contractors; 17 (CTR), Chasing Light/James Stone/Moment/GI; 17 (LO), RanMarine Technology; 17 (litter), Cube29/SS; 17 (cog), EPS/SS; 17 (fish), Akevi/SS; 18 (UP), Sipa US/AL; 18 (LO LE), Javier Brosch SS; 18 (LO RT), Krafla/AD; 19 (UP LE), backup/SS; 19 (CTR LE), Tatyana Vyc/SS; 19 (LO LE), Ljupco Smokovski/AD; 19 (RT), John W. McDonough/Sports Illustrated/GI; 19 (clown), Lenin Graphics/SS; 20 (UP), GAGAnuma/SS; 20 (LO), GI/Sankei; 20 (house), 90miles/SS; 20 (cat), Puckung/SS; 21 (UP), Imaginechina Limited/AL; 21 (CTR), REUTERS/AL; 21 (LO), Michele Falzone/AWL Images; 22, Willy Barton/SS; 22 (house), 90miles/SS; 23 (UP), cineuno/SS; 23 (LO), VYCHEGZHANINA/IS/GI; 24 (UP), Images & Stories/AL; 24 (LO), Duangkamon Panyapatiphan/IS/GI; 24 (jellyfish UP), frozenbunn/SS; 24 (jellyfish LO), AAVAA/SS; 24 (paw print), AAVAA/SS; 25 (UP), Neil Bromhall/SS; 25 (CTR), Sandesh Kadur/Nature Picture Library; 25 (LO), Fred Bavendam/Minden Pictures; 26 (UP), Robert Harding/AL; 26 (LO), Sylvain Cordier/Minden Pictures; 26 (paw print), AAVAA/SS; 27, Stephane Bidouze/SS; 28, Babak Tafreshi/National Geographic Image Collection; 28 (camera), CAPToro/SS; 29 (UP), Steven Kovacs/Biosphoto; 29 (CTR), Massimo Brega/Science Photo Library; 29 (LO), domnicky/IS/GI30 (camera), CAPToro/SS; 30-31, David Fleetham/Nature Picture Library; 32-33, Lucas Ottone/Stocksy; 34 (UP), Newscom/AL; 34 (CTR), NOAA Office of Ocean Exploration and Research; 34 (LO LE), dpa picture alliance/AL; 34 (LO RT), REUTERS/AL; 34 (newspaper), T-Kot,SS; 35 (UP), EQRoy/AL; 35 (CTR), ITAR-TASS News Agency/AL; 35 (LO LE), Emmanuelle Bonzami/AD; 35 (LO RT), Igor Avramchuk/AD; **CHAPTER 2:** 36 (UP), Luis Javier Sandoval/VWPics/AL; 36 (CTR), Sonsedska Yuliia/SS; 36 (LO LE), Vacclav/SS; 36 (LO RT), Paul Sarosta/Stone/GI; 37 (UP LE), Minden Pictures/AL; 37 (UP CTR), Six Flags; 37 (LO CTR), Cheri Alguire/SS; 37 (LO LE), All Canada Photos/AL; 37 (RT), dpruter/IS/GI Plus; 38, Kasefoto/SS; 39 (UP), Mircea Costina/SS; 39 (LO LE), Dotted Yeti/SS; 39 (LO RT), matis75/AD; 40 (UP), Mauricio Collado/Xinhua/Alamy Live News40 (LO), Cheri Alguire/SS; 41 (UP), Gunter Marx/HI/AL; 41 (LO), Life on white/AL; 42, Rick & Nora Bowers/AL; 43, Six Flags; 44 (UP), Norman Pogson/AL; 44 (LO), Carlos Sanchez Pereyra/AWL Images; 45 (UP), Sergii Figurnyi/Dreamstime45; (CTR), Jordan Banks/AWL Images; 45 (LO), Walter Bibikow/AWL Images; 46 (UP), Prisma by Dukas Presseagentur GmbH/AL; 46 (LO), Peter Conner/AL; 47 (UP), Laurie Ulster; 47 (LO CTR), Melissa Kopka/IS/GI Plus; 47 (LO LE & LO RT), Dmitri Stalnuhhin/AD; 48 (UP), Michael R Brown/SS; 48 (LO), CBS Photo Archive/GI; 49, Carsten Peter/National Geographic Image Collection; 50-51, Fractal7/SS; 51, Daria Rybakova/SS; 52 (UP), Mark Sykes/AWL Images; 52 (LO LE & LO RT), Brian Cahn/ZUMA Press Wire/AL; 53 (UP), Mmuseumm; 53 (LO), Gopher Hole Museum; 54 (UP), Vacclav/SS; 54 (CTR), Pete Souza/The White House; 54 (LO), Brendan Smialowski/AFP/GI; 55 (UP LE), Manuel Balce Ceneta/AP/SS; 55 (UP RT), Paul Damien/National Geographic Image Collection; 55 (CTR), Library of Congress Prints and Photographs Division; 55 (LO), Robert Eastman/SS; 56, Zaheer Mohammed/SS; 56 (inset), Isabella/IS/GI; 57, David Hoffmann/SS; 58 (UP), Citizen of the Planet/AL; 58 (LO), Bill Keough/AFP/GI; 59 (UP), Cow Chip Committee; 59 (LO), Just Another Photographer/SS; 60 (LE), Bill Keough/Florida Keys News Bureau/GI; 60 (RT), Six Flags; 61 (LE), Walter Bibikow/AWL Images; 61 (RT), Alex Petrenko/AD; 62 (UP), Chris Hadfield/NASA; 62 (CTR), Claus Lunau/Science Photo Library; 62 (LO), Danita Delimont Stock/AWL Images; 63 (UP), John Coletti/AWL Images; 63 (LO), Mark Ralston/AFP/GI; 64 (UP LE), Nick Hawkins/Nature Picture Library; 64 (UP RT), Alexandre Meneghini/REUTERS/AL; 64 (LO), Nick Hawkins/Nature Picture Library; 65 (UP LE), Tod Pusser/Nature Picture Library; 65 (UP CTR), Joseph Beck/IS/GI; 65 (LO CTR), Yva Momatiuk & John Eastcott/Minden Pictures; 65 (LO RT), Vaclav/AD; 66 (UP), Bob Kaufman/Alaska Channel; 66 (LO), Design Pics Inc/AL; 67 (UP), Wall Media Limited/Yap Wickedest Productions Inc; 67 (LO), Andre Jenny/AL; 68 (UP), Inspired By Maps/SS; 68 (LO), Michele Falzone/AWL Images; 69 (UP), CassielMx/IS/GI; 69 (LO), Danita Delimont Stock/AWL Images; 70 (UP), dpruter/IS/GI Plus70 (LO), Laura Storm/AL; 71 (UP), Gunter Marx/HI/AL; 71 (CTR), Life on white/AL; 71 (LO), Stan Tekiela/AD; **CHAPTER 3:** 72 (UP), iFerol/IS/GI; 72 (CTR), Claudio Contreras/Nature Picture Library; 72 (LO LE), hipokrat/IS/GI; 72 (LO RT), Alex Robinson/AWL Images; 73 (UP LE), Robert Oelman, Moment/GI; 73 (UP RT), C.DANI/I.JESKE/DEA/GI; 73 (LO LE), phototrip/AD; 73 (RT), Raphael Alves/Stringer/GI; 75 (UP), imageBROKER/AL; 75 (LO LE), Robin/AD; 75 (LO RT), Mari_art/AD; 76 (UP), Papichev Aleksandr/AD; 76 (CTR), Google Maps/Google Earth; 76 (LO), Karol Kozlowski/AWL Images; 77 (UP), Jorge Ivan Vasquez Cuartas/IS/GI; 77 (CTR), Ricardo Ribas/AL; 77 (LO), baibaz/AD; 78 (UP), Pedro Alexander Lasso Cortes; 78 (LO), Andres Conema/SS; 79 (UP), James Brunker/AL; 79 (LO), Smithsonian Institution, National Museum of Natural History, Department of Vertebrate Zoology, Division of Mammals; 80-81, Olga_Gavrilova/IS/GI; 81 (LE), ImageBROKER/AWL Images; 81 (RT), Karol Kozlowski/AWL Images; 82 (UP), Natura Vive; 82 (CTR), Natura Vive; 82 (LO), Stefan Havadi-Nagy/IS/GI; 83 (UP), Walter Bibikow/AWL Images; 83 (LO), Uilo Huilo/SIPA/Solent News; 84, worldclassphoto/SS; 84 (inset), Tristan Tan/SS; 85, Brooke Brisbine; 86 (UP), Pawel Toczynski/The Image Bank/GI; 86 (LO), W. BUSS/DEA/GI; 87 (UP), Ksenia Ragozina/SS; 87 (LO), Jonathan Chancasana/SS; 88 (UP), Christian Pinillo Salas/IS/GI; 88 (LO), Moment Open/GI; 89 (UP), webguzs/IS/GI; 89 (LO), John Coletti/AWL Images; 90 (UP), Pete Oxford/Minden Pictures; 90 (CTR), Claudio Contreras/Nature Picture Library; 90 (LO), Patrick Landmann/Science Photo Library; 91 (UP LE), imageBROKER/AL; 91 (UP RT), George Grall/AL; 91 (LO), Francisco Gomez; 92, Jukka/AD; 93 (UP), Javier brosch/AD; 93 (CTR LE), Lukas/AD; 93 (CTR RT), Maridav/AD; 93 (LO LE), zanna_/AD; 93 (LO RT), natursports/AD; 94 (UP), Alex Robinson/AWL Images; 94 (LO), Barry King/AL; 95, videobuzzing/SS; 96-97, Stringer/AFP/GI; 98 (UP), renelo/IS/GI; 98 (LO), Interfoto/AWL Images; 99 (UP), ephotocorp/AL; 99 (LO), Diego Grandi/AL; 100 (UP), Aleksandar Tomic/SS; 100 (LO), Rodrigo Soldon; 101 (UP), Nigel Pavitt/AWL Images; 101 (LO), Yesica Fisch/AP/SS; 102 (UP), Luis Echeverri Urrea/SS; 102 (LO), Media Drum World/AL; 103 (UP), Alexandr Vorobev/SS; 103 (LO), Robert Oelman/Moment/GI; 104 (UP LE), Nigel Pavitt/AWL Images; 104 (UP RT), Coulanges/SS; 104 (CTR), Nature in Stock/AL; 104 (LO), Bence Mate/Nature Picture Library; 105 (UP LE), Kseniia Mnasina/SS; 105 (UP RT), Konrad Wothe/Nature Picture Library; 105 (LO), Amazon-Images/AL; 106 (UP), Nigel Pavitt/AWL Images; 106 (LO), Uilo Huilo/SIPA/Solent News; 107 (UP), Ksenia Ragozina/Nature Picture Library; 107 (LO), Kseniia Mnasina/SS; **CHAPTER 4:** 108 (UP), Milllda/Dreamstime; 108 (CTR), blickwinkel/AL; 108 (LO LE), ImageBROKER/AWL IMAGES; 108 (LO RT), James Morris/Moment Open/GI; 109 (UP LE), Eva Bocek/Dreamstime; 109 (LO CTR), Leonardo Papera/AWL Images; 109 (LO LE), Jim Monk/AL; 109 (RT), fhm/Moment/GI; 110 (UP), dennisvdwater/AD; 110 (LO), Steve Allen/SS; 111 (UP), Rafael Ben-Ari; 111 (LO LE); Susan Schmitz/AD; 111 (LO RT), Uros Petrovic/AD; 112 (UP), Leonardo Papera/AWL Images; 112 (LO), Marko Ignjatovic/IS; 113 (UP), Alex Mustard/Nature Picture Library; 113 (LO), sjhaytov/IS; 114 (UP), Nick Ledger/AWL Images; 114 (LO), Eva Bocek/Dreamstime; 115, Stefano Brozzi/4Corners; 116 (UP), ClickAlps/AWL Images; 116 (LO), blickwinkel/AL; 117 (UP), Endless Travel/AL; 117 (LO), Jasius/Moment/GI; 118 (UP LE), AA World Travel Library/AL; 118 (UP RT), Mariusz Cieszewski/Ministry of Foreign Affairs of the Republic of Poland118 (LO), dirk94025/AD; 119 (UP), Kiev.Victor/SS; 119 (CTR), Massimo Borchi/4Corners; 119 (LO), emperorcosar/AD; 120 (UP), Design Pics Inc/AL; 120 (LO), Moment/GI; 121, Karl Hausammann/AL; 122 (UP), Jim Monk/AL; 122 (LO), Patryk Kosmider/SS; 123 (UP), Hervé Lenain/AL; 123 (LO), rusm/IS/GI; 124 (UP LE), Sipa/SS; 124 (UP RT), Museo Miniaturas de Ordino; 124 (LO LE), Fairy Tale Museum, Cyprus; 124 (LO RT), Ryan Gemmola/AL; 125 (UP), By Pavel L Photo and Video/SS; 125 (CTR), Adam Eastland/AL; 125 (LO LE), Anna Krivitskaya/SS; 125 (LO RT), Peter van Evert/AL; 126 (UP), Stephen Davies/AD; 126 (LO), Chiara Salvadori/Moment/GI; 127 (UP), PA Images/AL; 127 (LO), James Morris photography/Moment Open/GI; 129 (UP LE), Mattuzzi Francesco/leapfactory srl; 129 (UP RT), Henrik Lindvall/AL;

Since 1888, the National Geographic Society has funded more than 14,000 research, conservation, education, and storytelling projects around the world. National Geographic Partners distributes a portion of the funds it receives from your purchase to National Geographic Society to support programs including the conservation of animals and their habitats. To learn more, visit natgeo.com/info.

For more information, visit nationalgeographic.com, call 1-877-873-6846, or write to the following address:

National Geographic Partners, LLC
1145 17th Street NW
Washington, DC 20036-4688 U.S.A.

For librarians and teachers: nationalgeographic.com/books/librarians-and-educators

More for kids from National Geographic: natgeokids.com

National Geographic Kids magazine inspires children to explore their world with fun yet educational articles on animals, science, nature, and more. Using fresh storytelling and amazing photography, *Nat Geo Kids* shows kids ages 6 to 14 the fascinating truth about the world—and why they should care. **natgeo.com/subscribe**

For rights or permissions inquiries, please contact National Geographic Books Subsidiary Rights: bookrights@natgeo.com

Hardcover ISBN: 978-1-4263-7331-2
Reinforced library binding ISBN: 978-1-4263-7452-4

The publisher would like to thank the book team: Claire Lister, Kathryn Williams, and Kath Jewitt, project editors; Julide Dengel, senior designer; Lori Epstein, photo manager; Kate Ford, designer; Anna Claybourne, Richard Mead, and Sara Stanford, contributing writers; Paige Towler, acquisition editor; Alix Inchausti, production editor; and Anne LeongSon and Gus Tello, associate designers; and the packaging team at Dynamo Limited.

Printed in Hong Kong
22/PPHK/1